LANFORD WILSON

CASEBOOKS ON
MODERN DRAMATISTS
(VOL. 7)

GARLAND REFERENCE LIBRARY
OF THE HUMANITIES
(VOL. 960)

CASEBOOKS ON MODERN DRAMATISTS
(*General Editor*, Kimball King)

LANFORD WILSON
A Casebook

edited by
Jackson R. Bryer

GARLAND PUBLISHING, INC. • NEW YORK & LONDON
1994

Library of Congress Cataloging-in-Publication Data

Lanford Wilson : a casebook / edited by Jackson R. Bryer.
     p.   cm. — (Casebooks on modern dramatists ; vol. 7. Garland
reference library of the humanities ; vol. 960)
  Includes bibliographical references and index.
  ISBN 0-8240-0648-8 (alk. paper)
  1. Wilson, Lanford, 1937–   —Criticism and interpretation.
I. Bryer, Jackson R. II. Series: Garland reference library of the
humanities ; vol. 960. III. Series: Garland reference library of
the humanities. Casebooks on modern dramatists ; vol. 7.
PS3573.I458Z74   1994
812'.54—dc20   93-31584
                                             CIP

Printed on acid-free, 250-year-life paper
Manufactured in the United States of America

CONTENTS

GENERAL EDITOR'S NOTE

For *Lanford Wilson: A Casebook,* Jackson R. Bryer has commissioned and edited ten original essays on Wilson's work, providing an invaluable record of a major American playwright's achievements. While Wilson has earned the Pulitzer Prize, two Drama Critics Awards, and two Obies, as well as Guggenheim fellowships and Rockefeller grants, he has been underrepresented in critical writings on modern drama. His forty-two produced plays as well as his wide range of subject matter and varied theatrical techniques make him one of the twentieth century's most prolific and innovative dramatists. Professor Bryer is well qualified to bring together wide-ranging, in-depth studies of Wilson's major work. He is presently the vice-president of the O'Neill Society and has edited two books on Eugene O'Neill, including the widely acclaimed *"The Theatre We Worked For": The Letters of Eugene O'Neill to Kenneth Macgowan.* He is also director of the annual William Inge Conference and has edited *Conversations with Lillian Hellman* and *Conversations with Thornton Wilder.*

Lanford Wilson: A Casebook includes Bryer's meticulous chronology of Wilson's life and the most thorough annotated bibliography of primary and secondary works yet assembled on the playwright. Both scholars of contemporary drama and theatergoers who have enjoyed Wilson's attempt to depict significant issues concerning American life will welcome this volume.

Kimball King

INTRODUCTION

As this volume goes to press, Lanford Wilson's newest full-length play, *Redwood Curtain*, is about to open on Broadway, after earlier productions at the Seattle Repertory Theatre and the Philadelphia Drama Guild. Assuming that this takes place, as scheduled, in late March 1993, it will be almost exactly thirty years since Wilson's first play, the one-act *So Long at the Fair*, made its debut at the off-off Broadway Caffe Cino in August 1963. As he enters the fourth decade of his career, Wilson has written forty-two produced plays, thirteen of them full-length; probably no contemporary dramatist of his stature—with the possible exceptions of Sam Shepard and Neil Simon—has been more prolific.

Stylistically, his work has ranged from the brutal naturalism of *Balm in Gilead* and the gritty realism of *The Hot l Baltimore* and the Talley plays to the highly imaginative experimentalism of *Lemon Sky*, *The Rimers of Eldritch* and many of his one-acts. He has set plays in California, in his home state of Missouri, in New York City, in Baltimore, in New Mexico, in downstate Illinois and in Chicago. He has written for casts of thirty-two (*Balm in Gilead*) and fifteen (*The Hot l Baltimore*), as well as for one (*The Madness of Lady Bright*) and two (*Talley's Folly* and *The Great Nebula in Orion*).

Wilson has been honored with the Pulitzer Prize (for *Talley's Folly*), two New York Drama Critics Awards (for *Talley's Folly* and *The Hot l Baltimore*), two Outer Critics Circle Awards (for *Talley's Folly* and *The Hot l Baltimore*), two Obie Awards (for *The Hot l Baltimore* and *The Mound Builders*) and the Drama Desk Vernon Rice Award (for *The Rimers of Eldritch*). He has received two Guggenheim Fellowships, two Rockefeller Grants, an American Institute of Arts and Letters award, an ABC-Yale Fellowship in motion picture writing, the first State of Missouri

Outstanding Artist's Award, an honorary Doctor of Letters from
the University of Missouri and the Brandeis University Creative
Arts Achievement Award for Theater (previously won by
Tennessee Williams, Arthur Miller and Thornton Wilder).

While Wilson's plays have certainly not received universal
praise from critics and reviewers (Edith Oliver and Gerald
Weales have been especially lukewarm over the years), he has
been called by John Simon (a commentator hardly known for
excessive praise) "our soundest, most satisfying dramatist. . . .
more disciplined and dependable than Sam Shepard; more various and productive than Tina Howe, Marsha Norman, David
Rabe; less autobiographically obsessed than any number of others; and far less quirky, mean-spirited, puny than David
Mamet." Simon adds, "To people who want eccentricity or ma-
nia from their playwrights, he may seem a bit bland [this
comment predates *Burn This!*]; to those who value comprehen-
siveness, comprehension, and compassion, his pre-eminence is
perspicuous." As early as 1970, Martin Gottfried had proclaimed
Wilson "one of America's most accomplished and significant
playwrights"; while, more recently, Frank Rich in 1982 described
him as "one of the few artists of our theatre who can truly make
America sing." David Mamet has been quoted as considering
Wilson the "contemporary playwright I admire the most."

When one considers this praise, the honors he has received, and the number of plays he has written, Lanford Wilson
has been the subject of very little serious and extended critical or
scholarly scrutiny. There are only two book-length studies, one
by Gene A. Barnett (1987) in the Twayne United States Authors
Series and the other a monograph by Mark Busby (1987) in the
Western Writers Series. (Philip Middleton Williams's *A
Comfortable House: Lanford Wilson, Marshall W. Mason and the
Circle Repertory Theatre* is announced for spring 1993 publication.) Gerald M. Berkowitz, Harold Branam, Ruby Cohn,
Gautam Dasgupta, Ann Crawford Dreher and William Herman
have devoted brief sections to Wilson in survey volumes on
modern or contemporary American drama. The handful of
scholarly articles dealing entirely or even in part with Wilson
includes pieces by Martin J. Jacobi on his comic vision, by Gary
Konas comparing plays set in Missouri by Wilson and Tennessee

Williams, by Henry Schvey on images of the past in Wilson's plays, by James F. Schlatter examining *Fifth of July* alongside family plays by Preston Jones and Sam Shepard and by Barry Witham looking at Wilson's vision of America in *Fifth of July* in comparison with that found in plays by Michael Weller and Israel Horovitz. The overwhelming majority of critical comment in print on Wilson appears in first-night reviews, profiles for mass-circulation publications, and interviews.

This collection seeks to be a first step in filling this regrettable void by presenting ten original critical essays written especially for this volume and never previously published. Their authors have chosen their subjects from the full extent of Wilson's career through *Burn This* (1987) and view that career from a variety of viewpoints. Befitting a book on a playwright whose theatricality is praised as often as his dialogue, its contributors include persons with practical theatre experience—as actors, directors and dramaturgs—many of whom are in addition widely published as academic critics and are conversant with the broader expanse of modern drama and thus can locate Wilson knowledgeably in this context. Several have written about Wilson previously and their essays in this volume represent rethinkings and extensions of their earlier work. The book also contains two in-depth interviews—with Wilson and with Marshall W. Mason, co-founder (with Wilson and others) of the Circle Repertory Company and director of most of his plays since *Balm in Gilead* (1965). The Wilson interview includes comments by the playwright on some of the key contentions made by essayists in this collection. Bracketing the volume are a detailed chronology of Wilson's life and writing career and a bibliography of his works and a selected annotated listing of writing about him.

Place is generally acknowledged to play a central role in Wilson's work; the opening essay in the book, by Thomas P. Adler, explores how the use of settings both real and imagined is related to theme. Adler, Professor of English at Purdue University and author of a book-length study of contemporary American playwright Robert Anderson (1978), as well as of *Mirror on the Stage: The Pulitzer Plays as an Approach to American Drama* (1987) and *"A Streetcar Named Desire": The Moth and the*

Lantern (1990), also locates Wilson's dramas among those of such contemporaries and predecessors as Wilder, Williams, Miller, Brecht and Pirandello.

Barry B. Witham, Professor and Executive Director of the School of Drama at the University of Washington, has published extensively in the fields of American and English theatre; he has also served as Dramaturg for the Seattle Repertory Theatre, where he worked with such contemporary American playwrights as Herb Gardner, William Mastrosimone and Richard Nelson. His essay reflects this experience in the professional theatre by reaching back to Wilson's earliest work and relating it to the techniques of the alternative theatre movement out of which it grew. Witham pays particular attention to performance techniques created originally by groups within the counterculture theatre and subsequently assimilated into Wilson's *The Family Continues, Balm in Gilead* and *The Rimers of Eldritch*, as well as into the work of John Guare and Sam Shepard.

Another central concern of Wilson's plays—families— occupies the attention of the next two essays. In the first of these, James J. Martine, who is Professor of English at St. Bonaventure University, author of *Fred Lewis Pattee and American Literature* (1973), and editor of *Critical Essays on Arthur Miller* (1979), of *American Novelists, 1910–1945* (1981) and of *Critical Essays on Eugene O'Neill* (1984), covers all of Wilson's major works. Martine's focus is on the playwright's portrayal of dysfunctional families and on the changing role of women in Wilson's dramas. Robert Cooperman's essay is narrower in its concentration on Wilson's trilogy of plays dealing with the Talley family (*Fifth of July, Talley's Folly* and *Talley & Son*). Cooperman, currently working on his doctorate in English at Ohio State University, is the author of *Clifford Odets: An Annotated Bibliography, 1935–1989* (1989) and of scholarly publications on Wilson, Eugene O'Neill and Marsha Norman. He has also acted lead roles in productions of *Talley's Folly* and *Fifth of July* and is a playwright whose work has been produced off-off-Broadway and regionally. He begins with Tom Scanlan's 1978 study of *Family, Drama, and American Drama* and shows how Wilson's trilogy documents the evolution of the American family and dramatizes "the history of family life in modern America."

The next two essays, by Richard Wattenberg and Susan Harris Smith, both deal with *Angels Fall* (1982), the play which followed the Talley trilogy in Wilson's career and has received virtually no serious attention other than from reviewers. Wattenberg and Smith, interestingly enough, come to almost diametrically opposed conclusions (neither had access to the other's essay). Wattenberg, who is an Assistant Professor of Theatre Arts at Portland State University, is currently working on a study of the impact of the frontier western myth on selected nineteenth- and twentieth-century American plays. Portions of this work have appeared as articles on Sam Shepard, Robert E. Sherwood, William Saroyan, David Belasco, Marsha Norman and on contemporary women's plays about women pioneers. Here he uses Emerson's "Self-Reliance" as his basic text for studying *Angels Fall*, in which he sees Wilson "attempting to reawaken American audiences to the democratic faith of their 'grandfathers'—Emerson, Thoreau and Whitman." Smith begins with a quite different premise—*Angels Fall* "is not a Jeffersonian agrarian or Emersonian transcendental romance"—and her examination of the women characters in the play leads her to conclusions quite different from those put forward on the same subject in Martine's essay. Smith is harsh in her judgments and it is of interest to note Wilson's responses to her argument in the interview in the collection. Smith is an Associate Professor of English at the University of Pittsburgh and the author of *Masks in Modern Drama* (1984), along with scholarly pieces on Charles Gordone, Eugene O'Neill, Sam Shepard, Mary Shelley, F. Scott Fitzgerald, Arthur Miller and Lulu Vollmer.

Wilson's debt to Chekhov has frequently been cited by critics and reviewers and also has been freely acknowledged by the playwright himself in interviews. Felicia Hardison Londré brings to her analysis of Wilson's 1984 translation of *Three Sisters* extensive experience as a translator of French, Spanish and Russian dramatic texts. Londré, Curators' Professor of Theatre at the University of Missouri-Kansas City and Dramaturg for the Missouri Repertory Theatre, has published books on Tennessee Williams (1979), Tom Stoppard (1981) and Federico Garcia Lorca

(1984), and *The History of World Theater—Volume 1: From the Beginnings to the Baroque* (1991), as well as many articles on English, American and continental drama. In her essay, she compares Wilson's translation very closely with Chekhov's original and with other standard English texts, showing what sets his version apart from the others. But she also goes well beyond this comparison in showing how translating Chekhov led Wilson to *Burn This*, the Chekhovian elements of which Londré identifies.

A trio of essays on *Burn This* (1987) concludes the critical pieces in the collection. Martin J. Jacobi, Associate Professor of English and Director of the Writing Lab at Clemson University, who has published previously on Wilson, and on William Faulkner, on rhetorical theory and on professional writing theory and instruction, is concerned with the play and its author's "personal strategies." Jacobi is especially interested in the play's "personal advice to its author" and to its audience, particularly with respect to the role of the artist in society. His focus is on the Anna-Pale-Burton triangle as it relates to the various alternatives presented to the artist.

Henry I. Schvey is also intrigued by the play's romantic triangle, but he views it against a background of the similar three-sided relationship depicted in Emily Brontë's *Wuthering Heights*. Schvey, Professor of Drama and Chairman of the Performing Arts Department at Washington University in St. Louis and author of numerous essays on contemporary American, British and European drama, begins where his earlier essay, "Images of the Past in the Plays of Lanford Wilson" (1981), left off and sees *Burn This* as its author's return, after a hiatus with *Angels Fall* and the Talley trilogy, to the "dangerous and 'unruly' sensibility of his earlier work."

Like Schvey, Daniel J. Watermeier sees the similarities as well as the differences between *Burn This* and Wilson's earlier unlikely love story, *Talley's Folly* (1979). Like Schvey also, Watermeier invokes other lovers as context for Wilson's play, but his are more Teutonic and mythic in origin, specifically the Flying Dutchman myth, the Romantic hero and heroine and the mythic mother archetype, and he views Wilson's story in epic terms. Watermeier is Professor of Theatre and Drama at the

University of Toledo and has edited *Between Actor and Critic: Selected Letters of Edwin Booth and William Winter* (1971) and *Edwin Booth's Performances: The Mary Isabella Stone Commentaries* (1990). His essays have appeared in *Theatre Journal, Theatre History Studies, Theatre Research International* and *Shakespeare Quarterly*, and he has directed over two dozen stage productions, including, in 1989, *Talley's Folly*.

The remainder of the volume is devoted to lengthy interviews with Wilson and with his longtime friend, director and collaborator Marshall W. Mason and to a Wilson bibliography. The Wilson interview to some extent focuses on issues raised elsewhere in the collection, while the conversation with Mason stresses the extent and nature of his collaboration with Wilson. Martin J. Jacobi's Wilson bibliography contains a detailed listing of the playwright's publications and of the first productions of his plays, followed by a selected annotated listing of the major research, reviews, criticism and interviews which deal with him and his work.

A word must be inserted here regarding when these essays and interviews were prepared. With the exceptions of the Chronology, the Introduction and the Bibliography, material in the volume was completed before *Redwood Curtain* was either produced or published.

For generous assistance and patience in the preparation of this book, I wish to thank Kimball King, the General Editor of the Garland Casebooks on Modern Dramatists series. Our friendship of more than thirty years was surely tested by the extended gestation of this project, but he remained cheerfully encouraging throughout the process. Caleb King did an expert job of preparing the manuscript for publication, pointing out inconsistencies and problems and solving many of them. Lanford Wilson is much more than the subject of this book; he has been supportive of it from the outset. He interrupted a busy schedule to agree to an interview, then read through and corrected the transcript of the interview; and he extended himself further by assisting with the Chronology and the listing of his works. Marshall W. Mason similarly gave of his time for the interview and the transcript thereof; and he also helped with the Chronology. Robert Cooperman shared his expertise in Wilson bibliography with me whenever asked; the Chronology and the Bibliography are much better due to his generosity—and that, indirectly, of Bridget Aschenberg, Wilson's agent. Drew Eisenhauer performed a variety of unglamorous tasks with dispatch and unfailing good humor, most notably the transcribing of the two interviews. Mary C. Hartig improved my writing. Jack Gates prepared the Index, which he dedicates to the memory of Bowden Anderson.

In a recent interview with Toby Silverman Zinman, Wilson describes "a Lanford Wilson play": "There are people talking. . . . people come together and talk about their problems and work out or don't work out their immediate situation." It is my hope that the voices which come together in this collection to talk about Lanford Wilson and his plays will have the effect of directing some long overdue attention to one of America's finest contemporary playwrights. And if the conversation we have begun is even half as stimulating and engrossing as that to be found in a Lanford Wilson play, then we will have succeeded in our intention.

Kensington, MD
1 March 1993

CHRONOLOGY

1937   Lanford Eugene Wilson born on 13 April, in Lebanon, Missouri, to Ralph Eugene and Violetta Careybelle (Tate) Wilson.

1942   Wilson's parents divorce; he moves with his mother to Springfield, Missouri; his father moves to San Diego, California.

1951   Wilson's mother remarries and the family moves to Ozark, Missouri, later to a farm outside Ozark.

1954–55 Wilson attends Ozark High School; sees productions of *Brigadoon* and *Death of a Salesman* and falls in love with theatre; plays Tom in a high school production of *The Glass Menagerie*.

1955   Wilson graduates from Ozark High School and attends Southwest Missouri State College during summer.

1956   Wilson goes to San Diego and lives with his father; attends San Diego State College; works as a riveter in Ryan aircraft factory where his father is employed.

1957   Wilson goes to Chicago and works as an artist at an advertising agency.

1959   Wilson enrolls in a playwriting class in the adult education program of the University of Chicago.

1962   Wilson arrives in New York City on 5 July.

1963 Wilson sees Ionesco's *The Lesson* at the Caffe Cino: "It was the first theatrical experience I'd had in New York City. That is what I thought theatre was going to be, not Broadway. . . . it was the first time I was engaged by something and probably the madness of that play influenced my plays at the Cino a little bit"; Wilson's *So Long at the Fair* and *Home Free!* are presented at the Caffe Cino in August and October respectively.

1964 Wilson's *No Trespassing* as well as a revival of *Home Free!* are presented at the Caffe Cino in January; *The Madness of Lady Bright* opens there in May. In August, Wilson meets director Marshall W. Mason.

1965 Wilson's first full-length play, *Balm in Gilead*, directed by Marshall W. Mason, opens at the Cafe La Mama Experimental Theater Club in January; Mason also directs the professional debut (off-Broadway) of *Home Free!* at the Cherry Lane Theatre in February; *Ludlow Fair* opens at the Caffe Cino in February; *This Is the Rill Speaking* is presented at the Caffe Cino in July; *The Sand Castle* opens at the La Mama Experimental Theater Club in September; *Miss Williams: A Turn* is presented for one benefit performance at the La Mama Experimental Theater Club on 3 November; *Days Ahead* and *Sex Is Between Two People* open at the Caffe Cino in December.

1966 Wilson's *Wandering* opens at the Caffe Cino in April; a revival of *This Is the Rill Speaking* opens in April at the Martinique Theatre (off-Broadway rather than off-off-Broadway as the Cino and La Mama were) as part of the *Six From La Mama* program; *The Rimers of Eldritch*, Wilson's second full-length play, opens at the La Mama Experimental Theater Club in July.

1967 Wilson receives a Rockefeller Grant; a revival of *The Rimers of Eldritch* opens at the off-Broadway Cherry Lane Theatre in February, runs for 32 performances, and the play receives a Drama Desk Vernon Rice Award; Joe Cino commits suicide on 1 April; in the spring and summer, Wilson, Rob Thirkield, Claris Nelson and Michael Powell join Ellen Stewart's La Mama troupe's tour of Europe; Marshall W. Mason and Tanya Berezin join them in the summer in Copenhagen and Wilson and Mason leave the troupe and tour southern Europe together while Wilson writes the libretto for the opera version of *Summer and Smoke*.

1968 *Untitled Play* (with music by Al Carmines) opens at the Judson Poets Theatre in January; Wilson receives an ABC-Yale Fellowship in motion picture writing; his full-length play *The Gingham Dog* is staged as a showcase production at the New Dramatists in New York City in February; during the spring and early summer, Marshall W. Mason, Claris Nelson, Charley Stanley, David Groh, Tanya Berezin and Michael Powell form the American Theatre Project and present highly successful revivals of *Home Free!* and *The Madness of Lady Bright* at London's Mercury Theatre in April and in Edinburgh in May; as a result, the two plays are published in England by Methuen; a staged reading of Wilson's full-length play *Lemon Sky* is given at the Eugene O'Neill Theatre Foundation in Waterford, Connecticut, in July; *The Gingham Dog* receives its first professional production in September at the Washington Theatre Club in Washington, D. C.

1969 Wilson receives his first Broadway production when *The Gingham Dog* opens at the John Golden Theatre on 23 April, but it is poorly reviewed and closes after five performances; on 14 July, Wilson, Marshall W. Mason, Rob Thirkield and Tanya Berezin announce the formation of a new theatre company, later to be called the Circle Repertory Company, at 2307 Broadway—between 83rd and 84th streets; on 28 November, Wilson's *Stoop* is presented as part of *Foul!* on the New York Television Theater (WNET, New York City).

1970 Wilson is awarded a Guggenheim Fellowship; Wilson's *Lemon Sky* opens at the Buffalo (NY) Studio Arena Theatre in March; in April, his full-length play *Serenading Louie* premieres at the Washington Theatre Club; on 7 April, *The Sand Castle* is presented on New York Television Theater (WNET, New York City) and is repeated on 13 April; *Lemon Sky* opens at the Playhouse Theatre on Broadway on 17 May but runs for only ten previews and seven performances.

1971 Wilson's first Circle Rep production, *Sextet (Yes)*, opens in February; *The Great Nebula in Orion* receives its first production at the Stables Theatre Club of Manchester, England, in February; in June, *Summer and Smoke*, Lee Hoiby's opera version of Tennessee Williams's play—with a libretto by Wilson—opens in St. Paul, Minnesota.

1972 Wilson receives a second Guggenheim Fellowship; in January, *Ikke, Ikke, Nye, Nye, Nye* is presented at the Yale Cabaret in New Haven, Connecticut; *Summer and Smoke* opens at the New York City Opera in March; *Three New Plays by Lanford Wilson* (*The Great Nebula in Orion, The Family Continues* and *Ikke, Ikke, Nye, Nye, Nye*) opens at the Circle Repertory Theatre in May; on 4 November, *The Rimers of Eldritch* is presented on Theater in America (PBS television) and is repeated on 27 August 1975.

1973 Wilson receives his second Rockefeller Grant; his full-length play *The Hot l Baltimore* opens at the Circle Repertory Theatre in February and moves to the Circle-in-the-Square Theatre (where it runs for 1166 performances) in March; *The Hot l Baltimore* receives the New York Drama Critics Circle Award for Best American Play, the Obie Award for Best Play and the Outer Critics Circle Award, and it is printed in the *Ten Best Plays* of the year.

1974 Wilson receives a $3,000 award from the American Institute of Arts and Letters; on 3 February, *The Migrants* by Wilson and Tennessee Williams is presented on Playhouse

90 (CBS television); in October, the Circle Repertory Company moves to the Sheridan Square Playhouse in Greenwich Village.

1975 Wilson's *The Hot l Baltimore* becomes the basis of a weekly television series on ABC which premieres on 24 January and runs until 6 June (Wilson is not involved in the writing of the series); his full-length play *The Mound Builders* opens at the Circle Repertory Theatre in February and receives an Obie Award for the Best Off-Broadway Play.

1976 Wilson's *The Mound Builders* is presented on Theater in America (Great Performances) on PBS television on 11 February and is repeated on 3 August 1977; *Serenading Louie* opens at the Circle Repertory Theatre in May.

1977 Wilson's *Brontosaurus* opens at the Circle Repertory Theatre in October.

1978 Wilson's teleplay *Taxi!* is presented on the Hallmark Hall of Fame (NBC television) on 2 February; the first Talley play, the full-length *5th of July*, opens at the Circle Repertory Theatre in April and runs for 159 performances.

1979 Wilson's ten-minute *Bar Play* is presented by the Actors Theatre of Louisville, Kentucky, in January; the second Talley play, the full-length *Talley's Folly*, opens at the Circle Repertory Theatre in May; *Victory on Mrs. Dandywine's Island* is presented at the Circle Rep Workshop; in August, *Fifth of July*, a revised version of *5th of July*, opens in repertory with *Talley's Folly* at the Mark Taper Forum in Los Angeles.

1980 Wilson's *Talley's Folly* opens at Broadway's Brooks Atkinson Theatre on 20 February, runs for 277 performances and is awarded the Pulitzer Prize for Drama, the New York Drama Critics Circle Award for Best Play and the Outer Critics Circle Award; in September, a revival of *Balm in Gilead*, presented by the Steppenwolf Theater

Ensemble and directed by John Malkovich, opens at Chicago's Steppenwolf Theatre and wins seven Joseph Jefferson Awards; on 5 November, *Fifth of July* opens at the New Apollo Theatre in New York and runs for 511 performances.

1981 Wilson's *A Tale Told*, the third full-length play in the Talley cycle, opens at the Circle Repertory Theatre in June, and in October is given a second production at the Mark Taper Forum in Los Angeles; in September, Wilson receives the first State of Missouri Outstanding Artist's Award and an honorary Doctor of Letters degree from the University of Missouri; *Thymus Vulgaris* opens at the Lee Strasberg Institute in Los Angeles in October.

1982 Wilson's *Thymus Vulgaris* opens at the Circle Repertory Theatre in January; his full-length play *Angels Fall* premieres at the New World Festival in Miami, Florida, in June; *Angels Fall* is presented at the Saratoga (NY) Performing Arts Center in August and at the Circle Repertory Theatre in October; on 15 October, *Fifth of July* is presented on Showtime cable television.

1983 Wilson's *Angels Fall* opens on Broadway at the Longacre Theatre in January and runs for 64 performances; on 10 May, *Fifth of July* is presented on PBS television; *Say de Kooning* opens at Southampton College, Southampton, New York, in August.

1984 Wilson's *Serenading Louie* is revived by Second Stage and presented at the Public Theatre in January; his translation of Chekhov's *Three Sisters* opens at the Hartford (CT) Stage Company in March.

1985 Wilson's *The Bottle Harp* (written in 1963) and *Sa Hurt?* (written in 1968) are performed at the Circle Rep Lab in February; *Talley & Son* (revised from *A Tale Told*) opens at the Saratoga (NY) Performing Arts Center in July; a revival of *Lemon Sky* opens at the Second Stage Theatre in New

York in November; *Talley & Son* opens at the Circle Repertory Company in November.

1986 Wilson's translation of *Three Sisters* opens at the Equity Library Theatre in New York in April; in July, Rob Thirkield commits suicide; *A Betrothal* opens at the Man in the Moon Theatre in London in September; in September, Marshall W. Mason announces that, effective in July 1987, he will resign as Artistic Director of the Circle Repertory Company; *Burn This*, a full-length play, opens in Saratoga (NY) in August.

1987 Wilson's *Breakfast at the Track* is presented in a benefit performance for Circle Repertory Theatre at the Lucille Lortel Theatre; *Burn This* opens at the Mark Taper Forum in Los Angeles in January; in March, *Burn This* is presented at the Circle Repertory Theatre; in July, Tanya Berezin becomes Acting Artistic Director of the Circle Repertory Company and in August is appointed Artistic Director; *Burn This* opens on Broadway at the Plymouth Theatre on 14 October and runs for 487 performances; in December, *A Betrothal*, *The Bottle Harp* and *Say de Kooning* open at the Sanford Meisner Theatre in New York City.

1988 Wilson's *Lemon Sky* is presented on American Playhouse (PBS television) on 10 February; in May, an opera version of *The Great Nebula in Orion*, with music by Ken Fuchs, is presented at the Circle Repertory Theatre; *Sam Found Out*, a skit by Wilson, is presented as part of a Liza Minnelli TV special on ABC television on 31 May; *A Poster of the Cosmos* opens at the Ensemble Studio Theatre in New York City in June; *Abstinence* is performed at a Circle Repertory benefit in October.

1989 In March, the original cast of *The Hot l Baltimore* re-assembles for a benefit for the Circle Repertory Theatre at the Lucille Lortel Theatre in New York; an opera version of *A Betrothal*, with music by Ken Fuchs, is presented at the Circle Repertory Theatre in November.

1990 Wilson's one-act plays *The Moonshot Tape* and *A Poster of the Cosmos* are presented at Humboldt State University in Arcata (CA) in August; in December, Wilson's full-length play *Redwood Curtain* is read at Circle Rep.

1991 In March, *Redwood Curtain* is read at the Seattle Repertory Theatre; in June, Wilson's one-act play *Eukiah*, co-winner of the Actors Theatre of Louisville 1991 National Ten-Minute Play Contest and the Heideman Award, premieres at Actors Theatre.

1992 *Redwood Curtain* opens at the Seattle Repertory Theatre in January; in March, *Eukiah* is presented at the Actors Theatre of Louisville's New Play Festival.

1993 *Redwood Curtain* opens on Broadway at the Brooks Atkinson Theatre on 30 March.

Lanford Wilson

The Artist in the Garden: Theatre Space and Place in Lanford Wilson

Thomas P. Adler

In his essay "Writing for Films," William Inge—whose plays share with several of Lanford Wilson's a distinctively midwestern setting—comments on the spatial limitations that would seem to restrict the dramatist's art: "In the theatre," Inge asserts, "one is always confined to the dimensions of the stage. . . . Writing for the theatre has its own satisfactions, but mobile geography is not one of them" (1). Such overstatement—some would argue inaccuracy—is understandable if one equates serious drama with a realistic set (the traditional room with an imaginary fourth wall separating audience from acting area) that allows for unity of place, at least within the acts. From Inge's perspective, the fluidity of moving from locale to locale and the possibility for simultaneity of action are properties associated with the freer medium of film rather than with theatrical realism.

And yet, from another perspective, just as the world in realistic film continues outside the boundary of the frame, the place in even a realistic play need not be contiguous with the stage space it inhabits but can be made to extend beyond it. As Bert O. States argues, "what the drama, of all the arts, requires is a way of allowing the stage to contain things outside of it and to make visible things that are invisible" (65). If it is true, as States says, "that the characters explicate the setting in their dialogue as one explicates a painting—at the same time, of course, [that] the setting is explicating character pictorially" (67), it is equally true that characters can create scenery rhetorically, out of nothing but words, that is unseen except in the mind's eye. Indeed, one of the characteristics—almost peculiarities—of Wilson's dozen full-length dramas is how frequently important places, rather than being visually represented, remain noticeably absent from the stage set.

In *Burn This* (1987), Wilson's most recent long play, the central character Anna, herself a dancer, defines choreographers by remarking: "They make the dance. You have bodies, space, sculptural mass, distance relationships; if they're lucky, they might even discover they have something to say" (36). Anna's comment could apply just as easily to the challenge facing the dramatist, who must take people and inanimate objects and position them in space, and move them through space, in such a way that the visual form will carry at least part of the play's meaning. The action of *Burn This* occurs in a *"huge"* white-walled Manhattan loft that features *"an exercise barre on one mirrored wall"* and *"a large framed dance poster"* (2) as the only decoration. The loft was home to Anna, to Larry, a gay advertising designer, and to Robbie, also a dancer like Anna who drowned in a boating accident with his homosexual lover before the play opens and whose sleeping loft is an element of the setting, making the absent present. During the play, Anna's lover Burton, a Hollywood filmwriter who has just returned from Canada where "land [that] looks like the moon, all gouged out," did not prevent his feeling a connection with "something" and inspiring a new story (10), will be displaced from Anna's life by the intruder Pale, Robbie's brother and a rather unlikely Jersey restaurateur.

In this work about dance, however, no dancing—not even practice or warm-up exercises—is ever seen. Though insinuated on the audience by the barre and mirror, dance in any traditional sense is relegated to unseen places (a rehearsal space, a recital hall stage) to indicate the divorce between art and life that Anna undergoes when she suffers the loss of her partner/mentor. When Anna turns choreographer, though, the connection reasserts itself as she draws upon the sexual maneuvering of her relationship with Pale for the subject of her dance, which can only be created once she, like any artist, has the essential "life experience to draw from" (59). As Larry who is present at the recital remarks to Burton, "The dance she's done is Pale and Anna"; his power to render that sculptured movement into words fails, however, since "you might as well try to describe a piece of music" (107). Pale, too, understands "That was me and [Anna] up there" on stage (112), and they seem powerless to stop in life an impulsive and intensely charged affair which may or may not end tragically but that has now been formalized through art.

The title of Wilson's play makes explicit the desired intersection of life and art: Burton advises Anna to "make [her dance] as personal as you can. . . . tell the truth, and then write 'Burn this' on it" (67)—words which Wilson himself etched on each page of his manuscript-in-progress. The playwright's injunction to himself, then, tacitly attests to the artist's frightening power, indeed necessity, to eradicate the line between life and art. Anna's dance is analogous to Wilson's play: both are representations that mysteriously transcend the thing being represented. Because the theatre audience never actually sees the dance performed, they, however, become aware that for them the disjunction between the life and the art remains. For the spectator there will always be an absence, a something unseen, at the very center of any work of art. It is the urge to fill this void which occasions the interpretive act.

No single visual element—unless it be the *"intense"* and blast-like "white-hot sunlight" (3) streaking into the interior of a mission in New Mexico—points to the unseen places in close proximity to this small church that dominate Wilson's *Angels Fall* (1982): a uranium mine where an accident has just occurred; the reactor at Los Alamos; the missile base at White Sands; an already polluted water supply; plus the prospect of a new dump for waste nearby. Turned back by the army from their westward journeys, several travelers arrive at this hallowed "sanctuary" seeking succor and protection, some of them finding renewed direction for their lives. The anomaly of a mission church surrounded by things nuclear and radioactive points to the worship of energy, the fascination with—even for some the attraction of—humankind's power to unleash apocalyptic destruction, as the new god in an age of unfaith.

As is true of one's response to art, faith requires a suspension of disbelief. So when Niles, a professor of art history (ironically hailing from Providence), undergoes a questioning of the increasingly "dogmatic" way in which he plied his vocation, sensing "a disturbance in [his] willful suspension of disbelief that allowed [him] to see what [he] had done for what it was" (35), Father Doherty deems Niles's "crisis of faith" as "right in [his] wheelhouse" (93). Doherty himself seems to be experiencing some disillusionment with his efficacy as priest: when the dozen or so Indians come to mass, he reports, "I mumble sincerely, they mumble sincerely, and they shuffle out. . . . Nothing on their faces, probably nothing on mine. In and out. Shuffle—shuffle" (63). He regards much more religiously his role as father-figure to Don Tabaha, a young Indian doctor ready to choose a lucrative and potentially noteworthy life as a medical researcher over ministering to his people.

Niles becomes the teacher of Doherty, counselling him that it might be his own vanity and selfishness that want Don to remain rather than answer the "call" of his "very special talent for research" (102). For everyone—teacher, artist, priest, doctor, athlete—"is called"; and, as Zappy the professional tennis player says, when one hears the call, "magic . . . happens and you know who you are" (96). This notion of calling or vocation is central to *Angels Fall*, which has to do finally with how we live, "what manner of persons ought [we] to be" when our daily existence is punctuated with "these rehearsals for the end of the world" (94–95). The disembodied voice from a helicopter announcing "'The road is clear'" (98) may recall the biblical injunction to make straight the path. The immediate threat may be ended, but the all-pervasive danger of annihilation in the blast of white light is still present. The pilgrims must leave their temporary sanctuary and go out into perilous places to live and work.

If the New York of *Burn This* and the New Mexico of *Angels Fall* were once places (east and west) of promise, they have now been blighted by urban unease and nuclear dust, and their "artist" inhabitants, that is, all those following their special callings, must now pursue those vocations outside the garden, so to speak. But in *5th of July* (1978), the garden, this time in the midwest and in the process of being restored—albeit offstage—is still an operative image. Several strains apparent in the two later plays appeared earlier in *5th of July*. Shirley, the youngest member of the Talley clan, has vowed to become a writer, even if this means the loneliness of never marrying; she stresses the link between one's life experiences and creativity, proclaiming: "I happen to, am going to be an artist, and an artist has no age and must force himself to see everything, no matter how disgusting and how low!" (27) Her uncle Ken, a double amputee who felt uneasy about coming home alive from the Vietnam War and who has sensed the invisibility imposed upon veterans when others refuse to "look" at them out of shame or guilt, overcomes the temptation to give up teaching and recommits himself to his calling, to his "mission" in life. And her great aunt Sally asserts the need for not succumbing to negativity and despair, opting for the continuation of life in the face of aloneness and death: "I've always had the feeling death wasn't all it was cracked up to be. . . . Matt [Friedman, her late husband] didn't believe in death and I don't either. . . . There's no such thing. It goes on and then it stops. You can't worry about the stopping, you have to worry about the going on" (114).

These characters resist the lure of other places (Shirley of Nashville, Ken of St. Louis, Sally of California) for the pull of the ancestral Talley home, *"a prosperous southern Missouri farmhouse built around 1860"* (5), whose family room and porch function as the setting for the play. Jed, Ken's lover, who has gradually been replanting the property in the manner of a traditional English garden that will take years and years to mature, recently rediscovered a lost rose which will "once again be propagated and grown" at Sissinghurst Castle in England, "the greatest rose garden in the world" (82–83). If necessary, Sally herself will buy the Talley "place" so that it will not go out of the family and to save it from those who would build an airstrip on the property—especially now that she and Jed have spread Matt's ashes in the rose garden. So the remains of this man who thirty years ago had been rejected by Sally's father and brother for his Jewishness and liberal political views will now, as Gene A. Barnett suggests (112), fertilize the soil, just as the commitment of the younger generation to, in Shirley's words, "find your vocation and work like hell at it" (128) will renew the Talley clan. Jed, in his planting of the garden and his caring for and loving the disabled Ken, is the new Adam inspiring a sense of purpose and restoring a feeling of community after the fall. On all planes, the archetypal, the natural, the familial, the individual, the movement in *5th of July* is from death to resurrection and rebirth.

No similar sense of restoration from the diminution that has overtaken the past pervades—or is even the least bit apparent in—Wilson's *The Gingham Dog* (1969); this play about the desolation of an interracial marriage is among the darkest of the dramatist's works, precisely because it shows the breakdown in community without any subsequent rebuilding. The decline of Gloria and Vincent's young marriage into a battlefield of invective where both have lost the capacity for caring can be charted largely through imagery of unseen places described by the characters. Unlike the warm and lived-in Talley home in *5th of July*, the *"compulsively clean"* yet "sterile" apartment painted "refrigerator white" (4–5) in *Dog* is denuded, the emptiness signaling the breakdown of a marriage. Although not nearly as upscale, the flat in which they first lived was affectionately called "the Hutch," since it was the site of spontaneous parties after basketball games on the street outside; that sense of community and camaraderie has vanished, and among the props only *"a deflated basketball"* (33) remains from those days. Vincent describes the room at the "Y" into which he has moved as an insult to the Christians, "a renovated chicken coop" spray-painted "speckledy-spackledy" to look like "pigeon droppings" (50–51); and Gloria recalls that in Harlem where she "lived in misery . . . every apartment is wall-to-wall screaming and filth, every pore of the rotting building you live in is death" (27).

By far the major symbols undergirding Wilson's overt social commentary are the buildings that Vincent designs. Whether an "architect" (that is, an artist) as he claims, or simply a "draftsman" as Gloria insists, she describes his structures in terms that explicitly connect the urban ghettos with the genocide committed in the Nazi concentration camps: "a crematorium . . . uninhabitable brick ovens. Hi-rise slums" with "the physical dimensions of hell" that, rather than "elevate the spirit," only "elevate the floor" (28–29, 32). Although Vincent can try to rationalize away the result by claiming a good intention, Gloria judges that motive vitiated by a heartless system which feeds the rich at the expense of the poor. Not only is there no garden here, but no artist either.

This same contrast between the past and a somehow diminished present (and future) informs two of Wilson's plays that, rather than employ offstage or only talked about places, feature highly symbolic settings. The more straightforward of the two in its handling of theatrical space is *The Hot l Baltimore* (1973), set on Memorial Day in the lobby of a once *"elegant"* railroad hotel now *"scheduled for demolition"* (xi). Similar in atmosphere to the set of a theatre under the wrecking ball created by Boris Aronson for the Stephen Sondheim/Jerome Weidman musical *Follies* (1972), the scene design of *Hot l* calls not for an absolutely realistic rendering but for a somewhat impressionistic *"lobby . . . represented by three areas that rise as the remains of a building already largely demolished: the Front Desk, the lounge, and the stairway"* (xiii). Wilson's extra-dramatic comment that *"The theater, evanescent itself, and for all we do perhaps itself disappearing here, seems the ideal place for the representation of the impermanence of our architecture"* (xiii) clues the reader into change and decay as central motifs of his play.

The work builds not only on the dichotomy between past and present, but on those between country and city, permanence and progress, and, as in Chekhov, beauty and use. The young call girl listens ardently for the whistle of the train that could whisk her away into "the country. That's still beautiful; some of it" (30). The trains, however, have declined, so that "you have to close your eyes on [one]," they never run on time anymore and "they've let the roadbeds go to hell" (30). If the machine in the garden was not at first a destructive intrusion, the symbiotic balance between technology and culture has long since been lost. Jackie, one of the hotel's temporary residents, decries processed foods and environmental pollution and, in her urge to rediscover some connection to rootedness with the earth, wants to go west, though the piece of land she is swindled into buying in Utah is worthless.

At one time, urban areas could be "beautiful," as were hotels such as the Hot l; now all that is changed, not only through neglect but through "the vultures" (129) who honor materialism and greed more than the cultural heritage of the past and the quality of life in the present. The play's symbolic network, then, hardly supports the note of affirmation that Wilson inserts at the end: although the prostitute April Green—whose "symbolic" name indicates a "life-loving and life-giving. . . . earth-mother/mistress" (Barnett 92)—enters into a ritual dance with Jamie, the brother Jackie has left behind, and although her gutsy, non-defeatist attitude that you must have "the convictions of your passions" and that "the important thing is to *move*" (142; 145) might echo other Wilson characters like Niles and Sally, this glorification of the down-but-never-outs of society as "repositories of its wisdom" (Kalem 96) here seems forced and hollow.

On the other hand, closure in *Serenading Louie* (1970; revised version, 1984) grows organically from all the dramaturgical elements, including Wilson's inventive handling of locale. *Louie* crosscuts between the disintegrating marriages of two suburban Chicago couples, for most of the play jumping back and forth from one living room to the other with blackouts in between the scenes. Wilson's ingenious use of theatre space by having *"one set, which should look like a home, not a unit set, . . . serve as the home of first one couple, then the other, with no alterations between"* (9) is by no means just a device or trick designed to save time or money. Rather, it indicates a flattening or sameness about comfortable, upwardly mobile, upper middle class Americans: the tired (the time is fall and autumnal imagery abounds) married lives of Carl and Mary and of Alex and Gabrielle are, except in the particulars, virtually identical. They are an in-between generation, not only in chronological age, but also in looking back to past values as they blunder into the future. Three of the four were students together at Northwestern, and they recall nostalgically a time and a place (the campus before the days of landfill) and relationships that were radically different; as Mary says of Carl in the play's most subtly poignant line, "I love him then now" (68). Diminishment is the leitmotif, expressed most forthrightly by the men: by Carl, who insists that his marriage, now scarred by his wife's affair, "WAS GOOD THEN" (49) and who pleads to "have it back the way it was" (107); and by Alex who, feeling emasculated by his wife's incessant sexual demands, yearns to be eighteen again when things were not all "falling apart" (27).

In the middle of Act Two, Wilson breaks the spatial convention that he established at the outset by jettisoning the blackouts that signaled a shift in locale between living rooms and then bringing the second couple onto the stage before the first has exited. The increased intricacy in the characters' movements and configurations that results from this new handling of spatial conventions emphasizes the interchangeability of these people. Carl, in desperation to preserve what he has already lost, literally kills his wife and daughter and then takes his own life. Yet any possibility for a sustained relationship between Alex and Gabrielle is equally dead, as the final *"sound of her leaving"* (63) underscores.

If the jumping between the two couples and the blackouts that separate the scenes in *Louie* might be seen as reminiscent of certain filmic devices, the handling of space in two other Wilson works depends even more heavily upon cinematic techniques adapted to theatrical use. Critics customarily classify the heavily populated ensemble plays, such as *Hot l* and *Balm in Gilead* (1965), as examples of documentary realism—*cinéma vérité* for the stage rather than the screen. As William Herman remarks in this connection, "The aesthetic reproduction of a milieu is redemptive and salvational" (201). And yet, Wilson is careful to indicate that the cafe in *Gilead*, for example, is only "represented, or suggested, in the center of a wide, high stage" (3), just the first of many ways in which he thwarts audience expectations of a naturalistic setting for this collection of prostitutes and addicts and dealers and hustlers who often talk in overlapping conversations.

Along with several Pirandellian or Brechtian or Wilderean distancing or illusion-breaking devices (such as the fictive play assuming a life of its own, out of control of the participants; direct address to the audience in the form of various songs, jokes, and moralizing or prophetic commentary; characters starting the play over, making metacritical comments about its plot deficiencies, or calling for the intermission; actors lining up across the stage to indicate the facade of a building), there are specific techniques more closely associated with the film medium. Spotlights picking out or highlighting individual characters replicate on the theatre stage the screen close-up. Having *"the people in the café silently lift every stick of furniture, the 'set,' about three feet off the ground and turn the set—as a turntable would—walk the set in a slow circle until it is facing the opposite direction"* (42) creates for the audience the effect of a camera doing a 360–degree pan, resulting in something akin to the shot/reverse shot. Finally, the two repetitions of the scene of Joe's murder at the end create an instant replay of the senseless yet pervasive urban violence directed against someone who got in deeper than he should have. The traditional home away from home for society's misbegotten is no longer a sanctuary.

If the distancing techniques keep the audience at *Gilead* from sentimentalizing these "riffraff, the bums, the petty thieves, the scum, the lost, the desperate, the dispossessed, the cool" (3)—in a way that nothing prevents such romanticizing of the characters in *Hot l*—the devices approximating the cinematic pan and instant replay force the spectators to think about their role as perceivers, to become more aware of the emotional and ethical dynamics of the look and the gaze, to consider their responsibility to move from being onlookers to engagement, to act upon what they see. As Darlene, the all too brief love of Joe's life, says, "aren't we even moving?" (69)

The Rimers of Eldritch (1966), Wilson's tapestry or mural of the meanness, hypocrisy, petty flaws and larger sins of small town middle America, would adapt itself easily to readers' theatre, since it is essentially a play for voices. A stage production of *Rimers* demands absolute fluidity in time and space, as it moves back and forth through three seasons (spring to fall) and from one minimally suggested locale to another. Such shifts are effected largely through lighting, "the most important single scenic element" (4). Because "a scene continues— sometimes two or more in separate areas of the stage si- multaneously—until the lights dim on the scene and focus at- tention elsewhere" (4), the transitions between segments would be similar to the fade outs/fade ins of the cinema. Furthermore, the sometimes simultaneous action with its overlapping dialogue would create a variation on the split screen technique. Finally, late in the play, the threnody of voices coming *"from all over the stage"* with its mournful refrain of loss, "Gone, gone, gone" (57–58), is like a montage sequence in film.

As in *Gilead*, the events leading up to the climactic violation and murder are repeated—a rerunning of the camera—so that the shock of the event in which another of God's harmless creatures is victimized and sacrificed to uphold the mask of respectability is indelibly etched. No one could ever mistake Wilson's Eldritch for Wilder's Grover's Corners: the rime, the hoarfrost, has blighted this garden where innocence has been either lost or corrupted.

Two of Lanford Wilson's short plays, the very early *Madness of Lady Bright* (1964) and the fairly recent *Thymus Vulgaris* (1982), exploit theatre *qua* theatre as an integral part of their meaning. *Lady Bright*, which occurs on a *"stage within a stage"* (75), traces the descent of a middle-aged queen into madness when memories summoned up from the past not only fail any longer to ward off loneliness but, more disastrously for the rememberer, point up the impossibility of the present reality ever measuring up to the past, as it existed either in fact or illusion. Place is handled flexibly (what is one moment an apartment window at the next *"become[s] the doorway to a symphony hall"* [78]); and the mirror before which Leslie applies his make-up and dons his costumes throws back at him the same image the viewers see: he becomes his own audience, watching himself. His mind serves as a theatre of sorts, where he (re)plays scenes from the past; his need, however, for something more than figments or memories, eventuating in his plaintive cry "TAKE ME HOME, SOMEONE!" (91), points to the inability of the imagination—of theatre, of art—to substitute adequately for a lived life and commitment to others.

In *Thymus*, withdrawal from contact with others into a solipsistic world is the characters' sought after end, and this equally entails a rejection of theatre, though for reasons other than illusion's failure to supply what reality cannot. This short work abounds in Pirandellian and Wilderean devices: from the *"raised platform . . . in the center of the stage"* (9) to suggest a house

trailer; to the characters' awareness of the audience and their
requests to the stagehands for adjustments in the lighting and
background music; to the actor playing the Albeesque American
Dream-like Cop who abandons fidelity to character to participate
in exchanges about not "want[ing] to blow [his] big scene" (22).
When the Cop brings the "good tidings of great joy" that the
man wanting to marry Evelyn will be "waiting at Schwab's
drugstore" (22–23) to take her and her mother Ruby off to a life
of relative ease, they choose instead a private existence alone
together. This decision was foretold by Ruby's earlier uneasiness
over being up on stage "with the lights on me and everybody
watchin'" (10)—an implicit desire to withdraw from the
audience's gaze even if it means a movement towards death,
since a dramatic character has no existence except through an
audience. Although Evelyn shies away from closure, believing
"all ends are bad. And we all come to a bad end" (26), she will
accompany Ruby to the ocean (here archetype of death rather
than birth, as is emphasized by the several repetitions of the
word "time" in the last few pages), exiting to a "slow fade out."
In choosing to reject the theatre space where audience and actor
meet and where something other than "bad ends" can be made
to happen, this mother and daughter reject the possibilities for
community with others that theatre art as ritual can inspire,
retreating instead into themselves.

   The potentialities of the theatre are precisely what
Wilson's Pulitzer Prize-winning *Talley's Folly* (1979) is all about.
The play's setting is architect/builder Everett (Whistler) Talley's
"folly," "*a Victorian boathouse constructed of louvers, lattice in
decorative panels, and a good deal of Gothic Revival gingerbread*" (3),
but it might just as well be the theatre itself, for here is a place
where "magic" (31) happens. That the stage space *is* a theatre is
emphasized for the audience by their first vision of the set: "*At
opening: All this is seen in a blank white work light; the artificiality of
the theatrical set quite apparent. The houselights are up*" (3). As Matt
Friedman, liberal Jewish accountant from St. Louis, and Sally
Talley, refugee from the anti-Semitic house up on the hill, meet
in the boathouse on July 4, 1944, the folly becomes a place for
storytelling since, as Matt implies, some tales like that of his own
past are too painful to be told in anything except a story or a fa-

ble. The play opens with Matt as narrator à la Wilder and
Williams, talking conspiratorially with the audience; filling out
the scene by description of what lies beyond; justifying the
chosen scenic conventions ("We could do it on a couple of
folding chairs, but it isn't bare, it isn't bombed out, it's rundown,
and the difference is all the difference" [4]); and establishing for
the audience the type of play they are about to witness: a
"valentine," "a waltz. . . . One-two-three, one-two-three" (6), a
"once upon a time" romance (5) that will run exactly "ninety-
seven minutes . . . without intermission" (3) and that could only
happen in quite this way in the theatre.

Unacceptable to Sally's prejudiced father and brother as a
beau or future husband for her, Matt is exiled to the boathouse
where Sally furtively joins him; much like a Shakespearean
couple loving in opposition to parental authority or prevailing
social mores, they leave the established society for a gar-
den/green world where their love will be tested, obstacles will
be overcome, and goodwill prevail—though not without some
prestidigitation by a providential artist-like force (Matt's refusal
to bring another child into a world torn by nationalistic hatred
dovetails perfectly with Sally's inability to conceive a baby).
They cannot, however, effect an immediate rejuvenation of their
society and so must go elsewhere rather than return to the house,
though in time they will have a positive impact, as seen in the
next generation whose story is told in *5th of July*. Their journey
away from society to reside briefly in a realm of story or tale is
analogous to the audience's temporary respite from reality,
coming into the theatre for entertainment and enlightenment,
and then going back out as a more generous community into the
everyday world. So the boathouse/folly in the garden is the
theatre, and what appears to be somewhat improbable romantic
foolishness can elucidate the truth.

The confessedly autobiographical *Lemon Sky* (1970), generally considered Wilson's *Glass Menagerie*, assuredly is reminiscent of Williams's "portrait of the artist as a young man" in its
memory structure and handling of theatre space; yet—as others
like Barnett (152) have noticed—it is just as surely influenced, in
its use of a skeletal house with *"no walls but indicated divisions of
rooms"* (339) as well as in the dynamics of its father/son conflict,

by Miller's *Death of a Salesman*; Douglas, the dad in *Lemon Sky*, even echoes the tone of Willy Loman's rhetoric when, blind to the reality of the relationship, he exclaims ecstatically of his son, "Hugged me, by God" (368). Wilson's alter ego Alan, twenty-nine years of age in the present when he finally succeeds in "get[ting] . . . down" the story of his seventeenth summer, at times employs his narrative passages metacritically, addressing the audience about his problems with recalcitrant characters, admitting the play's possibly confusing structure, apologizing for "the plot . . . such as it is" (345), or, rather like Sabina in Wilder's *Skin of Our Teeth*, commenting facetiously on the playwright's (that is, Wilson's) skills, as when he glosses "compromise purple" as "the funniest line in the play" (358). Like memory, the theatre is unbounded by time or space and can preserve the "continually young and alive and beautiful," which is part of its "magic" (356). From the beginning, the other characters are all *"on stage"* in this house of memory waiting for the light of recall to make them visible, and Alan shares the narration with them, which accomplishes a closer approach to omniscience than Miller's strategy of being locked much of the time inside the mind of Willy allows.

The emotional coloration of Alan's visit to his father and then his abrupt departure—after the macho Douglas murders any chance for love not only by rejecting the "effeminate" artist/son whose example threatens to make "sissies" of his younger boys but by his sexually abusive inclinations towards one of the foster daughters living with them as well—is underscored by the extensive imagery of place. In search of a father, Alan "left Nebraska to come to the promised land" at the far western "edge of the continent" (362, 364), yet California is no new Eden of infinite possibilities. Under the peculiar lemon sky, "the color green does not occur in California naturally"; rather than "that bright eye-breaking, bright-sun-shining-through-oak-and-maple-and-elm-unto-bright-green-ferns-and-grass-green," the dominant hues are "the colors of perpetually early autumn: umber, amber, olive, sienna, ocher, orange: acres and acres of mustard and sage" (356–57). Relationships that lack care and concern are as sterile as the fallen garden that Alan escapes, although his final cry for "LIGHTS!" (368) will not be able to erase from his mind what he flees from in space.

Virtually the last line in *Talley & Son* (1985; revised version of *A Tale Told* [1980]), which is set in the ancestral home on the same day (July 4, 1944) as the action in *Talley's Folly* occurs, reports that "The garden's pretty bad" (114). The speaker, Timmy, exemplifies yet another of Wilson's variations in the handling of his narrators, since Timmy has been killed in the Pacific just before the play opens. The presence of this "ghost" on stage, acknowledged only by his Aunt Lottie who has been engineering the relationship of her niece Sally and Matt Friedman behind the scenes, is in ironic contrast to the absolutely realistic stage setting, with no mitigating sense of the play as existing in the mind of Timmy or being filtered through his eyes. Without reducing war's horror ("splatted is more like" what happened when he was hit [85]), Timmy attempts to de-sentimentalize and de-heroicize it, claiming that "somebody has got to take this thing lightly" (86), since attitudes like his father Eldon's about the glory of getting the enemy before one dies are responsible for perpetuating war and killing off society's sons. Civic-minded and philanthropic Talleys like Everett who gave land to the city for a park have been replaced by those petty and materialistic ones who run off people of different backgrounds and gouge the government on war supplies. As Timmy exits, he remarks that those who won the war for America will not "recognize" her when they come home, since "the country's changed so much" (115). That such change is for the worse remains unsaid, but Timmy is yet another of Wilson's innocents to whom life in an earthly garden is denied in order to prove something for an increasingly cutthroat society.

Although presenting a dead narrator who converses with a sympathetic character, as Wilson does in *Talley & Son*, may be novel, the dramatist's most sophisticated handling of narrative technique and of theatrical space, as well as the most complex treatment of his recurrent themes, appears in *The Mound Builders* (1975). The action essentially occurs in the *"mind's eye"* (4) of Professor August Howe as he recalls an archaeological dig of the preceding summer, and so Wilson's dramaturgy here approximates even more closely that of Williams in *Menagerie* than *Lemon Sky* had. Since *"the back wall serves as a screen onto which are back-projected slides from the previous summer"* (3), the playing area might be seen as August's mind, with the pictures as promptings to his memory; yet if Williams employed a similar device not only to replicate how the mind functions through association but in a Brechtian fashion to decrease mawkish sentimentalism, Wilson does not exploit the technique for emotional distancing.

The slides picture the artifacts of the Temple Mound People, remaining "evidence of . . . craft, of a subtle skill and imagination, of . . . care and conscientiousness" (107) now threatened by developers bent on turning the area into a vacation resort. So the conflict is between preservation of a culture's heritage, on the one hand, and commercial progress and destruction on the other; between the past age of poetry—primitive art whose "truth is in dreams and nightmares" (54)—and the present age of facts—as represented in photography and the "compulsive compilers. . . . digging . . . evidence, piecing together shards, fragments, sherds" (102) as if these could provide some final answer. The scientists stand poised between commercial promoter and creative artist, capable of bending either way. When the young scientist Dan holds the death mask from the burial mound of the god-king *"up to his face, and almost inadvertently it stays in place"* (121), it is perhaps an act of hubris revealing his lack of appropriate awe for the primitive culture and leading to his death by the sexually jealous and money-crazed Chad.

The artist in this midwestern garden that is unearthed only to be forever destroyed by the encroaching waters is August's sister Delia. The author of one successful novel, she has been unable to summon up from "the cold depths of some uncharted secret currents" into "the light some undiscovered color" (104) that would have been a second book. The source of her creative block was the death of her father and separation from what might be seen as the garden of the paternal home, "the whole place filled with sunlight. Especially in the winter" (105). If the heritage of the past—the childhood home, the ancient burial mounds—serves as a creative spur to the artist, then once these garden places are lost or defiled, judged as worthless or anachronistic, the imagination atrophies, and all that remains are "syllables, not sense" (56).

In the history of drama, from the time of the Greek ampitheatre open to the heavenly abode of the gods to the closed, insular drawing room of the bourgeois well-made play with its stratified manners and mores, there has been a link between theatre space and ideology. As an undergraduate, Wilson majored in art history, which taught him "what we have done, what our heritage was, and what we are doing to it" (quoted in Busby 20) and must undoubtedly have awakened him also to spatial dynamics and imagery of place. Throughout the history of art and literature, one of the central archetypal images has been that of the garden. Unfallen gardens are, however, difficult to come by in Wilson's world. In many of his plays—*The Gingham Dog, Serenading Louie, Balm in Gilead, The Rimers of Eldritch, The Mound Builders*—the garden has receded or is in process of disappearing, destroyed either by violence or by a materialistic progress that cares not for the culture of the past; in some—such as *The Hot l Baltimore*—it remains as only a fading memory or—as in *Lemon Sky*—as a now sterile place from which the writer/artist must flee. If fortuitously discovered, the garden can be a conducive space for the artist's creative energies, as Delia's paternal home in *Builders* was for her, or as those other gardens where imagination can grow—that is, theatres—prove to be for such characters as Anna in *Burn This* or Matt and Sally in *Talley's Folly*.

One of the most thematically charged spaces in Wilson's entire canon is the mission church setting in *Angels Fall*, a sanctuary or an oasis in the midst of a desert place whose inherent beauty has been threatened by contemporary man's idolization of technological progress at the expense of human values. The space around the mission is the nuclear garden of post-Hiroshima man in which everyone must become an artist, each by embracing his or her vocation or calling, to survive. If it is humankind's fate now to inhabit that "garden," Wilson neither forgets nor denies that another one—Jed's new Eden in *5th of July*—beckons those with the vision and courage to plant and nurture it. For Wilson, despite the dark realities that his plays chart, still clings, as Mark Busby notes, to "the pastoral ideal" that through a commitment to "work and art or artifice" (15) human beings in concert with one another, joined in a community, can have an ameliorative and restorative effect.

REFERENCES

Barnett, Gene A. *Lanford Wilson*. Boston: G. K. Hall, 1987.

Busby, Mark. *Lanford Wilson* (Western Writers Series 81). Boise, ID: Boise State Univ., 1987.

Herman, William. *Understanding Contemporary American Drama*. Columbia: U of South Carolina P, 1987.

Inge, William. "Writing for Films." Manuscript Collection, Independence Community College, Kansas.

Kalem, T. E. "Transient Souls." *Time* 23 April 1973: 96.

States, Bert O. *Great Reckonings in Little Rooms: On the Phenomenology of Theatre*. Berkeley: U of California P, 1985.

Wilson, Lanford. *Angels Fall*. New York: Hill and Wang, 1983.

——. *Balm in Gilead and Other Plays*. New York: Hill and Wang, 1965.

——. *Burn This*. New York: Hill and Wang, 1987.

——. *5th of July*. New York: Hill and Wang, 1978.

——. *The Gingham Dog*. New York: Dramatists Play Service, 1969.

——. *The Hot l Baltimore*. New York: Hill and Wang, 1973.

——. *Lemon Sky*, in *Best American Plays*. 7th Series 1967–73. Ed. Clive Barnes. New York: Crown, 1975. 337–68.

——. "The Madness of Lady Bright," in *Rimers*, 73–91.

——. *The Mound Builders*. New York: Hill and Wang, 1976.

——. *The Rimers of Eldritch and Other Plays*. New York: Hill and Wang, 1967.

——. *Serenading Louie*. New York: Hill and Wang, 1984 (revised).

——. *Talley & Son*. New York: Hill and Wang, 1986.

——. *Talley's Folly*. New York: Hill and Wang, 1979.

——. "Thymus Vulgaris." *The Best Short Plays 1982–1983*. Ed. Ramon Delgado. Garden City, NY: Doubleday, 1983. 3–26.

The Playwright Continues: Lanford Wilson and the Counter Culture

Barry B. Witham

Two theatrical moments inspired this essay and inform its design. The first was the Living Theatre Company in 1968 standing in front of and among a slightly hostile audience reciting, individually and collectively, the words on a dollar bill. The second, a few years later, was an actor playing the part of Jack Argue in John Guare's *Muzeeka* confronting a more docile but still expectant audience and singing to them the words on a penny. The point here is not deflation but rather that the avant-garde, collective theatre movement of the 1960's and 1970's was to a large extent co-opted by the very figure whom they threatened for a time to replace: the playwright. And Lanford Wilson was one of the writers involved in that transaction.

Richard Schechner has written that his generation "destroyed the idea that the playwright is the only, or main, originator of a theatrical event" (16). Indeed for Schechner and many of his contemporaries the playwright was the "absentee landlord" in the theatre of the late 1960's and early 1970's. While this kind of generalization tends to neglect or obscure the ongoing activities at places like Caffe Cino or La Mama, Schechner's point is certainly well taken. Playwrights were under attack not just because of the renewed interest in actor improvisation and collective creation, but because they represented a conventional notion of theatre that was increasingly at odds with the counter culture.

By 1970, for instance, critic and playwright Sam Smiley announced that "modern drama is dead," and went on to explain that

> . . . the kind of theatre conceived by Eugene O'Neill, Maxwell Anderson or Arthur Miller; directed by Guthrie McClintic, Harold Clurman or Elia Kazan; designed by Robert Edmond Jones, Mordecai Gorelik or Jo Mielziner; and performed by Alfred Lunt, Luther Adler or Marlon Brando—that sort of modernism, although admirable in its struggle for verisimilitude, belongs strictly to history . . . some of the most exciting work and pertinent drama of our society now comes from improvisational groups. (36)

There were still "well-made" plays, of course, throughout the 1960's and an ongoing Broadway season which frequently seemed oblivious to the alternative theatre that was flourishing in churches, cafés, streets and fields. But the notion that a theatrical event could be created through group improvisation without the necessity of a prepared script was one of the most invigorating and creative ideas of the period.

A decade later, however, the playwrights were back, re-claiming their ground with a vengeance. Sam Shepard abandoned much of the surrealism of his earlier work and wrote three plays about the American family. David Rabe did the same for Vietnam. Michael Weller wrote three more about the counter culture while others, no longer comfortable with individual plays, experimented with entire dramatic trilogies. Preston Jones detailed life in rural Texas while Israel Horovitz's *The Alfred Trilogy* transported *The Oresteia* to Wakefield, Massachusetts. John Guare and Lanford Wilson threatened to explode even the boundaries of dramatic trilogies into whole sagas about the Lydie Breeze clan or the Missouri Talleys. The "absentee landlord" had not only returned but had re-established a dominant position in the theatrical scene.

How could this have happened so quickly? There are a number of important issues here but certainly one of the most fascinating is the way that writers were able to adapt the ideas and techniques of the alternative theatre movement and thus prosper in a theatre that had threatened to banish them. In *American Alternative Theatre*, Ted Shank argues that during this period

> An autonomous method of creation became the typical means of making new plays. Instead of the two-process method of the conventional theatre—a playwright writing a script in isolation and other artists staging it—the autonomous method involves a single process wherein the same artists develop the work from conception to finished performance. (3)

This is a difficult landscape to negotiate because the process of collaboration varied frequently from group to group as did sometimes the definition of improvisation. I recall Jean-Claude van Itallie, at a Conference on the Open Theatre at Kent State University in December 1983, refuting a scholar's contention about group improvisation in *Interview* by announcing that he sat at home and wrote the scene by himself.

What I am suggesting here, in response to Shank's observation, is that there was at least a third dynamic at work in this very complex genealogy whereby playwrights assimilated the techniques of the group creation and produced scripts which had the feel of collective creation but which were crafted by a writer. And this skill, in part, paves the way for a return to the semi-isolation of the two-process method. In the following pages, I examine this notion paying specific attention to some of Lanford Wilson's early works.

When the traditional playwright was kicked out of some theatres in the 1960's, with what was he/she replaced? This is not the place to construct a "poetics" of the counter culture, but a few generalizations are important for clarity. The Becks, Chaikin, Schechner and others wanted to sweep the American theatre clean of "well-made" plays which comfortably explained the puzzling events of human existence and forced the theatre into an embrace of the visceral, the irrational and the spontaneous. They wanted to revitalize the theatrical experience by redefining both the audience-actor relationship and the purpose of theatre in our society. In their rejection of an Aristotle-Stanislavski model, however, they clearly offered not chaos, but another model.

How can we characterize this model? First, there seems to have been a rather widespread abandonment of traditional narrative. The story was not nearly as important as a structure which sought its unity or organization from other ingredients. The separate events of the Becks' *Mysteries and Smaller Pieces* (1967), for example, coalesced around notions of lifestyle and politics rather than story and even in cases where story was still a discernable thread (*Dionysus in 69, Frankenstein*), the emphasis was on image-making in particular scenes or actor interaction with the text. Meditation was a fashionable phrase in much of the counter culture and the dramaturgy of a number of theatrical pieces was inspired by meditations on such issues as violence, death or fame rather than by formal narrativity.

Second, there was a pronounced shift away from the idea of dramatic or literary imagery to the concept of visual/aural or theatrical imagery. This was partially inspired by the newly acquired familiarity with Artaud and notions of "Cruelty" as well as the French Absurdists. The theatrical image became, in a sense, the building block for much of the avant-garde and the plays or "pieces" of this period abound in unique and striking images: the plague sequence in *Mysteries* with its rigid actors stacked like cords of wood and empty shoes neatly paired along the proscenium line; the red strips of tape which signify the rising flames in Bread and Puppet's *Fire* (1965); the Bread and Cake sequence in *Tom Paine* (1968); the monster coming to life in *Frankenstein* (1968); and the gruesome embalmings of *Terminal* (1969). Many theatrical pieces were built by improvising such powerful images around central ideas or motifs. The successful images were then rehearsed, adding connective links as needed. *The Serpent* (1967), *Commune* (1970) and the Becks' *Antigone* (1968) and a number of others were created in this manner.

Third and certainly concomitant with the first two was a view of acting which rejected ideas about orderly explications of human behavior—and psychological "truths"—and replaced them with an improvisational attack which, in the broadest sense, encouraged multiple transformations from one moment to another. The playing of many characters and frequently not "hiding" behind any of them often matched the impressionist structuring of the plays. Examples of this are abundant, most obviously in the Open Theatre's "transformational" style and in such free-flowing events as *Paradise Now* and *Dionysus in 69* where performers alternate between themselves and characters. In addition there was a questioning of much traditional acting theory with its stress on "personality." In fact, character—that hallowed concept of most Stanislavski-based acting—was now defined by some as "bundles of actions" and was being redefined in light of contemporary psychology, sensitivity exercises and Spolin-induced games.

Fourth, there was a certain abandonment, if not rejection, of much conventional scenic practice. While a lot of the theoretical base came from Grotowski's concept of a "poor" theatre, in practical terms there was a move towards bare stages, simplified technical demands and scenic design which was often environmental, found and inventive. There was, as always, some discrepancy between the ideal and the actual—costumes might be simple street clothes or elaborately constructed puppets, and lighting effects were often striking and theatrical—but platforms, scaffolding, empty boxes and benches frequently constituted the design of many plays. Moreover, this rejection of the "theatre of the machine" can also be seen in the emerging popularity of street theatre, productions in gyms, churches, basements and open fields.

And, finally, there was a feeling among many of the groups that the theatrical event should somehow draw from, if not participate in, ritualistic and/or communal experiences. There was a great deal of concern about myths and celebrations, sometimes in awkward or silly ways, but often in the context of making the theatre a more meaningful experience, striking the audience or participants with an immediacy and impact muted by traditional drama. Bread and Puppet asked us to break bread in communion; the Becks sought the magical power of reinventing classical tragedy; and the Open Theatre asked us to contemplate the fundamental ritual of death that we all share. Some took up the Artaudian challenge of finding new myths for our times and audiences relived the Kennedy assassination as well as the rise and fall of James Dean, Marilyn Monroe, Charles Manson and a variety of versions of the American Dream.

There are other elements of the alternative theatre that could be examined—such as the largely New Left stance of many of the groups—but these should be sufficient to focus the material and allow an investigation of the impact of this movement on Lanford Wilson and others who were coming to the theatre at a turbulent time. Margaret Croyden believes that the unifying characteristic of the entire non-literary outburst was a "departure from the System's concept of theatre" (xxi). And she is right to remind us that there was an entire cultural revolution in progress which questioned not only the origins of authority but the very nature of the written and spoken word as sources of truth. Playwrights, of course, were aware of the swirling debates and changing times. After all, they were part of a larger milieu where the notions of creation and performance were no longer as clearly defined as they had once been. In rock music, for example, the Beatles (icons for much of the alternative culture) had ceased performing other composers' songs and were now creating their own material. And the enormous publicity surrounding the Happenings had further blurred the distinctions between those who wrote the material and those who "performed" it. Small wonder that John Guare discovered that the logic and good construction taught at Yale would no longer serve him in New York (Hewes 48) or that Sam Shepard would later observe about this whole period:

> The movement toward a collective ensemble type of theatre came on strongest when the Living Theatre barnstormed the country after their exile in Europe. They copped everybody's mind with their incredible energy and sense of immediate desperation. Nobody was left untouched, least of all the playwright. For some playwrights it had a defeating effect. They felt impotent and saw the Living as a true, radical, revolutionary force and their own efforts to write plays

> seemed futile and self-indulgent in the face of that.
> For other playwrights it opened up their own possi-
> bilities and they started experimenting with groups
> and even trying their hand at directing or acting. . . .
> After a while you find out that you're not the Living
> Theatre but something else, something that's equally
> valuable in its own right. (26–27)

Confronted with a theatre that embraced and prized a "non-literary" model, writers played on the landscape of this new world
with a variety of techniques and experiments.

One of the most striking experiments in Lanford Wilson's
work is a one-act that he wrote in 1972 called *The Family Continues*. Dedicated to the Circle company and their director
Marshall Mason, *Family* is according to Wilson an "exercise in
swift characterization and ensemble co-operation" (*Great Nebula*
30). It is a ritualized account of the life of "Steve" who goes
through various stages from birth to death accomplishing little.
He attends school, goes AWOL from the Army, works in a gas
station, kills a young boy in an automobile accident, marries a
girl over her parent's objection, fathers a son and, finally, dies.
The events are mostly ordinary, even banal at times, as Steve
tries to adjust to a life which is swiftly passing him by. School,
dating, marrying and failing are the ingredients of the narrative,
but the story line is far less interesting than the structural devices
and performance conventions which give the piece a feeling of
spontaneity and communal improvisation.

The play is written for a company of eight and its ensemble demands, where the actors play a variety of roles, recall the
transformational quality of a lot of the improvisational work of
the 1960's. Wilson specifies in the introduction to the text that
with the exception of Steve—and perhaps the Narrator—the
twenty-six roles should be divided among the actors with some
playing five or more. In addition many of the parts are written to
be spoken at the same time with different voices overlapping. In
production, Wilson notes, they found that when two people
spoke simultaneously they had a tendency to raise their voices
but when speaking naturally both could be heard and

understood. (I recall the Open Theatre doing a warm-up exercise where you could observe this same phenomenon.)

This transformational quality is underscored by the disruption of the traditional linear flow. Past and present are constantly interwoven and various events from each phase of Steve's life are repeated at appropriate times in the text. Critical moments like the time he insulted a customer at the gas station or stole a car at school are replayed throughout as the performers transform both their characters and their "time." This impressionistic structure, which Wilson had already experimented with in *The Rimers of Eldritch*, gives the play a wonderful theatrical presence and allows for the kind of acting that was popular in so many of the off-off-Broadway companies.

The improvisational quality of *The Family Continues* is also underscored by Wilson's careful directions about the physical playing of the piece. "The text is printed here with minimal stage directions to encourage directors and actors to work as unfettered as possible: any decisive activity based on observed behavior is permissible." Wilson further specifies that there should be no furniture or props and that the performers should take as many liberties with the text as they wanted: "It is not at all necessary, or even intended, for all words to be heard" (*Great Nebula* 30). The effect here is a kind of joyous spontaneity which places a considerable emphasis on "play" and imaginative abandon. Yet the script itself is carefully prepared in terms of the placement of lines and the choral effects. When I spoke recently to Trish Hawkins who was a member of the revival cast in October 1972 (five months after the premiere), she confirmed this impression: "We had a good deal of leeway in terms of certain kinds of business, but we also had to listen very closely so that we could get the lines in the places they needed to be."

Wilson also describes the actor's creation of the physical imagery of the car accident recalling the image making and physical activity which was so prevalent in the "alternative theatre." In the play there are numerous echoes of an incident in high school where Steve stole a car and accidentally killed a young boy. Wilson suggests that in performance the actors created the car with their bodies and then Steve "rode" in it as it sent the boy hurtling through the air. Apparently the moment was very effective and Wilson recalls that "the actor playing the kid went flying through the air landing splat! on the floor" (*Great Nebula* 30). In other plays, as we shall see, he repeats these strong theatrical images stressing their importance as building blocks in the structure of the pieces.

Finally, the whole notion of ritual is continually reinforced by the play's reenactment of the human journey from birth to death. The audience accompanies Steve through the various stages of recognizable human (actually male, middle-class) behavior climaxing in the birth of his son and his own calling to death. Like Everyman, Steve is taken unaware and the rush to hold off the inevitable, while he seeks some relief from his guilt over the death of the boy, forms the dramatic basis for the last few moments of the play. This sense of ritual is also reinforced by the circular structure in which we see the son undergoing an almost identical process of growing up, and by the title of the piece which suggests that life will continue with its attendant human rites and rituals.

Wilson never wrote anything as clearly a product of the late 1960's as *The Family Continues* but his early work continually exhibits the features of the counter culture and it is intriguing to examine the resonances of that aesthetic in his plays. A great deal has been written about the influence of the French Absurdist theatre on Wilson and I am not suggesting that that is not accurate but there were other forces which are also significant. Like Guare and Shepard, Wilson co-opts much of the improvisational theatre with a masterful writer's eye. The transformational playing in *Wandering* (1966), for example, and the dramaturgy of *Untitled Play* (1967) are intriguing in this regard but of his better known works probably *Balm in Gilead* (1965) is the most revealing.

Like *The Family Continues*, *Balm* is written with careful attention to creating a sense of improvisational spontaneity. Conversations are repeated, overlap and run simultaneously. There is an ebb and flow of action in which scenes materialize and disappear rather than a traditional plot. Even though the actors only perform a single "character," there is a real sense of company creation in the apparently random structure of the events. And yet the dialogue and stage directions are precise and carefully scripted. Wilson suggests places where actors may "improvise" nightly but the free flowing spontaneity and sense of improvised language and behavior is only achieved after a very rigorous writing/rehearsal process.

What is even more striking about *Balm*, however, and what links it to the experimentation of "off-off-Broadway" is the way that Wilson uses the actors' bodies as physical elements of the production, not just as their own presence but *literally* as sculpting to create an environment in the same way that the Living Theatre and other groups created theatrical imagery. The most striking example of this process is in Act One when Joe and Darlene leave the café and walk to her room. Wilson specifies in the stage direction how this is accomplished:

> *Dim almost out on café interior. Patrons inside walk to the front of the café and stand in a line across the stage, back to the audience, forming a "wall." There is a space about four feet wide at the center of the wall, forming a doorway. JOE and DARLENE walk down the wall slowly.* (*Balm* 33)

After entering the *"door"* to her apartment it *"closes"* behind them and a moment later the *"wall"* disperses showing us the interior of Darlene's room. This imaginative, non-realistic use of the actors to create theatrical imagery is a hallmark of a lot of improvisational theatre and recalls a variety of exciting moments from that period such as the creation of the monster in *Frankenstein* or the various body tableaus in *Mysteries and Smaller Pieces* and *Paradise Now*.

This disruption of realistic conventions is also apparent in other places where Wilson not only creates a startling image but repeats the image—in the manner of an instant replay—to heighten and maximize its effect. In Act Two, at the climactic moment of Joe's death he blends the horror of a knife assault with the mock horror of a children's Halloween party in a stunning moment. As a spotlight tightens on the stranger stabbing Joe underhand in the heart, the Halloween costumed children *"run out with the paper sacks flapping over their heads. They are screaming and yelling joyously. . . . They circle around the café, and enter from the back and run through again"* (*Balm* 68). This entire sequence is then repeated twice as the realistic time frame of the dramatic events is violently skewed recalling a number of similar episodes in the plays of the 1960's such as the Kennedy assassination sequence in *The Serpent*.

These repeated moments also give the play a sense of ritual that is reinforced by the constant street life environment. Unlike most of Wilson's rural pieces, *Balm* captures the very essence of New York City with its pushers, pimps and prostitutes. Each day they hang out in the same places, pursue their "tricks" with the same urban jargon and play the power games that give meaning to their lives. Wilson's notes for the actors are explicit in detailing the authenticity of these daily rituals such as his insistence that everyone looks up to check out any newcomer to the café or his repeated use of circular blocking and movement patterns to suggest repetition. Part of the theatrical effectiveness of the play is its authentic depiction of these dozens of vividly re-enacted rituals.

Balm also has numerous echoes of the "poor" theatre in the way that Wilson undermines the conventions of the realistic stage and uses his actors to change the settings in full view of the audience. Although the play relies upon more than the minimalist conventions of *The Family Continues*—or even *Rimers* for that matter—the benches of the *"café"* are positioned by the performers and the whole "set" is turned to allow a different viewing angle by the audience. These conventions—along with the creation of Darlene's room—are again resonant of theatrical conventions which were decidedly counter culture.

The "improvisational" feeling of *Balm* is also evident in the continually overlapping dialogue, the apparent randomness of the entrances and exits, the frequent simultaneous playing and the direct address to the audience, which recalls the actors in the improvisational theatre speaking "outside" their roles. Wilson specifies when simultaneous events are required or when the dialogue is to be overlapped, thereby creating a sense of spontaneity and randomness which tends to obscure the narrative structure of the play. Of course there is the story of Joe and Darlene which functions as a rudimentary kind of plot but the design of the play is much closer to a collage with different threads or patterns emerging from the mosaic. This structure, which Wilson later employs to wonderful effect in *Rimers of Eldritch,* is reminiscent of a lot of the improvisational theatre of the 1960's and again exhibits his skill in appropriating and manipulating the traditions of "collective creation."

Rimers, which was written and performed two years later, is in many ways more traditional than *Balm* but it too is shaped by similar aesthetic notions. There is still the same kind of mosaic quality about the events, although a story line about Skelly's murder eventually emerges. In this sense the play is less random and more accessible as a theatre piece. But many of the features discussed above are evident in *Rimers.* The simultaneous action and overlapping dialogue suggest the same kind of spontaneity as in *Balm* and recall a great many of the improvisational pieces of the period. And while the transformational playing is not identical to Wilson's other early pieces—as in *Balm* the actors mostly play just one identifiable character—there is a clear feeling of the company transforming the space from one place to another. See, for example, the stage direction where Wilson indicates that *"The town becomes alive everywhere. . . . the effect should be of the entire cast moving in a deliberate direction with lines coming in sequence from all over the stage"* (*Rimers* 14–15).

But most striking again is Wilson's use of people as scenery and the device of repeating striking theatrical images. Here, however, instead of actors as "walls" they double as "trees." In Act Two Robert and Eva wander in the forest as a prelude to their sexual encounter and Skelly's death. The stage direction reads: *"The people have wandered to random, scattered positions about the stage. They stand still and isolated, ROBERT and EVA moving about them as though walking through the woods"* (*Rimers* 50). A few moments later Wilson repeats the actions with the exact dialogue recalling the stabbing moment in *Balm.* These techniques are a powerful connection to Wilson's off-off-Broadway apprenticeship. As his work became more linear and narrative bound, these touches of the counter culture diminish but in *Rimers* they persist like traces of a dramaturgy nurtured in another time.

Rimers is also evocative of the "poor theatre" with its platforms and railings which can transform to specific locales such as the court, the street, the store and the church. I don't mean to suggest that this kind of staging is unique to Wilson—Shakespeare is an obvious forerunner!—rather that it echoes a fascination with a kind of "poor theatre" that was popular in many of the counter culture productions. There are numerous examples of it off-off-Broadway and the fascination with open staging can also be seen in a lot of the scripted work of Shepard, Guare and others.

Finally, *Rimers* has clear traces of Wilson's fascination with ritual and, like *The Family Continues* and others, the play is informed by his sense of the daily routines of small town life. The loves, births and deaths are richly recorded in a lot of Wilson's plays and *Rimers* participates with its evocations of the church choir, front porch gossip, teen romance and growing old. Of course, there is a dark side in *Rimers* and that too contributes to the mosaic, giving the play a sense of ritual participation in human existence.

There are other places in Wilson's work where we can see the traces of the counter culture—such as the transformational chorus characters in *The Madness of Lady Bright* or the use of bare stage and multiple voices in *This is the Rill Speaking*—but the traces diminish as his plays become increasingly situated in narrative and traditional story. *Talley's Folly*, for example, is a remarkably crafted piece of theatrical writing, so well-crafted in fact that Matt Friedman can assure us that it will run only ninety-seven minutes and that it will be a waltz. And it does and is. And *5th of July* is so rooted in notions of "realism" and acting as replicating human behavior that theatregoers may as well be watching Sidney Howard. Although both plays bear the stamp of Wilson's remarkable gifts, they are distinctly distant from some of his earlier dramaturgy. It is important in viewing them, however, not to see them as distinct but rather as products of an ongoing American theatre that was at war with itself in the late 1960's. The good *writers*—the ones who wouldn't be discouraged—persisted and grew with their theatre. If by co-opting a lot of the radical agenda they found their way back to rather conventional, formal structures, it is perhaps no different from a society that lurched from the irrationality of the 1968 Democratic Convention to the recent Republican "coronations" of the Reagan-Bush years. Nor is it very different from the countless traditional careers pursued by the children of radical parents who sought the good life in communes from Provincetown to Haight-Ashbury.

In his book on Lanford Wilson, Gene A. Barnett says of *The Family Continues*, "It also seems likely that a theatre piece like Richard Schechner's *Dionysus in 69* and the work of the Living Theatre, so popular in the late 1960's, left their mark on this little round" (67). This is an acute observation and one which needs to be stressed. But, as I have argued in this paper, that influence is not limited to the "little round" but rather is resonant in much of Wilson's early dramaturgy, as well as in the work of John Guare, Sam Shepard, Irene Fornes and others. Seeing these plays in the context of a revolutionary time not only enriches them but reminds us how some writers reclaimed their voices in an American theatre that often seemed bent on silencing them.

REFERENCES

Barnett, Gene A. *Lanford Wilson*. Boston: G. K. Hall, 1987.

Croyden, Margaret. *Lunatics, Lovers and Poets*. New York: McGraw-Hill, 1974.

Hewes, Henry. "The Playwright as Voyager." *Saturday Review* 20 November 1973: 48.

Schechner, Richard. "The Decline and Fall of the American Avant-Garde." *Performing Arts Journal* 15, 3 (1981): 9–19.

Shank, Theodore. *American Alternative Theatre*. New York: Grove, 1982.

Shepard, Sam, et al. "Symposium on Playwriting in America." *Yale/Theatre* 4, 1 (1973): 8–27.

Smiley, Sam. "Actor Creativity." *Players* 46, 1 (1970): 36–40.

Wilson, Lanford. *Balm in Gilead and Other Plays*. New York: Hill and Wang, 1965.

———. *The Great Nebula in Orion and Three Other Plays*. New York: Dramatists Play Service, 1973.

———. *The Rimers of Eldritch and Other Plays*. New York: Hill and
Wang, 1967.

Charlotte's Daughters: Changing Gender Roles and Family Structures in Lanford Wilson

James J. Martine

There is no inconsistency in the fact that serious and important writers can be placed in a literary tradition while the contribution of their artistic originality is applauded. It is possible to appreciate Lanford Wilson's literary affinity to Luigi Pirandello, Thornton Wilder, Tennessee Williams and Arthur Miller in matters of form; his relation thematically to William Faulkner and John Steinbeck as a confirmed humanist; an added indebtedness to Williams; and acknowledge concerns leading eventually back to Henrik Ibsen.

Audiences of several of Wilson's plays recognize, for example, the influence of the more celebrated playwrights in his use of the engaged narrator—some more engaged, or engaging, than others: Alan in *Lemon Sky*; Matt Friedman of *Talley's Folly*; and Timmy Talley in *Talley & Son* who is a synthesis of both the Stage Manager and Emily from *Our Town* (1938) which was on stage when Wilson was one year old. An examination of the autobiographical aspects of *Lemon Sky*, and perhaps other Wilson plays, must await another and different essay. The play's theatrical techniques, however, in which characters move down halls and into rooms yet at other times cut across the entire stage paying no heed to room "divisions" are reminiscent of *Six Characters in Search of an Author* (1921). If the temptation is to see in Wilson's engaged narrator a character like Alfieri in Miller's *A*

View from the Bridge (1955), one is better advised, in an attempt to understand the perspective of *Lemon Sky*, to recall Williams's *The Glass Menagerie* (1945) in which the play is Tom Wingfield's memory or that Miller's approach in *Death of a Salesman* (1949) may be summed up in the play's draft title "The Inside of His Head." *Lemon Sky* is such a memory play.

None of this is to suggest that Wilson's work is derivative. It is, for the most part, not. His relationship to other world-celebrated writers properly places him in a context of themes and techniques that have attracted other first-rate minds. In the end, perhaps, the bromide remains valid: an author does not choose his topics, they choose him. This may apply to Lanford Wilson, and all of us. Yet it is not comparisons here which are most interesting, but contrasts. As Wilson is of the great modern dramatic traditions, he is unique. If he has taken from the pool of themes and techniques, he has contributed to it in that his major work may be seen as a watershed in its engagement of the applicability of age-old questions of the heart and mind to provide a record of new challenges and changing roles, especially for modern women. It may be that, as reflected in Wilson's plays, people fundamentally have not changed much in their needs and aspirations, but their relationships and roles have changed. Since World War II, the ways we relate to one another in a family—and out—have changed, and the role of women especially has evolved precipitously.

Lemon Sky (1970) is one man's recollections of his search for a functioning traditional family. This play concerns an especially contemporary American family: a second wife; two "wards of the state" who are living with a family which takes their $60 per month; two young stepbrothers of Alan, an engaged narrator; and Douglas, a loathsome, repellent and repulsive father figure. Alan may conclude that "we're all of us selfish" (52), but none are quite so selfish as Douglas or Ronnie, his wife, who puts up with Douglas's philandering and wandering eye (and hands) because "I have two kids to think about" (57). Alan is not one of those kids. He is the son of Douglas but he is not Ronnie's son. Alan recalls having come to California in his need for a functioning family unit and discovering there really isn't one.

His search for a father turns up a lecher. There's no further west to go, young man. America ends in California.

A brief examination of the purposes of the techniques used in the play may be informative. Characters cross boundary lines and they cross "times" as well. They can converse of the past as in the present. There is a double sense of time which suggests that Alan, the engaged narrator, does more than provide exposition, but that he has the entire play, like Willy Loman, inside his head. So Alan continually cries out for what once was and is gone. As he walks off at the play's final curtain, Alan cries out, "LIGHTS!," yet everyone in the play follows after him *"before Alan can escape them"* (68)—which are the play's final words. Thus the repetition of the lines which open the play in the play's concluding scene suggests the entire play is to be seen as having taken place in Alan's mind:

> DOUGLAS. Hugged me, by God. By God you can't—
> PENNY. Pleased to meet you, I've heard a lot about you.
> DOUGLAS. No matter what anybody anywhere says, you can't separate a kid from his father. (68)

Moreover, it is Carol, the seventeen-year-old ward of the state living with Douglas's family, who continually reminds the audience that it is a *play* they are witnessing: "Nothing but big cars in this play" (37). After slinging a cigarette all the way off into the wings, Carol explodes: "I hope it burns down the theatre" (43). The "characters" all float in and out of the play. When they drift too far from the subject, one of the "actors" must call them back as when Penny, the other ward of the state, reminds them "Weren't we doing a play a while back?" (44) Carol again and again in Act Three insists that she *is*, she exists, only in the theatre, but she provides a history, a reality for herself beyond the theatre. Yet she always serves to remind the audience that this is a "story." One must make out the theatrical function of all the asides to the audience. Because Alan and the play project forward in time, and within that play Carol can further violate an established sense of reality, the audience's interest is focused not upon *what* happens but *why*. Moreover, the asides blur the demarcation between illusion and reality throughout. These are, after all, actors playing actors in what is effectively a play within a play, and as they drop "roles" the audience is tempted to forget that they are in roles still. It further heightens the blurring of illusion and reality. Here technique serves theme perfectly in a play set in California about an American family, which is what Alan seeks and which is, finally, an illusion.

There are a number of curious aspects to *Lemon Sky*, not the least of which is the title. A great deal is made of color in the play in which ". . . as many scenes as possible are bathed in bright cloudless sunlight" (4). The stage directions insist "There is no green in set or costume . . . nothing green" (4). This suggests that the audience is to see no hope, no possibility of fruition or regeneration. Moreover, Carol comments that "the color green does not occur in California naturally" (43) which restates and amplifies the intention of the earlier stage directions. Alan addresses the audience directly about California and Californians: "They're insane—well, you've seen the movies they make out here, they have no idea at all what people are like— well, it's not their fault; they've got nothing to go on—they're working in the dark" (32–33). This is more than an enterprising playwright making sport of the dream factory in a play which is to have its first production in Buffalo, New York, for this image of darkness is pressed even further. While Act One ends with the family's smiles at riding out an earth tremor as though it were a ride on Space Mountain at Disneyland, it is fire, "something that the Californians *do* fear" (58), that opens Act Three, a far more serious act. Alan's opening address to the audience at the beginning of this final act is drawn in red and black, the red of fire and the black of ashes. He describes the California landscape in terms reminiscent of a wasteland: ". . . ashes six inches deep" (58). Wilson's literary figure is not lost on his audience. There is little hope for any of the play's characters: Carol will become a violent "highway statistic" (59) and Alan, the controlling consciousness, will never be rid of his continual "incredible headache" because those he cries out for—"Where are they! Penny! Carol! Jerry! Jack!" (16)—are all gone, except as each member of the family is inside his head inextricably intertwined in his memory. *Gone* is the word which characterizes the most pervasive mood of the play.

For all of the somber colors and moods in the play, however, Wilson chooses *Lemon Sky* as his title. His stage directions are very explicit: the play's setting is "against a broad expanse of sky (which is never yellow)" (4). The lemon then is not to be taken as suggestive of light or brightness, nor even of the color yellow. Lemon is presented not as a color but in its suggestion of bitterness. Even in its slang connotation, a "lemon" is something or someone undesirable or inadequate, which is what Alan discovers in pursuing his horizons, the sky, in California, the land of sour fruit.

Lemon Sky celebrates an autobiographical reunion in San Diego with a father from whom he had been separated since his parents' divorce when Wilson was five years old; the recreation in art is a bitter memory, if not for Wilson, then certainly for Alan, his protagonist. The interaction of character, actor and audience striving for the illusion of life on the stage, a technique redolent of Pirandello, is perfectly appropriate for this bitter *Lemon Sky* which insists on its own existence as an illusion. Alan, the youthful American "hero" who has gone west in search of his American dream, has discovered that there is no further west to go. As Nathanael West had suggested in *The Day of the Locust* (1939), the American dream had ended. It is illusion. As Alan informs his audience in a direct address:

> ALAN. It's beautiful. It is. I always wanted a big old
> family like this, it's just great. And it's not going to
> last. . . . (33)

The manner of the play is perfect for its matter. The play, insisting on itself as an illusion, presents the dream of "a big old family" as an illusion. Alan's need for a family and the fact that there really isn't one is demonstrated throughout. Alan's reiterated line "what am I supposed to do?" (67) articulates the dilemma for someone who wants a family, and a father, when there are none. The play's penultimate tableau is a sharp picture of the fragmented family:

*Douglas and Alan are very far apart. Jack beside Alan,
Douglas by Ronnie, Jerry alone outside. Penny and Carol
together near their room.* (67)

An Act Three exchange between Alan and Douglas stresses Wilson's point that this family is not atypical but to be seen
as symbolic of the average American family. Alan, nearly crying,
accepts that this family is "quite normal" (60) and Douglas's
"just ordinary" (60) is not self-delusion, but Wilson's
commentary on the new character of the contemporary American family. Wilson's next major play will show the development
of a new unit to replace the "big old family," and that play will
be far less bitter. It will, in fact, be delicious and will win the
New York Critics Circle Award as the Best American Play of
1972–73.

The Hot l Baltimore (1973), quite unlike *Lemon Sky*, observes
unity of time, place and action. In fact, here Wilson, while his
stage directions call for *"music popular during production"* (xiv),
carefully structures his drama by using the techniques of opera.
Wilson did, of course, provide the libretto to Lee Hoiby's music
for an opera version of Tennessee Williams's *Summer and Smoke*
which opened at Lincoln Center in March of 1972. *Hot l* itself is
composed of duets and double duets, and the grand ensemble
with Jamie stunned by the naked Suzy and everybody laughing
which ends Act One is *opera buffa* and gives the curtain of the
initial act the *"upbeat"* and *"positive"* conclusion which Wilson
wants (xiv). He even describes his *dramatis personae* as baritone,
tenor, mezzo and so forth. As Wilson likes to set some of his
dramas on national holidays, *Hot l*'s setting is a *"recent Memorial
Day"* (xiv). The world of the Hotel Baltimore is one in which
"you got to be crazy even to do anything good" (122). It is a
cynical, sardonic, down-at-the-heels, hard world, but "share"
(128) and "sharing" (130) are the words which best sum up the
theme of this play.

As in *Lemon Sky*, the principal concern is human, indeed
familial, relationships. The engine of the play is called simply
Girl, a call girl who at age nineteen has found reasons to reject
the associations of a surname and uses different given names
weekly: Billy Jean, Lilac Lavender, Martha (which may or may

not be her real name). Bill Lewis, the night clerk, cares for Girl, but cannot communicate his feelings for her. A telephone "call" for this call girl precipitates a scene in which Bill and Girl punish each other: Girl says, "Would you stop being a daddy to me" (55). Ignoring Bill's responses, she then concludes:

> One minute you're friendly and nice and the next minute you're . . . as bad as my own daddy. Worse. Because he at least didn't care what I did. He didn't even care if I was a hooker as long as I kept him in enough money to buy beer. That's why I left, only you're worse than he is. (57–58)

Her daddy may not care; Bill, who is only thirty years old, does care but cannot express it; but if there is one thing Girl does and can do, it is *care* and express her care. In Girl's relationship with her "daddy" there is an odd similarity to the situation of Carol who is accused of being a whore by Douglas, the failed father in *Lemon Sky*. Carol is promiscuous if not a pro like Girl. April Green, the large and pragmatic prostitute of *Hot l*, like Carol in *Lemon Sky*, has a wry, satirical and earthy comic sense, only April is far funnier than Carol and a more interesting character. One of her *bons mots* deserves special attention. It is April who says, "If my clientele represents a cross-section of American manhood, the country's in trouble" (108). In point of fact, generally speaking, if Lanford Wilson's male characters represent a cross-section of American manhood, the country is in trouble. In his major plays, it is Wilson's women who are more effective both as characters and as functioning people. It seems no coincidence that Girl and April are the most thoroughly likable characters in this play. Douglas, in *Lemon Sky*, by contrast, is all libido, who, to cover his own guilt for fumbling Penny, accuses Penny's boyfriend Phil of being "queer" and damns his son Alan as a "homosexual" (*Lemon Sky* 64). Many of Wilson's most effective males are, in fact, homosexual: Alan; Ken and Jed in *Fifth of July*; Larry in *Burn This* among them. It is almost always Wilson's women who are the voice of hope and regeneration. It is the women of *Hot l* who take the leadership roles; they are the most active persons in the pursuit of establishing a purpose in life and a new, functioning family unit.

There are several examples of malfunctioning families in *Hot l* in addition to Girl and her tale of her father. In Act Two, the audience learns that Paul Granger III has come to the Hotel Baltimore searching for his grandfather who was rejected by his parents: "He wanted to come live with Mom and Dad, and they wrote him they didn't have room for him. They didn't want him" (94). Paul, who has never met his grandfather, now says, "*I* want him! *I* have room for him!" (95) Paul, like Alan in *Lemon Sky*, wants to restore what he can of his fragmented family. In Paul's case, it is his grandfather, but like Alan, it is all too late; it is, like Paul's grandfather, gone.

The character of Jackie, age 24, with her name written on the back of her denim jacket, despite the fact that "her manner, voice, and stance are those of a young stevedore" (xii), wants nothing so much as to proceed to twenty acres of land she has purchased (having heard about it on the radio) in Utah and establish a "family" life there with her nineteen-year-old browbeaten brother Jamie. Jackie wants to raise organic garlic on land that in truth won't grow cactus. Neither Paul nor Jackie will get what they desire.

It is Girl, who never wants to hurt anybody, who inadvertently kills Jackie's dream (102–03), and Act Two ends with Girl pursuing Jackie in an attempt to make up for the hurt in the destruction of the dream. Jackie knows "instinctively" that she has been foolish to purchase land she has not seen but only heard advertised on the radio. Her "dream" is a misinformed illusion which can come to no good end. Jackie abandons her brother Jamie, and Paul abandons his search for his grandfather. Paul just gives up the search; however, it is now important to Girl that Paul find his grandfather or at least continue the search for him. Girl says, "I *like* getting involved" (139) in the face of Bill's wisdom that "you can't help people who don't want it" (139). It is the male voice that is hard and pragmatic, non-involved and finally selfish. Audiences will hear this male voice again in John Landis of *Fifth of July* and the trio of Mr. Talley, Eldon and Harley Campbell in *Talley & Son*. It is the female voice that is hopeful, that insists on "getting involved."

Many of the characters in *Lemon Sky* and *The Hot l Baltimore* are portrayed as having a need for a sense of family in an essentially rootless, shifting contemporary American society. When another prostitute who has been a denizen of the Hotel Baltimore, Suzy, moves out of the hotel to move in with one other girl and a black pimp, "Billy Goldhole," she, *super-emotional*," bursts back in and says, "We been like a family, haven't we? My family" (136).

Why doesn't the center hold? Why is everything being destroyed? Girl speaks Wilson's indictment: "That's why nothing gets done; why everything falls down. Nobody's got the conviction to act on their passions" (140). Girl does. One of her passions is trains, and she sends the "front office a telegram of congratulations—I honestly did" (124) when the Continental comes through on time. She likes things orderly and on time; moreover, she likes getting involved and she does in Paul's search for a grandfather, even when Paul, disillusioned, gives up and quits his search. Girl is no exceptional romantic. It is she who points out the reality of the condition of the Utah land to Jamie (120–21), not maliciously to disillusion him but to help him. As for Paul's abandoning his search and Jackie's abandonment of Jamie, Girl again seems to speak for Wilson: "I don't think it matters what someone believes in. I just think it's really chicken not to believe in anything!" (141)

She is more than the stereotypical whore with a heart of gold. She is the voice of hope (much like Steinbeck's Ma Joad in *The Grapes of Wrath*) who insists on being "involved." Whether she is successful in her attempts does not matter. In the world portrayed by Lanford Wilson, the attempts themselves are important. Even if no one makes it (Suzy's "escape" from the Hot l Baltimore may be into exactly what April and Girl suggest, a situation even worse), it is the effort that is important, the attempt, the involvement. April, who knows that Bill "aches" for Girl but will not pursue her, drives home the point when she says to him: "Bill, baby, you know what your trouble is? . . . You've not got the conviction of your passions" (142).

This is the world of the Hotel Baltimore; it is contemporary society and "the bulldozers are barking at the door" (145). It seems all about to come tumbling down unless someone somewhere keeps the "conviction of passions." Is it just the Hotel Baltimore? Is it just Baltimore? Trying to answer that would be like trying to ascertain the present location and identity of Twain's Hadleyburg. Notice the following exchange:

> GIRL
> Baltimore used to be one of the most beautiful cities in America.
> APRIL
> Every city in America used to be one of the most beautiful cities in America. (129)

April's comic, and true, observation is more than an expression of contemporary cynicism. It is an indication that Wilson uses Baltimore and the Hot l Baltimore as a symbol for every city, every town. Perhaps too many people are too self-consumed and in too big a hurry. As Suzy says as she exits, "the whole fuckin' country is double parked" (134–35).

The final scene of the play suggests that from the ashes of the disintegration of old units of relationships a phoenix of a different sort arises. Bill, Millie, Girl and April now will adopt Jamie into their family unit—the larger unit of mankind. April expresses her concern for Jamie. Has he had anything to eat? Then, keeping her hope, she brings Jamie into the group by dancing with him: "Come on; you're so shy, if someone doesn't put a light under your tail, you're not going to have passions to need convictions for" (144). This is not sexual innuendo. When Jamie says that he doesn't know how to join in the dance, April insists, "Nobody knows how. What does it matter; the important thing is to *move*. Come on" (145). The dance is the dance of life. No one really knows *how* to do it; the important thing is to do it, live it. Why? Because "they're gonna tear up the dance floor in a minute; the bulldozers are barking at the door" (145). *Hot l* is, in some ways, a modern call to *carpe diem*.

Mr. Morse, the grandfather figure adopted much earlier in the play into the family of the Hot l Baltimore, has not, in the play's conclusion, touched the celebratory champagne Suzy has provided. He blurts out, "Paul Granger is an old fool! . . . He's an old fool" (143). Both Paul Grangers are fools—grandfather and grandson—the grandfather for making it difficult if not impossible for his grandson to find him, and the grandson for "giving up" the search for the father figure in his grandfather.

Morse, his wife long dead, settles into his new "family" which consists of Bill Lewis, Girl, April and Millie and is now a "grandfather" to Jamie who has been abandoned by his sister Jackie. If the old family unit malfunctions, a new unit is formed. Steinbeck expended an entire novel so that Ma Joad could learn that it used to be that the "fambly" was first. It "ain't" so now. It's anybody. This is called, in the cliché, the family of man. And like Steinbeck's characters, it is misnamed, for it is womankind who are the repository of hope, of endurance. Now, finally, in the last lines of *The Hot l Baltimore*, Mr. Morse *"sips the drink and watches o n"* (145), as April shows Jamie how to survive in the dance. Like the conclusion of *The Grapes of Wrath*, the important thing is not where they are going. "The important thing is to *move*" (145), to live, to believe in something, to keep the conviction to act on passions (140–41). Because people are like Suzy who needs love (133), they must, like Girl, get "involved" (139).

There are several points to note that make *Hot l* a far more hopeful, optimistic and comic experience than *Lemon S k y*. Wilson's bulldozers at the door bark on several levels. It is not just a philosophical expression encouraging people to eat, drink and be merry for tomorrow they die but a reminder that American society is changing. The important thing is to move, not out and away, but *into* the dance. Wilson's voice here asks to keep belief and to stay involved. Moreover, one notes the detached, cynical and dysfunctioning men. The women can be aware, alert and cautiously caustic yet remain hopeful, hopefilled and potent. Wilson's men? If this "represents a cross section of American manhood, the country's in trouble" (108). Wilson, like Steinbeck before him, observes the formation of the new family unit in contemporary American society. It doesn't look like the Victorian family. Then again, Wilson is not describing Victorian times.

Why is it the "e" that is missing in the Hot l Baltimore? Of course, it suggests the sleazy quality of a neon sign with a non-functioning part outside a seedy flophouse—that used to be a grand place—with some sexually *hot* residents. Is there anything else in that missing "e?" Steinbeck makes a good deal in *Grapes* about the movement from "I" to "We." Is this the "e" that

Wilson suggests is missing in "every city in America?" As *Lemon Sky* is a curious, brooding and troubling play, *The Hot l Baltimore* is the positive and upbeat song of a confirmed humanist.

Wilson has been concerned with the dysfunctional family unit and the changing role of women in *Lemon Sky* and *Hot l*; these elements will provide the thematic mainsprings for the plays of the Talley cycle: *5th of July* (1978; revised version, *Fifth of July* [1982]), *Talley's Folly* (1979) and *Talley & Son* (1985). All three plays are set on the Talley Place, a farm near Lebanon, Missouri. That they are set, wholly or in part, on Independence Day, in 1977 for the first play and in 1944 for the latter two, seems hardly a coincidence.

While the comic elements in *Hot l* are natural and organic, attempts at humor in *Fifth of July* seem strained and reached-for. Take for example this exchange involving June Talley, Sally Talley Friedman and Ken Talley:

> JUNE. I think that and Mahler are in a class by them-
> selves.
> SALLY. He loved swimming naked.
> KEN. Mahler? Loved swimming naked?
> SALLY. Your Uncle Matt, darling. (18)

Or consider this brief exchange between Jed, Ken's lover, and Aunt Sally:

> JED. And no botanist has ever known anything at all
> about gardening, or there wouldn't be mildew on
> the phlox.
> SALLY. Mildew on the phlox . . . What's the name of
> that novel? (20)

Neither the herb nor the George Eliot joke are organic here.

Early in the first act the audience becomes aware that *Fifth of July* is something different from *Lemon Sky* or *Hot l*. In 1974, Wilson collaborated with Tennessee Williams on a television filmscript for *The Migrants* which was nominated for an Emmy. Actually, Williams gave Wilson a story outline in 1973 and the credits for the *Playhouse 90* drama acknowledge a teleplay by Lanford Wilson, suggested by a story by Tennessee

Williams. *Fifth of July* seems to be written under the sway of Williams's influence. The play is loaded with eccentric, down-home dramatis personae who are "characters" and the drama is laden with "curiosities"—an overly dramatic fourteen year old smoking cigarettes with a cigarette-holder who climbs trees to witness a cunnilingus-masturbation scene (21); an apparently eccentric widowed "Aunt Sally" who carries her husband's ashes with her for a year, uses them to dry roses (23) and occasionally stores the ashes in the refrigerator (27); and a crippled Vietnam veteran, Ken Talley, and his lover, Jed Jenkins. It all begins to look like Tennessee Williams—bad Williams. Imitation may be the sincerest form of flattery, but not when it is bad imitation and seems to lead a younger writer away from his own genius.

Fifth of July's Act One curtain, with Jed picking up his crippled lover Ken—who has lost both legs in the Vietnam War—and carrying him up to bed is supposed to be moving, but, curiously, it is not. This might have been a powerful curtain but it isn't. There is no felt life here; the characters remain *curiosa*, curiosities for whom the audience senses they are being manipulated to feel . . . yet don't. There are some interesting moments and some funny lines, but no play. Even as a let's-get-together-ten-years-after-Berkeley-and-the-1960's exercise, this is just adequate. The physical damage (Ken) and the disillusionment (Gwen and June) subsequent to Vietnam are present; this is, after all, the fifth of July, the time *after* the major national event, and Wilson has a fecund title.

Much of the play is mired in a slough of *facetiae*. Sexual variants abound: Ken and Jed now; John and Gwen now; Ken and Gwen and John and June then; even, as children, John and Ken and June (57); and Ken in love with John (then)—quite a sexual *mélange*. John Landis is the newly constituted capitalist who keeps his spacey, ding-dong wife Gwen away from the companies she owns so *he* can run things; she is not "blind" (73). She's "gotta have John" (73). He, after all, performs "cunnilingus all over her and his face was all over mucus" while he masturbates (21).

Well, all's well that ends well and in the play's final scene (68–75) everything rushes together satisfactorily: Ken does not sell the Talley place and property and he will prepare to face the high school students as a teacher in the fall; Gwen will get a genuine singing career despite John's manipulative efforts and we're told (not shown) "she's really good" (73); Shirley, "the last of the Talleys" (75), will remain with her mother despite the threats of John who is sure he is Shirley's father; Aunt Sally will not go to California but remain on the Talley place; she and Jed have finally scattered the ashes of Matt "all over the rose garden" (70) to help things grow. No longer are the ashes of Matt Friedman to be used to desiccate roses, but as fertile matter to help them grow. Yet, as in *Lemon Sky* and more especially *Hot l*, a new and peculiar "family" unit is restored: Ken and Jed, Aunt Sally and Shirley and June. They will all live apparently happily ever after. Or as Ilya, the character played by Melina Mercouri in Jules Dassin's film *Pote Tin Kyriaki* (*Never on Sunday*), concludes after her viewing of *Medea*: they all went to the seashore.

The audience finally may be tempted to identify with Ken Talley in his reaction to the absurdity of the conversation about slugs: "Does anyone have something I could open a vein with?" (61) As the pieces of the Talley cycle fall into place, however, Aunt Sally and Matt Friedman, whose ashes will help things grow, will be of far more central importance than might appear here. For that, the audience will have to come forward one year in their time to 1979 and go back thirty-three years in Talley time from *Fifth of July* to the Fourth of July of 1944 on the Talley place for the events of both *Talley's Folly* and *Talley & Son*.

Set in an old boathouse called "Talley's Folly," an excessively romantic structure, a "genuine Victorian folly. . . . Constructed of louvers and lattice and geegaws" (4), which was built in 1870 by "Uncle Whistler," Everett Talley, *Talley's Folly*, this two-character drama played without intermission, opens with a monologue by the engaged narrator directed to the audience as in *Lemon Sky*. But this piece delivered by the same Matt Friedman whose ashes some thirty-three years later eventually decorate the roses in Jed's garden in *Fifth of July* is of greater uninterrupted length (3–6) than anything written for Alan in *Lemon Sky*. As Lanford Wilson is roundly praised by critics for his realistic and naturalistic dialogue (a good ear is an important appendage for a playwright), the small cost is that often in lengthy soliloquies the realistic lacks poetry. The advance here is that Wilson gives Matt Friedman language that is appropriate to his character yet is a full cut above the colloquial or prosaic. There is poetry here, and Matt is a more persuasive and charming interlocutor.

Again it is a musical figure which best serves to identify the play. As *Lemon Sky* is a fugue and *Hot l* is an *opera buffa*, this play is, as Matt insists several times, a waltz. Informed by more than the waltz or the level of diction, at once both realistic and poetic, *Talley's Folly* is a mature play with two real, likable characters. There is felt life, and the wit of Matt Friedman and the humor of the play are warm and human, not forced and stilted like much of *Fifth of July*.

The plot is simple, but America has a fresh Romeo and Juliet—a 42–year-old Jewish Romeo and a 31–year-old radical Midwestern Juliet from a Methodist family. Matt and Sally *will* live happily ever after for three decades. How they got that way makes a remarkable play. With only two characters, there is believable life here, two people an audience will like and care about. This is the stuff of which Pulitzer Prizes are made. *Talley's Folly* received its Pulitzer in 1980.

Matt is a wonderful storyteller; he tells tales to Sally to win her, and they are good stories. Even if they are tragic and may be true, they remain winning stories. In the play's lovely *sotto voce* ending, Matt has won his Sally Talley; they kiss and, finally, sit "perfectly relaxed" (60); then Matt says, "and so, all's well that ends . . . (*Takes out his watch, shows time to* SALLY, *then to audience*) . . . right on the button. . ." (60).

As Matt, whose wondrous abilities have won Sally, has promised the audience in the play's opening line, it has been "ninety-seven minutes here tonight—without intermission" (3). Matt has won Sally by telling her jokes and stories. At the same time . . . in the same time . . . he has presented a lovely, moving romantic waltz for the audience. And he has won them as well. At that same time, however, the ominous events of *Talley & Son* are occurring. It would be a mistake to underestimate a play because of its charm. *Talley's Folly* is, in the context of the Talley trilogy, about one woman's escape from an oppressive paternalistic family, and it comes exactly one hundred years after Nora slams the door on *A Doll's House* (1879). Sally will leave in

Talley & Son. She will not slam the door, but she will leave. Since Sally is the only character to appear in all the Talley plays, the *& Son* in the title of the last drama in the cycle is powerfully ironic, and she is far more significant than has been heretofore acknowledged.

An early draft of *Talley & Son*, then called *A Tale Told*, was presented during the Circle Repertory Company's 1980–81 season. In both versions, once again as in *Lemon Sky* and *Talley's Folly*, Wilson's tale is told by a narrator. This time it is Timmy Talley, who has just been killed in World War II. Timmy, like Alan and Matt, addresses the audience and provides exposition and asides, yet unlike them he does not interact with the play's other characters except through an extraordinary human empathy with Sally but most especially with Aunt Charlotte Talley, called Lottie in the play, at the play's conclusion. Even then he seems to speak Lottie's mind and through Lottie's character.

In *Talley & Son*, Wilson adds another impressive theatrical weapon to his panoply of dramatic tools, this time a Rashomon effect which Alan Ayckbourn had used so brilliantly in *The Norman Conquests* (1973), three plays which represent the same characters, events and instant in time seen from different places in the house and garden. Ayckbourn's accomplishment is duplicated by Wilson if with less comic intent. *Talley's Folly* and *Talley & Son* are indigenous entities that are perfectly satisfying if seen separately. Yet since they occur at the same instant in time, taken together each sheds new lights on the other and creates a third, even richer, tapestry.

Aunt Charlotte, Lottie, is a fiercely independent person; she encourages Matt to continue his relationship with Sally who will be like her aunt in being not just liberal but radical. Lottie and Sally are the independent ones in the family in these plays set on the Fourth of July, and *Talley's Folly* is about, among other things, how Sally, who only appears briefly in *Talley & Son*, finally became "independent." There are many references in *Talley's Folly* that make it clear that Aunt Charlotte is the one who encourages Matt's pursuit of Sally (see pp. 9, 31–32, 50–51, 52). Aunt Charlotte has become great friends with Matt, and when we eventually meet her in *Talley & Son*, Lottie smokes and curses at a time when "ladies" like Olive, Buddy's wife, think it inappropriate for *men* to smoke in the house or curse in the presence of women. Olive, in calling her father-in-law, Eldon, "Dad" and her mother-in-law, Netta, "Mom" and "Mother," is trying to hold an old sort of family unit together. Olive is a throwback to Victorian times: annoyingly obsequious, in the way in the kitchen but in the kitchen nonetheless, and a desirous, if not desired, bed partner. Olive almost always exits to the kitchen or up to the bedroom. She acts the traditional female roles—in the kitchen, concerned with feeding "you men" (83)—and she talks in accepted stereotypical "female" fashion: she says to Lottie, "you're going to go straight to H-E-double-toothpicks" (84). Lottie, shackled by no such delicacy required in a lady's avoidance of the vulgar, responds as a male might: "Oh, kiss my ass" (84). Olive, who will make a concession to progress in Leclede County by wearing slacks (33), would never think of wearing them when her husband Buddy comes home. Women do not wear the pants in this family—at least not Olive's conception of the family.

The patriarch, Calvin Stuart Talley, whose circumstances and actions may remind some of Big Daddy in Williams's *Cat on a Hot Tin Roof* (1955), is dying, and a way of life will die with him. This good Methodist family will not allow inappropriate behavior for a woman—no smoking, drinking or cursing. Sally must surreptitiously go down to the boathouse as she does in *Talley's Folly* to sneak her cigarette and nip of gin. And none of the men would think of allowing a Jew to court a Talley family member. The anti-Semitism of the men (Eldon, Buddy and Harley Campbell) is blatant. It is the independence day for two women, Aunt Charlotte and Sally, that will allow for Sally's growth to happiness in marrying Matt Friedman. Sally (who is, recall, Aunt Sally in *Fifth of July*) is Aunt Charlotte's spiritual offspring—the independent, radical woman who escapes the decaying order of the Talley decline.

Charlotte never marries, but her spiritual child is Sally. Sally can never have children and Matt doesn't want them, but in *Fifth of July*, it is Shirley who says that not John and June, but Matt and "Aunt Sally" are the only real parents she has ever had. Sally has raised Shirley, and *she* will go on to be a great artist (or scientist, or whatever). In many of Wilson's major plays we see the disintegration of a dysfunctional family unit tied by blood, to be replaced by a new sort of family unit, one formed by selection, election and a shade of chance. Only in the declaration of independence from some kinds of blood ties could women be prepared to be the center of the new "family" unit. It may be why the audience of Wilson's plays has a slim sense of Steinbeck's Ma Joad (*Grapes*) as a new "fambly" structure develops. Wilson's men die or are wounded, and the women remain memorable. The men are the narrators, Alan, Matt and Timmy, but the strong characters are the women, like April and Girl in *Hot l* or Lottie and Sally in *Talley's Folly* and *Talley & Son*.

Some critics see the power of *Talley & Son* in the relationship of fathers and sons and that may in part be so, but it overlooks too much, especially the role of Wilson's women. Both Sally and Lottie are college-educated, independent women, and Sally, Lottie and Shirley have more in common than the fact that all three smoke cigarettes. The Talley cycle is about many things, and the individual plays are of varying merit, but the one consistent factor is Sally Talley Friedman who alone appears in all three plays. Lottie is an independent, college-educated woman who never marries, a life-long spinster. Her spiritual progeny is Sally, the radical, college-educated woman of the next generation of Talley women who has no natural children but raises Shirley of *Fifth of July* who believes, at age fourteen, that she can and will have it all. Both Sally and Lottie make it clear that they would not have returned to their individual father's home—Sally to Eldon Talley's—"I'm as eager to leave as they are eager to get rid of me" (*Talley's Folly* 26)—or Lottie to Calvin Stuart Talley's—"if there'd been another place to go" (*Talley & Son* 39).

It is in a consideration of all three women of the Talley cycle that we see two major themes come together: the changing nature of the American family and the evolution of the role of women and its part in that change. If the movement from Charlotte, the spiritual mother, through Sally to Shirley seems an incomplete matter, that may be because America has not yet written a conclusion to the evolving role of its women. One thing is certain, however. The culture will be quite different. Sally is committed to making the world a better place, and Lottie's concern is with the welfare of her fellow human beings (*Talley & Son* 39, 46). She has little concern with material "things" or with the male pursuits of wealth and power. Eldon Talley would leave everything to the sons Buddy and Timmy, who, as the audience knows, has already been killed, and nothing to his daughter Sally (49); Buddy, Sally's brother, agrees. Wilson's women are excluded from male obsessions.

The only thing a woman is good for according to the men in the Talley family is to have children, and because tuberculosis has descended to Sally's fallopian tubes she can have no children; that is what broke up the engagement between Sally and Harley Campbell (*Talley's Folly* 58). A woman who cannot bear children would be no good in a match between two rich and powerful patriarchal families. It is the modern man, Matt Friedman, who loves the woman because she is like him. She's a worthy mate. The woman's child-bearing is unimportant. She is his equal. It's a match. In these plays set on Independence Day, it is only certain women who are independent. The Talleys have, as Eldon says, "got to have one in every generation" (*Talley & Son* 49), and Lottie has influenced "that girl [Sally] since the day she was born" (*Talley & Son* 49), as Sally, in her turn, will be the major influence in raising Shirley.

The women are far more admirable human beings than the men portrayed here. Harley Campbell, for example, has little humanity or social concern, especially for women, in sharp contrast with Lottie and Sally. Harley would sell the firm of Talley & Son, in which he is a business partner, to the Delaware conglomerate. He has no concern for the workers or what would happen if Talley & Son were to close: "Divorced women, unmarried mothers. The town would be better off without them" (55). Calvin Stuart "Granddaddy" Talley agrees about the women who work in the mill: "Moral corruption. Never trusted those women. Broken homes and moral weakness" (55). Moral corruption? Moral weakness? At the curtain of Act One, Avalaine Platt arrives, claiming to be Eldon Talley's illegitimate daughter; almost at the same moment the news arrives of Timmy's death. It is the arrival of an unwanted daughter and the death of a son for whom all the dreams were held which concludes Act One. Buddy Talley apparently has several times tried to seduce Avalaine who is the illegitimate and unacknowledged daughter of his father Eldon, who brusquely dismisses Avalaine as he had dismissed her mother Viola earlier in the play. Buddy, who throughout Act One has avoided sex with his wife Olive, is moved to go upstairs with her only by the thought of begetting a son.

Women are clearly second-class citizens and good only to provide sons—in a play about Talley and son. It is *grandsons* who "mean more to" Granddaddy Talley "than almost anything" (70). Sally, who is at this moment down in the boathouse (*Talley's Folly*) with Matt, has been forgotten by everyone. Timmy is, after all, Sally's brother, and she is the grandchild of Talley, whose concern is with grandsons. Just Lottie and Netta even think of her, and Netta does because Sally is "so strong" (72). Netta's concern for Eldon at the loss of his son is because "he's not resilient like we are" (71). Since she speaks this line to her daughter-in-law Olive, someone she does not especially like, the "we" must mean women. Lanford Wilson's women—like Steinbeck's women—are, in fact, more resilient than Lanford Wilson's men. Moreover, Lottie, like April in *Hot l*, has vision and wit in addition to her concern for the well-being of her fellow humans. It is noteworthy that Carol in *Lemon Sky*, April in *Hot l* and Lottie have the readiest wit in each play. Among the men, only Ken, a legless homosexual in *Fifth of July*, has the same combination of vision, intelligence, sardonic wit and concern for his fellow man that the women do.

The exchange between Talley, a war-profiteer, and his daughter Lottie (*Talley & Son* 79–81) establishes firmly that with her education, assertiveness and independence of mind, she is perceived by her father as having acted in ways generally reserved for males. It is further evident that men like Talley, Eldon and Harley prefer their women "frail and beautiful" (80). Lottie's bitter revolt concludes with the response which suggests that the lack of choice relative to contraception killed her mother: "Well, Momma, bless her, didn't live that long. Doctors told him she wasn't strong enough; it's not like we're Catholic. Didn't they have rubbers back at the turn of the century?" (*Talley & Son* 80) Even minor characters reflect changes in gender behavior:

Viola Platt is disposed to acquiesce, to be submissive while her daughter Avalaine, though nasty and eventually succumbing to the power, ruthlessness and superior negotiating skills of Talley, is more than assertive—she is aggressive in her attempt to stand up to the Talleys.

Sally finally exits from the action of *Talley's Folly*, enters directly back into *Talley & Son*, and Lottie's identification with Sally is complete and total. Sally makes peace with her father and makes her escape to fulfill Lottie's thwarted hopes and dreams. Lottie conspires with her, lies to protect her and insists upon her escape which is the fulfillment of prohibited ambitions.

In the penultimate lines of *Talley & Son*, Timmy says that returning servicemen will find "the country's changed so much I don't imagine they'll recognize it" (115). The play's final line, Lottie's "I know" (115), seals the theme of the country's changes, in the role of women, in the nature of the family unit and the implications both will have for the country itself. The custodianship of the Talley garden which has become "pretty bad" (114), nourished by the ashes of the liberal and liberated man Matt, will fall to Jed in *Fifth of July*. "Women's work" will no longer be work for women, and behavior once reserved for men will no longer be the exclusive domain of the male.

What has Wilson captured in his play cycle? He has caught in mid-flight and permanently fixed very real and significant accommodations and adjustments in social continuity. What had wrought the changes in the family and the role of women? An answer is found in two allied forces—independent, liberated women who are educated and the immutable fact of World War II. That is the importance of 1944 and the background of the war to the plays. Is there other evidence of the changes and their impact? There is, perhaps, one massive symbol: in *Talley & Son*, the one thing that will tempt Buddy to bed with his very interested wife Olive is the thought of fathering a son. That son turns out to be Ken, who thirty-three years later will be the veteran who has lost both legs in another war, this time Vietnam. Ken, a homosexual, will father no son since he is, if we are to trust Wilson's genealogy provided in *Talley & Son*, married to his lover Jed. With Timmy Talley, the hope for effective male progeny, at least as recognizable to the Talleys,

has died on Guam. In stark contrast to this pre-war insistence on
fathering a male heir is the sex act described in *Fifth of July*. John
Landis performs cunnilingus on his wife Gwen as he
masturbates himself. What changes had World War II, the 1960's
and Vietnam brought? They are depicted in the comparison of
the sexual relations between John Landis and his wife Gwen,
who has been liberated by Berkeley and the 1960's, and Buddy
and Olive Talley. The contrast of these two sex acts is significant.
They are a potent set of decades, those thirty years. Men had
changed, women had changed perhaps even more, the family
structure even more than that, and gender expectations had
changed to an even greater degree. The end result to date of this
evolution is Anna, whose last name appropriately is Mann, the
central protagonist of *Burn This* (1987). Anna is the figure of
modern, educated, liberated, talented, urban woman—the
achieved person.

Burn This is a slick piece of New York (or Los Angeles,
where it premiered) dramaturgy. It is sure-fire, fast, funny and
hip. Like most Wilson drama, it plays well. By 1987, this man
who knows theatre in its many aspects well enough to write excellent drama, knows the commercial theatre well enough to
write a Broadway hit. It would be a mistake, however, to sell
Burn This short merely because it has all the schtick to generate a
decently long run on Broadway. *Burn This* is less experimental—
no crossing boundary lines; no blending times, no narrator,
engaged or otherwise; just straightforward theatre that the
matinee lady can cope with. The traces of Pirandello, Wilder and
Miller are gone, only a touch of Williams remains, and a fair
dollop of Neil Simon has been added; but Ibsen's Nora is still
looking for a comfortable new residence where the price is not
too high.

At the play's opening, Anna is *"huddled on a sofa, smoking. . . . She is thirty-two, very beautiful, tall and strong. A dancer"*
(5). She is recovering from the loss of one of her gay roommates,
Robbie, who has been killed along with his lover Dom in a
boating accident. Wilson's audience may have been transported
to a huge loft in lower Manhattan, but they are on familiar
ground. Alan, who in *Lemon Sky* is in the process of discovering
his sexual identity, has grown through Ken and Jed in *Fifth of*

July, who are in some ways a fairly conventional married couple except for the fact that they're both male, to the character of Larry, Anna's remaining roommate. Larry is a gay who is quite comfortable and happy with who he is; he is very witty, funny and a winning character. Although he concedes what he calls his "protective sense of humor" (56), that just means he is human.

Early in the play, Anna describes her relationship with her mother—"all she wants is grandchildren" (11)—but Anna's expressions of self-doubt seem gratuitous, and like Larry's, are just indications of her humanity. She is, in truth, able and quite confident. She has quit dancing and is attempting to establish a reputation in choreography. Half seriously she tells her well-to-do suitor Burton that perhaps it is time for them to move to Martha's Vineyard "permanently" (19), which Burton would love. Yet Anna recalls that she did not fit in "with the women" at Robbie's funeral where she had been expected to join with his mother in "some little back bedroom, with all the aunts and cousins, with the women, right?" (20) in mourning. Anna, a contemporary woman, just does not fit in with yesterday's fashion for women. In addition, it is clear that Anna is beyond and above "prevailing opinions" (31). This educated and intelligent woman has no time for social mores or conformity to expectations relative to gender.

Robbie's brother, known as Pale, enters, and the major dramatic complication has been struck. Anna is, to use an appropriate colloquialism, a very "together" person—confident, strong and sensitive, perhaps too sensitive. At the beginning of the relationship, she does indulge Pale too much in what seems to her to be his grief. The audience suspects that he is high and on the make. After their initial one-night tryst, she is super-cool, unemotional and calm as Pale's possessions reveal a photo of his wife and children. She is unaffected by the knowledge that Pale carries a gun. She tells Larry that she went to bed with Pale after knowing him not even an hour because of the "bird-with-the-broken-wing syndrome" (47). Act One ends after Pale has left without so much as a "have a nice day" (47), and the audience is unsure which bird really had the broken wing. It is not Pale. It is certain, however, that this is a funny play and that its hero, Anna, is an exceptional woman.

Act Two reassures the audience. In the fight scene between Pale and Burton, Anna is the one who commands the situation. It is she who is most in control. She may say that Pale is "dangerous" (82) and that she's "frightened" (86) of him, but she is not intimidated by him. Anna says she's never had a personal life. There was no place for it. It wasn't important. All that is different now and she is "very vulnerable" (86), but she firmly indicates that she is not going to be prey to something she does not want. She is still in command of herself, and of the situation. Pale is impressed:

> PALE: You're a real different person in the sack than you are standin' up.
> ANNA: I know. (82)

She is a passionate, vibrant woman, but she is more than a horizontal being; there is also an upright, rational being to Anna. She continues:

> ANNA: I'm sick of the age I'm living in. I don't like feeling ripped off and scared. . . . I'm being pillaged and I'm being raped. And I don't like it. . . . If I can't have a life at least I can work. (87–88)

In fact, she wants it all—work and a life too. Earlier in the play, Anna delivers a speech on "mother love" (54). It has been proposed that she choreograph a piece the overall theme of which is to be mother love. Burton proposes that they should "have kids or something" (54). Anna hears "the sound of the biological clock or something" (55). Note the vague "or something" used twice. This is more than two people feeling tentative about entering a serious commitment. Parenthood and a child are *part* of what is wanted; they are not *all* that people are about. That would no more be enough to satisfy Anna than it would Burton. Her *art* is important, and it will take a different shape.

As this discussion is taking place, at 2 A.M. on New Year's Eve, Anna is preparing to go to bed with Burton in what is a quite conventionally romantic scene. The audience may be secretly cheering for Anna and the near-perfect, very rich, unmarried Burton. Yet she will choose Pale. Why? It is not merely animal magnetism. That is apparent in this scene with Burton, and to suggest her choice is based on only sexual attraction to Pale would be to cheapen the play to a cliché.

The opening dialogue in Act Two between Anna and Burton about the first few pages of a new script he has written is revealing, first of all, as a sly commentary on the previous act of Wilson's, not Burton's, drama:

> ANNA: Oh, I like it. It's so sad. God.
> BURTON: Sad? I thought they were having fun.
> ANNA: Oh no, sure. But underneath all that, God, they're so lonely. (51)

Late in the play, however, when Larry discovers that he and the others have been used as prototypes for characters in Burton's now completed script, he is pleased but surprised. Burton responds:

> BURTON: Nobody's safe around a writer. I thought you knew that. (90)

Burton no longer has written commercial science fiction but has taken real life and turned it into art as Anna turns her relationship with Pale into art in the dance she eventually choreographs. Earlier in the play, Anna has been reflecting upon a dance she is creating, and she says she thinks it is all getting a little too personal. Burton's response is crucial:

> BURTON: Good, it's supposed to be—make it as personal as you can. Believe me, you can't imagine a feeling everyone hasn't had. Make it personal, tell the truth, and then write "Burn this" on it. (60)

Lanford Wilson has, of course, so marked his play. He presents Anna as the achieved woman, all that Charlotte and Sally might have wished. What is the truth, then, upon which Wilson will write *Burn This*? It may be that having what Anna has leaves her wanting more. As Pale does, she wants something more than polite, civilized life ". . . like the ocean. That hurricane . . . those gigantic, citywide fires—Somethin' that can—like—amaze you" (38).

Something that can amaze you. Part of the irony is that this
is why the audience in some measure has come to the theatre. As
well, when the achieved person does achieve it all, he or she
wants even more. When one gets what life has to offer, there is
the need for something larger than life. Life does not have to be
life-size. Something to amaze you: there is no other way to
explain why Anna, beautiful, intelligent, mature, witty,
educated, talented, strong and tall, will enter into a relationship
with a vulgarian like Pale. That it is not merely animal attraction
is made clear. What moves Anna is to reach for that which is
beyond the pale. (Pale's name, after all, is really a mundane
"Jimmy.")

Burton too wants "something larger than life" (51) and
advises Anna to "Reach! Reach for something! God! Reach for
the sun! Go for it!" (52) Burton's own desires and his hopes for
Anna connect Anna's aspirations to all persons, people, humans.
For a woman to be accepted as a person is not the *end* of the journey; this acceptance, by society, and by the woman herself, is
merely the beginning. Anna Mann is an achieved person who
will reach for something, something larger than life yet something personal, something "amazing." She is not a symbol for
contemporary women. She is every man, . . . every person. The
choreographed piece she achieves finally is "phenomenal. It's
great" (91), according to Larry. "The dance she's done is Pale and
Anna" (92). Even Pale thinks the dance is "real good" (96).

Larry leaves a note which is read in the play's conclusion
that itself concludes: "This isn't opera, this is life, why should
love always be tragic? Burn this" (98). Thus the audience is reminded of Burton's earlier line and recognizes that Anna has
"made it personal" and has told the truth. She has turned her
relationship with Pale into art, into the dance she has choreographed.

In personal terms, as critics have said of the unlikely romantic couple at the play's conclusion, it would be injudicious to
see the ending as happy. It is not. This is not merely a love story.
Whether Pale and Anna could possibly live happily ever after for
longer than the six days that Pale's own marriage "was good"
(80) is unlikely, and perhaps unimportant. What matters, what is
beyond life, greater than life, better than life-size, that thing

which people seek that is personal and "amazing," is the art, the creation of Anna in the dance, the creation of Lanford Wilson in the play.

The last of Lottie's daughters is Anna Mann. In an evolutionary line from Charlotte through Sally and Shirley, it is Anna who is the achieved person. She is *the* dancer. That dance which April in *Hot l* has said nobody knows how to do, Anna has mastered. She can more than dance it, she can choreograph it, control it, shape it, mold it. At once concerned and committed, she strikes an almost perfect human balance between selfishness and selflessness. She wants it all. She has it all. Still, there is the curious irresolution of *Burn This*'s conclusion. Anna is the achieved person indeed. Yet there is always that something beyond—beyond the pale. This is part of the artist's condition as it is part of the human situation. No artist ever writes that one true sentence. All art is a sacrifice made upon the altar of intention. No one ever gets it all. So Anna Mann is the complete person, strangely incomplete, exactly the appropriate figure for the achieved person—male or female. Everyman, this time, is a woman.

REFERENCES

Wilson, Lanford. *Burn This*. New York: Hill and Wang, 1987.
——. *Fifth of July*. Rev. ed. New York: Dramatists Play Service, 1982.
——. *The Hot l Baltimore*. New York: Hill and Wang, 1973.
——. *Lemon Sky*. New York: Dramatists Play Service, 1970.
——. *Talley & Son*. New York: Hill and Wang, 1986.
——. *Talley's Folly*. New York: Hill and Wang, 1979.

The Talley Plays and the Evolution of the American Family

Robert Cooperman

I

In his 1978 study, *Family, Drama, and American Dreams*, Tom Scanlan outlines two idealized models of the American family which he labels the "family of security" and the "family of freedom." The "family of security" is "a molecule of independence, self-sufficiency, and progress, a repository of private property values, a place where one can reject society without foregoing the security and nurture of a social structure which would care for all" (30–31; adapted from Hector St. John Crèvecoeur's *Letters from an American Farmer*). This family is highly structured from within; it contains a hierarchy which protects, nurtures and governs its members. In short, it is what one might consider to be the traditional nuclear family consisting of (in its highly structured order) the father, mother and children (with male children "outranking" the female children), all interacting for the good of each other and the survival of the family business, which in the country's more agrarian days meant the family farm.

The "family of freedom" developed as America became less agrarian and more industrial. Scanlan based this model on the writings of Alexis de Tocqueville (especially *Democracy in America*) about the effects of democracy on family life in America (34). The family of freedom preserves the emotional solidarity of the family of security, but dispenses with its hierarchical structure and insular behavior. This type of family creates a more democratic atmosphere by allowing its members to grow as individuals and to follow their own course in life. "The emotional solidarity," Scanlan argues, "of the family of security can be preserved without hierarchy, without structure, in a spontaneous, unforced domesticity" (35).

Scanlan believes that the clash between these two models creates the tension which characterizes the American family play and the best family dramas are so crafted to show the friction between family members who embody these ideals. The members of a family of security often feel trapped and overburdened by the demands of family and are constantly seeking their individuality outside of the family. They resent the hierarchy of family life and consider the head of the household (usually the father) to be a tyrant who must be defeated. Members of a family of freedom long for the security of the past and seek the emotional, spiritual and financial stability lost when they embarked on their own. Theirs is the existential dilemma of determining their sense of being in an insecure and often hostile society. The disenchanted members of a family of freedom are quick to learn that it is extremely difficult to go home again.

Scanlan's work anticipates the 1983 sociological study "Contemporary Traditional Families: The Undefined Majority" by Sara B. Taubin and Emily H. Mudd. Taubin and Mudd describe two extreme beliefs regarding the American family (256). One describes the family as a limiting and inhibiting force which stifles individual growth, in essence the argument of Scanlan's family of freedom. The other view argues that the changes which have already occurred in the family are deplorable and that the established norms must be adhered to if America is to survive, similarly the argument of the family of security.

A brief survey of twentieth-century American drama reveals many examples of Scanlan's security vs. freedom model, and indeed some of our finest plays are family dramas which follow this very pattern. O'Neill's *Long Day's Journey into Night*, Miller's *Death of a Salesman*, Odets's *Awake and Sing!*, Shepard's *Buried Child*, Durang's *The Marriage of Bette and Boo* and Rabe's *Sticks and Bones* all depict the dilemma of a family caught between the forces of security and freedom which "vie with each other for a claim on the American imagination" (Scanlan 42). By contrast, the sentiment and nostalgia which characterize O'Neill's *Ah, Wilderness!*, Wilder's *Our Town*, Lindsay and Crouse's *Life with Father* and Horovitz's *Today, I Am a Fountain Pen* represent the rare family dramas that have successfully tempered the storm and managed to keep the opposing forces of security and freedom from disrupting family life.

What is lacking from the contemporary scene is the family drama that balances freedom and security without utilizing sentiment and nostalgia as a technique. Such would be the play which dramatizes Taubin and Mudd's "undefined majority" (quoted from the title): "contemporary traditionals." These are families that adapt to change while respecting custom and convention, a phenomenon which suggests that the forces of security and freedom have been equalized and that the family has undergone some type of ameliorating evolutionary transformation. As their title indicates, Taubin and Mudd see this new type of family as that which makes up the majority of American families. Lanford Wilson appears to be the only playwright who has been successful in dramatizing such a family in *Fifth of July* and, through *Talley & Son* and *Talley's Folly*, successful in showing the evolution of America as it becomes a nation of contemporary traditional families. Through his work with the Talley family Lanford Wilson proves himself to be uniquely in tune with modern America.

II

Between 1978 and 1985, Lanford Wilson completed three plays about the fictitious Talley family of Lebanon, Missouri: *Fifth of July* (originally *5th of July* [1978]), *Talley's Folly* (1979), and *Talley & Son* (1985). *5th of July* was revised in 1982, *Talley & Son* was the revised version of *A Tale Told* (1981) and *Talley's Folly* was never modified. Wilson has shown an uncanny ability to dramatize the evolutionary forces at work in America through the three completed plays. By studying the plays in their chronological order rather than in their order of composition, one can follow the steady progression of the American family as it dispensed with the formalities that characterized the family of security and became instead a family of "contemporary traditionals."

Talley & Son has been described as "a standard family package," and indeed its basic family structure is of the traditional nuclear type (Weales 500). The head of the clan is Eldon Talley, a middle-aged man who, for the last few years, has managed both the family finances and the family business because of the advancing senility of his octogenarian father Calvin. Eldon's wife Netta runs the Talley household and assumes all its domestic responsibilities. Eldon's son Kenneth (known throughout as Buddy) is, at least in Eldon's mind, the heir to the Talley dynasty, as is the younger son Timmy. Also living in the Talley house are Sally, Eldon's daughter; Lottie, Eldon's sister; and Olive, Buddy's wife. Together they form not only a traditional family, but, because of the four generations of Talleys living under one roof, a rather old-fashioned family as well (modern households are two-generational [Scanlan 18]). Theirs is a self-contained household with a direct hierarchy and with a family business that must be maintained internally. For Wilson, it marks "the only time I've written one of those families" (Cooperman 76). The Talleys are the consummate family of security and Wilson uses them to represent the traditional American family in all of its glory and shame. The fate of the Talleys will then, by extension, parallel the fate of family life in America.

The ultra-traditional Talley clan resides in a *"large and elegant farmhouse,"* and the house itself suggests a great deal about the family (5). Up until this cycle, Wilson has never made an issue out of the ownership of a house (or land) and its effect on the American psyche. His interest in the subject seems to be twofold, beginning with his well-documented interest in the past, and especially in the architecture of the past. There is some evidence of this in *The Hot l Baltimore*, when Girl laments about the imminent destruction of "the most exclusive medium-sized hotel anywhere on the Eastern Seaboard line" (10). In various interviews, Wilson has discussed his anger at city planners who "were tearing down a culture that I'd never had time to see," citing the designs of architect Louis Sullivan as a major victim of urban renewal (Berkvist 33).

Wilson's other interest in the architecture of the past is in the *act* of building itself and in why man builds. This is an issue he embraces thoroughly in *The Mound Builders*, but it is of no less importance in *Talley & Son*. Gene A. Barnett's discussion of this issue is particularly insightful: "As the mound builders created and built, trying to seize immortality through structure and wealth, so do we still seek status and a kind of immortality through building" (101). The Talley house, then, represents an attempt at immortality, and it is Wilson's purpose to debunk this powerful feeling. He depicts the Talley house as a place of entrapment and sorrow, of secrets and death; it is a house that serves as a dwelling but never as a home. He uses the house as a setting for the destruction of the Talleys, and, in extending the metaphor, an ironic representation of America just prior to war's end: proud, morally strong, seemingly indestructible and about ready to lead the Western world forward into the modern era. At the same time, her oldest and most cherished institutions such as the family are now rapidly heading for defeat by the forces of modern capitalism, war and the march of time.

Indeed, it is time's unrelenting march that does the most damage to the once-mighty Talleys. The family suffers from a blatant failure to renew itself, as evidenced by Calvin's senility and Eldon's inability to take full control of the Talley fortune. In addition, Timmy has been killed in the war, Sally is unable to produce offspring and Buddy has no interest in the family business whatsoever. This leaves Eldon presiding over a family that is in danger of becoming extinct through uncontrollable external forces and a fatalistic malaise which is embodied in the character of Eldon himself. Eldon's passive attitude to all events, an attitude that disgusts Calvin, is especially revealed by his decision to swap his share of the Talley factory for his partner Harley's share of the Talley bank, a magnanimous and money-losing gesture, motivated in part by the death of Timmy. Indeed, the deal is so unfavorable to Eldon that Harley (who will profit the most) finds it difficult to accept.

The inactivity that Eldon displays undermines his position as head of the household, a position he wrested from the incompetent hands of his father. Wilson has nothing but disdain for these traditional family leaders whom he characterizes as "feudal lords," and notes that *Talley & Son* represents "the loss of control of these controlling, patriarchal figure[s] who no one dared rob or offend" (Cooperman 78). That both Calvin and Eldon have lost control is unmistakable but Eldon especially represents "the end of the line" for the old conventions as there is no one to take over (either by force or by a peaceful transition) after he is gone. His children reject his lineage and the values associated with it, leaving Eldon as the captain of the sinking ship that is the American family structure.

Ironically, although Eldon's sons offer no tangible threat to his position as head of the household, Wilson sees the patriarchal figure as a man constantly threatened by his sons (or others who desire to rule). His interpretation of the traditional family is one in which "the father [is] in conflict with the son, in direct, physical conflict . . . that's the king must die. That's the family: the king must die" (Cooperman 77). *Talley & Son*, for all of its links to tradition, surprisingly offers very little in the way of father/son confrontations, although there are two relatively minor encounters. The lesser of these involves the more potent patriarch, Calvin, and his patriarch son. What could have been a real clash of Titans becomes a rather tame encounter, basically because Calvin is not mentally up to the challenge and Eldon is too passive and disgusted to care. Also, Eldon has usurped his father's "throne" out of necessity, thus the severity of their confrontation is lessened accordingly. At the height of their "showdown," Eldon lashes out at his father mildly: "Dad, why don't you go to hell. At least go to bed. You've done enough for one night" (111).

The clash between Eldon and Buddy is a more dynamic one, and, because of the mental and physical capabilities of both men, a more violent and degrading encounter. Their confrontation occurs, fittingly, in the same scene as the Calvin/Eldon struggle. Buddy is angry at his father for selling out the factory: "We'd be losing our shirts on a trade like that," he warns (108). Eldon reacts to this cynically, realizing that it is only greed that motivates Buddy, who never cared about the business that Eldon took so much pride in. Eldon taunts his son with the memory of Timmy, revealing a strong sibling rivalry between the brothers:

> ELDON: Timmy was there. I could count on him. You were never on my side in your life.
> BUDDY: Oh, bullshit. All Tim ever did was what-ever you wanted, so you'd maybe pat him on the head—which you never did. Timmy was his father's little puppy dog, just like you are.
> ELDON: Enough!
> BUDDY: God knows, I tried to shake some sense into him. Now the son-of-a-bitch's even died for you. (ELDON *slaps him across the face. . . .*)
> (110–11)

The cruelty of Buddy's remarks notwithstanding, this scene is all too brief and ineffective for the kind of father/son battle that Wilson generally has in mind; he offers a much more telling example in *Lemon Sky* between Douglas and Alan, or to some extent in *Angels Fall* between Doherty and Tabatha. The *Lemon Sky* clash in particular compares with the classic father/son confrontations in *All My Sons*, *Death of a Salesman* and *Long Day's Journey into Night*. If the king is to die in *Talley & Son*, it will be a slow wasting away and its effect will be much more long-term.

Passivity is one response to the inevitable powers that are shaping America and ruining the Talleys. A more active response involves escape and this choice is embodied most effectively by Timmy, Lottie and Sally, the only truly likable characters in *Talley & Son*. Wilson champions their separation from the family (Timmy and Lottie through death, Sally via abandonment) by making them the most worthy of our sympathy and respect. These three figures represent the dawn of the family of freedom, a family formed when members rebel and escape from the confines of the family of security. The character of Sally, primarily in *Talley's Folly* (where her role is greater than in *Talley & Son*), especially offers a hope for the rebirth of the American family in some new and workable form. Sally's departure demonstrates not only the radical changes that the American family is going through, but by having a woman lead the way to rebirth and a new future for the American family,

Wilson once again shows his intuitive knowledge of the trends and developments that have shaped modern America. Indeed, sociologists have recently determined that the movement from the authoritarian, sex-role system of family to a freer, less rigid system began in the mid-1940's (Taubin and Mudd 258).

III

If *Talley & Son* signals the end of the traditional American family, then *Talley's Folly* ushers in the new era of family life. Literally, *Talley's Folly* is not about a family at all; its focus is on two people, Matt Friedman and Sally Talley. On a larger scale, however, the play has everything to do with families and their effect on individual members. Matt and Sally are many things—lovers, misfits, loners—but they are, above all, victims of a corrupt and dying institution. The strength of their characters, and the strength of this play, come from their active decision to repair the damage that has already been done to themselves in particular, and to the family in general.

Sally Talley has disgraced her family. As an unmarried woman at age 31, she is subject to old-fashioned notions about spinsterhood. As a woman who cannot bear children she is of no value to the Talleys who, like all large and prestigious families, desire many capable heirs to continue the family line. But there is more at stake for the Talleys than the matter of children. As it is later revealed in *Talley's Folly*, Sally was engaged to marry Eldon's business partner, Harley Campbell, when she contracted tuberculosis and became barren. Her family hoped that a marriage between Sally and Harley would mean a major business merger between the Talleys and the Campbells, "a very prominent Laclede County family" and part-owners of the Talley garment factory (55). Sally's sterility rendered her "no longer of value to the merger" (58). After this, she began to teach Sunday school, but was promptly fired from that position for reading the work of economist and social critic Thorstein Veblen to her class (presumably to stir up pro-union sentiments which would be damaging to her family's business). Sally has done so much damage to her family, socially and economically, that she is, in business terms (certainly in terms of how the Talleys think of her), a liability.

These factors contribute to her deep-rooted feelings of estrangement from her family and entrapment: "You know I can't stand livin' there as it is," she tells Matt (8). Her feelings transcend any simplistic notions that a child will naturally seek to leave his family in order to find his individuality (although certainly there is some of this in Sally's thinking). Her need to escape from the "hypocrites and fools" that make up her family is so great that she will do almost anything to be free of them (11). This includes her rather unorthodox decision to run off with Matt Friedman who, being liberal, foreign, middle-aged and Jewish, is the least likely to be accepted by the conservative, WASP Talleys. She tells Matt: "You were very exotic to me. I reread the Old Testament" (28). Sally's determination to join Matt demonstrates her courage in challenging the evils of her family.

Despite her intense feelings of resentment toward her family, Sally nevertheless does harbor some warm feelings about the Talleys. She enjoys telling Matt about her great-Uncle Whistler (Everett Talley, Calvin's brother) who built the boathouse in which the action of *Talley's Folly* takes place. Sally feels a camaraderie with Whistler who also was an outcast of the family. In *Talley & Son*, Calvin wanders off to the family cemetery and remarks that Whistler "won't shut up. Dead and buried, still won't quit yammering" (59). Sally, by contrast, remarks that Whistler, because of his singing and toy-making, "was the healthiest member of the family" (19).

Sally also resents Matt's grotesque imitations of her family members and their accents: "Please don't do that. Don't make fun of the way we talk," she scolds him (13). She also appreciates the beauty of the land around her, saying that she will miss it when she leaves with Matt. Reactions such as these prove Sally to be a more sensitive and multi-dimensional person than her familial counterparts. While she cannot abide their greed, hypocrisy and ignorance, she has a fondness for their customs, speech and surroundings. She does not see the world in terms of economics as her family (and, in some respects, Matt) does. Rather, she sees America as a place of tradition and beauty which has been ruined by things like banks, factories and families. These feelings create a terrible dilemma within her. On the one hand, she knows she must leave her home; on the other, she would like to stay, if only she could be free of her family. She makes a slight, but needed, concession in her decision to go with Matt when she agrees to come back home once a year "so we don't forget" (60). Despite the social ramifications of her departure, and the fact that she is, indeed, leaving behind things that she loves, Sally goes off with Matt, and this truly is testimony to her bravery.

   Talley's Folly also offers an opportunity to examine the effects of both the biological family and the family of man on their particular members. These are the two types of families that Wilson is most interested in: "One is the family that's really a biological family, and the other is the 'catch-as-catch-can' family of man. When I use family, that's the context I use them in because I'm really talking about everybody" (Cooperman 73). It is obvious what a biological family has done to Sally. It is also clear what the family of man has done to Matt. While Sally must share some of the blame for her predicament (she does, after all, challenge tradition), Matt is a victim of forces completely beyond his control. In his touching scene of self-revelation, Matt tells Sally of his life as a "probable Lit" (Lithuanian) who, with his family, traveled all over a troubled and violently anti-Semitic Europe just prior to World War I (36). The subsequent murder of his parents and his sister at the hands of the German government left him alone to wander from "Norway to Caracas to America on a banana boat" (40).

   Matt's harrowing story painfully demonstrates human betrayal and inhumanity. Sally, appalled by Matt's revelations, asks in amazement, "They [the Germans] wouldn't kill their own people just because they knew something they might or might not tell—," to which Matt replies, "—Well, they didn't consider them their own, of course" (39). Matt's response points to a world, which, like a corrupt family, does not nurture its "children." In Matt's particular case, it is the German government, acting like a power-mad patriarch, that destroys its own children to prevent them from growing up and, possibly, usurping its power. Matt and Sally share this feeling of betrayal and this serves to strengthen their union.

What Wilson is arguing here is that the traditional family structure, with internal hierarchies and omnipotent rulers, is evil on any scale, small or grand. He has demonstrated this in play after play and in his own statements as well: "I don't have a good deal of respect for what we consider the family" (Cooperman 76). *Talley's Folly* is the first of his plays to present this as a world-wide dilemma and not strictly an American problem. Ironically, the play indicates that it is not "family" as an ideal that Wilson dislikes, but rather "what we consider the family." Destruction is therefore not the focus of *Talley's Folly* as it was in *Talley & Son*. Instead the focus is on rebuilding from existing bedrock, creating changes which are novel while simultaneously respecting the conventions of the past. This idea is clearly reinforced by Sally's desire to come home once a year.

Talley's Folly also answers the distress call of *Talley & Son*, for it proposes a possible answer to the predicament of a dying institution in America. Rather than surrendering to destruction, as Eldon Talley does, the ultimate survivors, Sally and Matt, join forces in order to start family life anew. Their dissimilar backgrounds and decision not to have children to impose a hierarchy on (of course, Sally cannot have children) leaves them in a non-traditional, but ultimately workable, family situation. However, they also will have some knowledge of tradition and plan to incorporate that knowledge in their unconventional union. This marks a step away from the general conception of a family of freedom, for in this new arrangement, the problem of the need to return to the past is solved. This brave new family design provides a non-sentimental balance between the forces of security and freedom and marks the genesis of Taubin and Mudd's "contemporary traditionals." In *Fifth of July*, Wilson will show exactly what the sociologists have proven: that this new family can be very successful.

IV

Following that apocalyptic Independence Day of 1944, all that is left is the mixed feelings of destruction and hope.

Apparently, Wilson is interested in dramatizing the devastation and the reconstruction of the American family, but not the painful process of adjustment in between, for thirty-three years separate *Talley & Son* and *Talley's Folly* from *Fifth of July*. There is no Talley play that explains what went on in their lives during the rest of the 1940's, the 1950's, 1960's or most of the 1970's. The optimism of *Talley's Folly* is the only evidence of the future of the Talley clan, but this is a fair indication of what is presented in *Fifth of July*. With this play, Wilson finally reconciles the forces of freedom and security in such a way that sentimentality is eliminated and longevity is achieved.

On its own, *Fifth of July* presents a "business as usual" family, with no indication that the events of July 4, 1944, ever took place. Wilson clearly wants this to be the case, as he does not see the Talley heritage as being a particularly important part of this new Talley family. About the issue of heritage he has said, "What do we know about any of that and what do we care. We all strike out on our own with no regard for any of that" (Cooperman 77). Indeed, *Fifth of July* takes place *after* a great many important events not only in the lives of the Talleys, but in America as well: the World War II victory, Korea, Vietnam, the troubled 1960's, etc. Even the title indicates that the action is after Independence Day, a day when there are explosions, either in celebration (as in *Talley's Folly*) or to signal annihilation (*Talley & Son*). Clearly, *Fifth of July* is the aftermath of a great many things, most of which are so troublesome that they are best left relegated to an unremembered past.

The title also is an indication of what the focus of the play will and will not be. Most important, it will not be about the Talley family as it has been presented heretofore. It is particularly noteworthy that the name "Talley" does not appear in the title. It can be safely assumed that the Talleys are no longer a family of any prestige or power, a situation that was prepared for in *Talley & Son*. By virtue of its title, *Fifth of July* could be about any family, or no family at all. By the same criterion, the 1944 plays could only be about the Talleys. Wilson's choice of title shows the dramatic shift away from the notion that family is of particular importance, or, rather, that a particular family is of particular importance in the grand scheme of things.

The family that is presented in *Fifth of July* blends elements of both old and new family structures. There are biologically related members: Kenny and June Talley (Buddy's children), Sally Friedman (Matt has died) and Shirley Talley, June's daughter. This is countered by non-related members: Jed Jenkins (Kenny's lover), John and Gwen Landis (friends of Kenny and June) and Weston Hurley, a friend of John and Gwen. The many generations that make up this clan point to a more traditional arrangement as well. Yet there is no structure or hierarchy to this throng and no ruling patriarch. Also, there is no one family business that must be sustained as every member of the household works at his or her "own thing." The traditional set-up has been replaced by homosexual pairings, single mothers and a diversified set of interests, ambitions and dreams.

This group, as presented, resembles other family groups found in Wilson's plays. For example, the fact that these related and non-related people will all be living under the same roof for a limited time—Gwen, John and Weston are there for a quick business meeting—recalls Wilson's surrogate family plays: *Balm in Gilead*, *Angels Fall* and, especially, *The Hot l Baltimore* (these are plays in which a group of people can be said to act cohesively as a family, yet are not necessarily biologically related, although some members may be). That most of these people are old school friends invites comparison with *The Sand Castle*. Finally, because there are such unfamiliar permanent members such as homosexual lovers and single parents, the wards of the state and the step-children of *Lemon Sky* come to mind.

In terms of temperament, *Fifth of July* most closely resembles the surrogate family structure found in *The Hot l Baltimore*. The play is a lively, comic piece whose fun derives from Wilson's mastery of character presentation. The eccentricities and outrageousness of characters such as Aunt Sally, Shirley, Gwen and Weston add to the atmosphere of joy in this household. In what amounts to a complete reversal from the technique used in *Talley & Son*, these comic characters are an integrated part of an already established lifestyle. Thus, there is no need for comic relief, as Lottie provides in the 1944 play. Rather, it is the character of John who brings to this household a sort of "tragic relief," for he represents the evil businessman trying to swindle both the Talleys and his lover Gwen for the sake of the almighty dollar.

In addition to the intrusion of John, this new Talley household has other serious problems. These predicaments are such that they focus on a particular individual, which is appropriate for a family of freedom founded on the principles of individuality. The problems in *Fifth of July* center around the main character, Kenny, and his struggle to find a purpose in life now that he is handicapped (thanks to the Vietnam War). The other major trouble in the play is directly related to Kenny's condition: he wants to sell the house, possibly to John and Gwen (who will use it as a recording studio for Gwen's music career).

Kenny's entertaining the thought to sell the house brings the element of family into the play. Selling the Talley house would mean getting rid of the last vestige of the Talley clan. Ironically, this is not what Wilson seems to think is the proper thing to do. He has applauded the survival of the mighty Talley mansion on many levels (not the least of which is his own interest in the architecture of the past). On one level, it marked the frivolity of the Talleys as builders of their own immortality. On another level, it serves as a lasting reminder that there is a need for family, or, at best, a family situation that is not corrupted by greed and the lust for power. The house therefore represents what the family could be (and is, in *Fifth*). On still another, and more personal level, it is Aunt Sally's link to her past, a past which she does not want to lose (as the ending of *Talley's Folly* shows). This being the case, it is Aunt Sally who bids against John for possession of the house, and eventually wins the property. Wilson makes it clear that it is Sally's passion as an individual that is the deciding factor of who shall own the Talley house. While he is not concerned with saving the family as an institution, Wilson nevertheless illustrates in the character of Sally a need for family and a need for a recognition of the past (i.e., a heritage).

The past, then, becomes an issue even in a play that in its title attempts to forget it. The past will always be a concern for Kenny, who was emotionally and physically victimized by it. He does remember his school days at Berkeley with some fondness: "All the old Berkeley days came back to wreck us last night.

Reminiscences, and camaraderie . . ." (15), but he is never nostalgic. June shares his feelings, also with no trace of nostalgia. She is adept at putting the past into perspective, although she wrestles with the results, as when she yells at Shirley, "You have no idea of the country we almost made for you. The fact that I think it's all a crock now does not take away from what we almost achieved" (40). The past for Kenny and June is something to be remembered but not sanctified. In addition, they could not be proud or even fond of their particular heritage, which would be the evil and corrupt Talleys of 1944. It is the Talleys themselves as particular people who must be forgotten, not the times in which they lived or the traditions which they corrupted. With this, Wilson avoids the sentimentality about the past that is found in other plays that manage to balance the forces of security and freedom.

What *Fifth of July* shares most with Wilson's other surrogate family plays is a sense of camaraderie. In one episode of the play, the characters sit around talking about their activist days in the 1960's. June, as always, adds a touch of cynicism and bitter realism to the proceedings when she describes the reaction of the stalled drivers on the freeway as she tried to hand them some flowers: "Unfortunately, they hated us. The traffic started moving; we nearly got run down" (57). Despite this, there is a real sense of togetherness in this scene, forcing Gwen (the only character in the play who is nostalgic) to say, "Oh, I loved us then" (57). Further evidence of such family-like togetherness comes late in the play when it is discovered that Sally fainted during the funeral services for Harley Campbell. Kenny, June, Gwen and Jed all tried to help Sally by giving her water, calling the doctor and making her sit down, demonstrating that a group of people can function as a family and care for each other without being utterly dependent upon each other. Both episodes demonstrate that togetherness and individuality are necessary components of any family situation; when they are conspicuously absent, as in *Talley & Son*, the family is left fragmented and on a steady course for destruction.

The obvious outsider in the proceedings is John. John is Wilson's typical American businessman, scheming mightily to make a quick dollar, but avoiding all contact with human emotion and spirituality. In that respect, he closely resembles the vicious hustlers of *Talley & Son*. Unlike that play, however, this corrupt character is clearly outnumbered by the forces of honesty and compassion, another reversal from *Talley & Son*, where Lottie was the outnumbered and dying embodiment of good.

Because he is so outnumbered, John loses twice: first, the house to Aunt Sally, and second, Shirley to June. John, it is revealed (although more hinted than actually stated), is Shirley's father. He wants to take her away from June, citing "the advantages for the kid" as his reason (71). Obviously, John is talking about the financial advantages for Shirley if she was to live with him. However, June wins out and in so doing wins a victory for motherhood, a traditional and American value. On a metaphorical level, John, the ultimate modern man, loses to tradition twice, and through him Wilson reconciles a return to the past with the need to break from it.

The basic theme of *Fifth of July*, like so many of Wilson's other plays, is survival. In a funny and revealing scene, Weston tells Kenny about an Eskimo folktale that he has read. It involves a starving family and their huge pile of frozen caribou meat. The hero of the story bravely farts on the meat, thawing it. However, the stench of his action renders the meat unappetizing, and so the family dies. When he is told this story, Kenny only senses the absurdity in it and drops the subject. In the second act, a more enlightened Kenny relates his version of the story's moral to Weston:

> KENNY. Oh, Weston, doll, I'm all in favor of your Eskimo hero. I think he was a man among men. I completely blame the family. You see, if you had said that the warrior was flatulent on the walrus blubber . . .
> WESTON.—caribou meat—
> KENNY. . . . Be that as it may, and it stank so bad that the family could hardly eat it, but they managed and survived, we could perhaps accept that. . . . (58–59)

Kenny also tells Weston that the "saving grace" of the story "would have been surviving. Don't choke on it, don't turn up your nose, swallow it and live, baby" (59). Kenny's response is typical Wilson; he blames the family for failing to sustain itself while championing the actions of an individual. Yet the point he is making is that survival should preclude any notions of family, especially in a family that cannot insure its own maintenance. The Eskimo myth, then, actually parallels Wilson's feelings, for it depicts the need of an individual to escape from a harmful family situation in order to survive. This is exactly what Sally and Matt did, thus insuring the survival of a new and enriched Talley family.

Along with the images of survival, *Fifth of July* also contains positive images of the future. Kenny is working on an audio tape made by a boy, Johnny Young, who cannot speak intelligibly. At the end of the play, Kenny finally is able to translate the boy's garbled speech. The result is a poignant paragraph about the future and one's need to become whatever one dreams to be. Kenny shares this optimism in the final line of the play: "I've got to talk to Johnny Young about the future" (75). With that, a determined Kenny walks off to ready himself for the coming school semester. Shirley, noting that "the whole family has just come to nothing at all so far" (75), decides that she will be "the greatest artist Missouri has ever produced" (41). Jed is cultivating an English garden on the Talley property which will take twenty years to mature, and he fully expects to wait it out (John, of course, wants to put a landing strip over Jed's garden). Jed comments that "the stupid herb garden is going rank. The lavender's all over the thyme, the angelica's flopping all over the germander" (7). This image of chaos is countered by Jed's meticulous care of the garden, which leaves the feeling that he will right its wrongs in the near future, just as this family has righted the familial wrongs of America's chaotic past. Perhaps the most telling action is Sally's sprinkling of Matt's ashes over Jed's garden (up until the very end of the play, they were going to be dumped in the river). This deed demonstrates the need for the past to fertilize the future without contaminating it.

In discussing this play, Wilson has said, "That's a family that could possibly work. That's a ramshackle, put-together family that could possibly work and feel some responsibility for the necessary traditions like cultivating the earth, and would not have any respect for all of the phony ones . . . all of the ones that really have no place" (Cooperman 75). His description suggests that the sociological phenomenon of "contemporary traditionals" has taken root in the soil of a renewed America. They are defined as a group of individuals who "respect and practice those conventions, customs and ideals that seem relevant and functional to their present well-being, while adapting those that no longer seem to fit. Politically, economically and socially they live in the present, while attempting to preserve the accumulated experience and wisdom of the past." The "contemporary traditionals" of Taubin and Mudd are equivalent to the modern Talleys of Lanford Wilson (Taubin and Mudd 256). *Fifth of July* is Wilson's greatest achievement as a dramatist, for he has created a rare piece of American drama: the family play that is neither mired in sentiment and nostalgia nor heavy with tragedy and sorrow.

V

The Talley plays, while interesting on their own, when discussed as a trilogy present a powerful vision of the American family. That Wilson dislikes the family as an institution is quite evident, especially in *Talley & Son*: "I don't think it particularly works. I think we survive in spite of it" (Cooperman 76). But that he acknowledges the need for some type of family structure in the lives of Americans is also unmistakable. Indeed, it has been suggested that he is always searching for a sense of family in his work (Haller 28). *The Hot l Baltimore* offers a glimpse of this, especially when Suzy, grieved at the thought of leaving her companions at the doomed hotel, cries, "We've been like a family, haven't we? My family" (65). Wilson concedes that Suzy's sentiments would be echoed by virtually every inhabitant of the Hotel Baltimore: "If you would say, 'who's your family?,' they'd all say, 'My family is here'" (Cooperman 73). Similarly, for all of their non-conformity, the Talleys of *Fifth of July* are basically a family, but, Wilson confesses, not the sort of family that is thought of as being typically American: "If you were writing about family and if you were taking the mid-Western American dream, that [the *Fifth of July* family] would be about as horrible as you could get" (Cooperman 76). The issue of family, then, as a basic human need is one that Wilson apparently has failed to reconcile in his own mind.

The issue of family life in America, however, is one that Wilson has quite astutely observed and recorded. If the Talley plays are nothing else, they are an honest look at a changing institution, and, ultimately, quite an accurate one. In three neat steps Wilson has been able to document an evolutionary process, based in fact, that operates at an almost unconscious level within and among the plays. It is an unseen thread that binds these plays together, yet allows them the freedom to exist independently of one another. The same could not be said of other contemporary family trilogies such as those created by Israel Horovitz or Neil Simon. These trilogies have no greater issues at work behind them. They are the continuing saga of the same family with the same members and a clichéd vision of a world that remains static as characters simply grow older. Wilson's view is greater and more worldly. He writes dynamically about evolution, death and rebirth and social, political and economic forces working slowly yet unceasingly, changing lives and changing the country. Lanford Wilson writes history.

The Talley plays, then, are the history of family life in modern America. "It's a history of America," he concedes regarding his purpose in writing the Talley cycle, and he shows considerable skill by using family as a leitmotif in writing such a history (Cooperman 83). Although he may not care for it, Wilson recognizes that the institution of family is inseparable from American notions of well-being and fulfillment. It is a major component of the fabled American dream and Wilson, like any American playwright, must grapple with family if he is to make sense of America. The Talley plays demonstrate that he has indeed made sense of America and has exposed its evils as well as its triumphs. Therefore, his choice of a family name is no accident; the Talleys represent America's "tally," its account, its reckoning, its coming to grips with itself. Lanford Wilson has allowed the American family an unprecedented opportunity to show itself corrected, having been left for dead just thirty years prior.

84 *Lanford Wilson: A Casebook*

REFERENCES

Barnett, Gene A. *Lanford Wilson*. Boston: G. K. Hall, 1987.
Berkvist, Robert. "Lanford Wilson—Can He Score On Broadway?" *New York Times* 17 February 1980, sec. 2: 1, 33.
Cooperman, Robert. "'We've Been Like a Family, Haven't We?': Lanford Wilson's Vision of the American Family." Thesis. Queens College, CUNY, 1989.
Haller, Scot. "The Dramatic Rise of Lanford Wilson." *Saturday Review* 8 (August 1981): 26–29.
Scanlan, Tom. *Family, Drama, and American Dreams*. Westport, CT: Greenwood, 1978.
Taubin, Sara B., and Emily H. Mudd. "Contemporary Traditional Families: The Undefined Majority." *Contemporary Families and Alternative Lifestyles*. Ed. Eleanor D. Macklin and Roger H. Rubin. Beverly Hills, CA: Sage, 1983. 256–68.
Weales, Gerald. "Flawed and Fascinating." *Commonweal* 11 September 1981: 500–02.
Wilson, Lanford. *Fifth of July*. Rev. ed. New York: Dramatists Play Service, 1982.
——. *The Hot l Baltimore*. New York: Dramatists Play Service, 1973.
——. *Talley & Son*. New York: Hill and Wang, 1986.
——. *Talley's Folly*. New York: Hill and Wang, 1979.

"Above Time" in the Present?: Emerson's "Self-Reliance" and Lanford Wilson's *Angels Fall*

Richard Wattenberg

After working for the better part of five years on his three Talley family plays, Lanford Wilson shifted direction with his next full-length play, *Angels Fall* (1982). Turning from fictitious family history, Wilson focused on issues that continue to have topical relevance. As Gene A. Barnett has written in his study of Wilson's plays, "*Angels Fall* may be Wilson's most obviously political play" (127). Touching on the problems of ethnic minorities and environmental mismanagement, Wilson gave his play an added sense of urgency by setting it against the background of a nuclear accident. Aware of the extremely precarious nature of our present technological society, the playwright addresses the very timely question posed by one of the play's characters: "Seeing that all this world shall be dissolved, what manner of persons ought we to be" (*Angels Fall* 101)—that is, given the possibility of a man-made end to human existence in the near future, how should we live today?

Despite the immediacy of Wilson's concerns in *Angels Fall*, reviewers and critics have generally not been very enthusiastic about the play. Initial responses were mixed. Wilson's dialogue and characters were praised,[1] and reviewers respectfully

---

[1]See Rich; Simon, "Too Much Heart?"; Simon, "Ideals Lost"; Gill.

commented on his handling of such questions as "how to find ways of living together or apart" (Simon, "Ideals Lost") and such themes as "the importance of finding a vocation" (Novick). Nevertheless, there was some reticence regarding the play's structure, which depends on the device of stranding a group of diverse characters and forcing them to interact. Reviewers like Frank Rich (*New York Times*), Julius Novick (*Village Voice*), John Simon (*New York Magazine*) and Robert Brustein (*New Republic*) pointed to the contrived and/or conventional nature of what Wilson himself has called a "locked-door play" (Savran 315). In a more recent assessment, Gene A. Barnett notes the earlier reviewers' concerns (125) but excuses the artificial nature of the play's structure by claiming that "sound construction, a sense of the importance of moral and spiritual matters, and a strong sentiment for people . . . are not bad materials for a dramatist" (132).[2] Barnett's defense of the construction of *Angels Fall* suggests, however, that while the play's subject matter meets with general approval, questions persist about its form.

In light of the play's origin, this kind of response is ironic. Wilson claims that the form and content of the play came to him simultaneously in a flash:

> I came back to New York from California in a panic and got an idea—bam!—in a bar. I saw a picture of New Mexico and I saw the entire play, all of the characters and the situation. The plays have often been a metaphor for where I think we're at, but usually I don't know that until I'm three-quarters of the way through them. This one I knew from the beginning, which is not as easy. If we're not people in a church that very few people go to, huddling

---

[2]Other recent critics have not only accepted the traditional nature of the play's structure but have discussed *Angels Fall* in terms of a particular "locked-door" genre. See Mark Busby's discussion of *Angels Fall* as an example of "one of the continuing frontier paradigms in American literature: the captivity narrative" (46) and Rudolf Erben's discussion of the play as an example of "a new dramatic genre, which we can call the western holdup play" (311).

> there in a minor nuclear emergency, I don't know
> where in the fuck we are. (Savran 314–15)

Form and content are closely linked in this metaphor for "where
we're at," this "church" suggesting spiritual possibilities—
possibilities to which "very few people" attend.

The nature of this unattended "church" can be clarified by
reference to a recurring Wilson motif: his concern with what he
sees as the destruction of the best elements of the American
heritage. Wilson has lamented that "America is trying to reverse
the myth of Jupiter; instead of the old man eating his children,
the children are eating their grandparents" (Haller 26–28). In
Angels Fall, this cannibalism is all too apparent. The barren
southwestern landscape surrounding the church or mission in
which this play is set is symbolic of the barren cultural landscape
of a nuclear age America that has lost contact with its spiritual
roots. In this play, Wilson seems to imply that these roots can be
found in the kind of democratic idealism expressed by
nineteenth-century men of letters like Ralph Waldo Emerson and
his equally well-known "disciples," Henry David Thoreau and
Walt Whitman. In *Angels Fall*, Wilson is more than just seeking to
awaken his contemporaries to the complexities of life in a
modern technological society, he is attempting to reawaken
American audiences to the democratic faith of their
"grandfathers"—Emerson, Thoreau and Whitman.

To be sure, an idealism akin to Emerson's pervades *Angels
Fall*, providing the play's "church" metaphor with secular significance. An Emerson-like faith in and hope for the individual
not only underlie the themes and ideas discussed in the play but
also the "locked-door" form which critics have judged conventional and/or traditional. The temporary isolation of the
characters as well as the nature of their diversity has added
meaning when viewed from an Emersonian perspective. Wilson
uses the play's situation and the motivations and actions of its
characters to imply that the manner of person one ought to be is
the manner of person Emerson described more than a century
ago under the heading of "self-reliance."

Called "the philosopher of democracy" by John Dewey
(76), Emerson consistently maintained that the common man/

woman was the measure of all meaning, the chief source of value in a universe which is "fluid and volatile" ("Circles" 302). In the essay "Self-Reliance" (1841), he announced: "Nothing is at last sacred but the integrity of your own mind. . . . No law can be sacred to me but that of my nature" (50).[3] Seeking to awaken his contemporaries to the necessity of living according to their "Spontaneity or Instinct" ("Self-Reliance" 64), Emerson was, however, also aware that few individuals could accept this challenge. He wrote:

> Man is timid and apologetic; he is no longer upright; he dares not say "I think," "I am," but quotes some saint or sage. He is ashamed before the blade of grass or the blowing rose. These roses under my window make no reference to former roses or to bet- ter ones; they are for what they are; they exist with God to-day. There is no time to them. There is simply the rose; it is perfect in every moment of its existence. Before a leaf-bud has burst, its whole life acts; in the full-blown flower there is no more; in the leafless root there is no less. Its nature is satisfied and it satisfies nature in all moments alike. But man postpones or remembers; he does not live in the present, but with reverted eye laments the past, or, heedless of the riches that surround him, stands on tiptoe to foresee the future. He cannot be happy and strong until he too lives with nature in the present, above time. ("Self-Reliance" 67)

According to Emerson, the individual would find his true abode in neither the past nor the future, but only in the present.

To be sure, Emerson's emphasis on the present is a mani- festation of a basically anti-historical sense of time.[4] He was not

---

[3]F. O. Matthiessen's discussion of Emerson's interpretation of individual consciousness is extremely relevant here. See Matthiessen 3-14.

[4]Matthiessen suggests that Emerson's interest in history was "unhistorical" (626).

concerned with the development of events in time—with the interrelationship of past, present and future—but with the individual's relation to eternal truth in the present. For Emerson, the past and the future have significance for the individual only insofar as they are subsumed within the present—a present in which the self-reliant individual lives harmoniously with his/her intuition of eternal values. Ironically, it is only by living in this fashion that the individual might accomplish deeds which would have historical significance in a world of flux and flow. As Emerson remarked: "Every true man is a cause, a country, and an age. . ." ("Self-Reliance" 61).

Emerson thus sought to define a kind of heroism which would depend on neither inherited wealth nor acquired education but was entirely appropriate to the democratic New World experience. In fact, Emerson's belief that the truly self-reliant individual lives fully in the present following only his/her own intuitive sense of moral and spiritual necessity is central to the development of American, democratic idealism. Other voices in this tradition, like those of Thoreau and Whitman, also call upon their contemporaries to anchor themselves firmly in the immediate present. At the start of *Walden*, Thoreau claimed that he was always anxious "to stand on the meeting of two eternities, the past and future, which is precisely the present moment; to toe that line" (18). Likewise, Whitman turned his back on the European past and sought to awaken his American contemporaries to the importance of exploring the moral and spiritual possibilities of the democratic present.[5]

While nineteenth-century Americans like Emerson, Thoreau and Whitman encouraged their contemporaries to live according to the eternal moral and spiritual truths inherent in the concrete present, twentieth-century American playwrights have been concerned with the problematic nature of this quest.[6] Even

---

[5]See Walt Whitman, "Democratic Vistas" and "Poetry To-Day in America—Shakspere—The Future."

[6]In her unpublished manuscript, "The American Drama and the New World Vision," Esther M. Jackson investigates in great detail the connection between the vision of nineteenth-century American men of letters—especially Whitman—and the vision

a playwright like Thornton Wilder, whose work was very much in the tradition of the democratic idealist Emerson, was concerned with the difficulties confronting the individual who seeks a life immersed in the present fully devoted to the expression of eternal truths. In *Our Town* (1938), Wilder's protagonist Emily learns during the climactic third act that the present moment has both temporal and eternal meaning, but she also learns how difficult it is for her fellow human beings to embrace this present, to "realize life while they live it . . . every, every minute. . . ." (62) Other early and mid-twentieth-century American playwrights like Eugene O'Neill and Arthur Miller have been even less certain of the place of true "self-reliance" in the modern world. Lacking both the faith in eternal truths and the strength to live fully in the present, their characters like the residents of Harry Hope's bar in *The Iceman Cometh* (1946) and Willy Loman's household in *Death of a Salesman* (1949) fail "to toe that line." These characters escape an unpleasant, present reality into either distorted memories of the past or baseless hopes for the future. Lanford Wilson's *Angels Fall* represents a more recent example of the continued preoccupation of twentieth-century American playwrights with the kind of "self-reliance" defined by Emerson. Wilson's play is significant insofar as he places characters torn between the moral and spiritual possibilities of the present and the allurements of either the past or the future within a context which is immediately relevant to the late twentieth century.

Set in a small mission located in a sparsely populated area of northwest New Mexico, the action of *Angels Fall* takes place during an extended moment of crisis. Because of the nearby nuclear accident, the play's characters find themselves temporarily taking refuge in Father Doherty's mission. All but the Father restlessly await the opportunity to continue on their separate ways, but at the start of the play, they hear *"a stentorian voice"* announce from a helicopter hovering over head: "The roads are closed. . . . The roads are temporarily closed" (19–20). Significantly, the "road" in this play has both literal and

---

underlying twentieth-century American drama. I am indebted to Jackson for the opportunity to read this manuscript.

metaphorical meaning. Indeed, the "road" for each character is not only his/her route but his/her evolving life. Consequently, for the six characters of this play, who have been forced, at least momentarily, to abandon their "roads," time has temporarily stopped. They thus live in an "extended present moment" which has clearly established eternal and temporal dimensions.

The seclusion of characters implied by the "locked-door" format of the play functions on a deeper level than mere plot device or structural short-cut. The play's form isolates the time of the play—freeing the represented "present" from past and future. During the play, the characters exist in a "present" which, on the one hand, is temporal insofar as this "present" represents only a brief interlude in the characters' lives—an interlude between their pasts and their futures—and, on the other, is "above time" insofar as the play's action articulates—and the mission setting suggests—the spiritual and moral possibilities of living fully in the present. Within this "extended present moment," each of the characters must decide how to live his/her life: whether he/she will seek to live a spiritually and morally fulfilled life in the "present" or escape into memories of the past or dreams of the future.

The Emerson-like spokesman for a spiritually and morally fulfilled life in the present is the mission priest Father Doherty. A witty Irish priest originally from Emerson's Massachusetts, Doherty is quite an unorthodox Catholic churchman. His life-style is surprisingly spartan. As Niles points out, his mission "is unrelentingly severe. No self-respecting Catholic should tolerate this degree of austerity" (5). Moreover, Doherty himself admits that the mass which he regularly performs for his Navaho congregation lacks spectacle:

> I'm afraid there isn't anything to watch. Not even picturesque, I don't imagine. Twelve, fifteen stoic Navahos shuffle in, kneel, I mumble sincerely, they mumble sincerely, and they shuffle out. Nothing to see. Nothing on their faces, probably nothing on mine. In and out. Shuffle—shuffle. . . . Oh, it's what we live for, but there's nothing to see. (63)

For Doherty as well as for his congregation, the mass which is mumbled in Navaho is less an expression of Catholicism and its particular dogma than a general celebration of eternal spiritual values.

The Father, who confesses to having "no concept of time" (10), actually lives "above time" in Emerson's sense of the words. Like Emerson, Doherty is completely aware of the "fluid and volatile" nature of worldly forms and occurrences. Speaking of the interstate, he comments on the transitory nature of worldly facts: "I-Forty. Used to be Route Sixty-six. I think they do those things deliberately. Don't want us to get too attached to anything" (64). Indeed, the "road," in its metaphorical sense, lacks substance for the Father. While the other characters reluctantly abandon their "roads" for the temporary shelter of the mission, the Father conveys a sense of the insubstantiality of temporal process in his very first speech. He enters reciting to himself: "And the road was a ribbon of moonlight over the purple moor" (12)—an ironic comment on the general preoccupation with temporal matters. To be sure, the passing of time hardly affects Doherty's way of life. Looking neither backwards nor forwards, he is totally committed to the present. Not even the command of his church superiors could draw him away from his present life among the Navahos. As he continually sings: "Wild, wild horses couldn't drag me away" (45). Firmly anchored in the present, he follows only his own inner voice, his own sense of "calling." Consequently, Doherty continues to work for and with the local Navahos, trying to open their eyes—as well as the eyes of the other characters of the play—to the moral and spiritual possibilities of a life immersed in the present.

Father Doherty, thus, provides the play's other characters with a standard for self-reliance. While he embodies an Emerson-like faith in the potentiality of the individual who lives fully in the present, other characters in this play have difficulty living up to this ideal. On the one hand, the art history professor Niles Harris "with reverted eyes laments the past," and on the other, the young scientist Don Tabaha "stands on tiptoe to foresee the future." In focusing on the past and the future, these two characters miss the opportunity for spiritual and moral fulfillment in the present.

Niles, an unstrung art history professor from an eastern college, who is traveling to a special clinic in Phoenix with his wife Vita, is conscious of the problematic nature of his adherence to the past. In fact, his present nervous condition stems from a sudden need to question his loyalty to past values. He is aware that in his scholarship and his teaching he has shown little interest in contemporary art. For Niles, as his wife Vita claims, no work of art created "later than the seventeenth century" (29–30) has had any intrinsic value. He confesses that as a young professor, he had dreamt of "a life of quiet reflection, strolling through the groves" (86–87) contemplating the great works of the past with scholars and students of like mind. In contrast to the Emersonian notion that the past has value only insofar as it is a "cheerful apologue or parable" of the living individual's "being and becoming" ("Self-Reliance" 66) in the present, Niles had committed himself to the past for its own sake. He had failed to see that, as Emerson wrote, the true test of historical research was whether it succeeded in making the past present—that is, he had failed to see that:

> All inquiry into antiquity, all curiosity respecting the Pyramids, the excavated cities, Stonehenge, the Ohio Circles, Mexico, Memphis,—is the desire to do away this wild, savage, and preposterous There or Then, and introduce in its place the Here and the Now. (Emerson, "History" 11)

Because of this failure, Niles had failed as a teacher as well as a human being.

Niles's attempt to live in the past has been shattered by the harsh intrusion of present reality. Unable to ignore the fact that seven of his brightest students had committed suicide in the last ten years and that countless others had been destroyed by drugs, overwork and academic pressure, Niles has had a breakdown of his "willful suspension of disbelief" (34). He has begun to understand that as a human being, he should not have buried himself in the past but confronted his pedagogical and personal

responsibilities in the present. Nevertheless, Niles continues to
evade present commitment by rationalizing his recent failures:

> If there were a way to survey my subject without
> comment, without comparisons. "This is a painting.
> What does it say to you? There will be no test. Make
> friends where you like." Oh dear. Given today's
> students, begging for structure, half the class would
> have breakdowns within a week. (89)

Niles struggles with his sense of inadequacy as a teacher and as a
human being but is apparently unable to commit himself to action in the present. Although he seems to have freed himself
from a preoccupation with the artistic achievements of the distant historical past, he is still obsessed with the failures of his
recent personal past.

While Niles, the academician, has devoted his life to
maintaining the traditions of his European ancestors, Don
Tabaha is determined to reject the traditions of his Navaho
ancestors. His decision not to continue the medical training necessary for him to become a doctor to the local Navahos but instead to work in Berkeley on the Lindermann cancer research
team is his way of cutting off his Navaho roots. Dr. Lindermann,
"one of those charismatic 'leaders of his field,'" who is "always
being interviewed on TV" (50) and by whom Vita and Niles have
been "less than impressed" (50), has provided Don "with such a
golden opportunity to make something of [himself]" (59) that he
is willing to ignore his past. Don thus pursues the kind of
activity that Vita Harris describes when she speaks of the
distribution of her father's possessions after his death:

> Dad kept everything. His dad's cavalry sword from
> the First World War. Old ribbons from high school
> track meets, his own Second World War stuff—
> snapshots of D-Day. We even found an old Western
> saddle stashed away. He had some secret cowboy
> fantasy, maybe. . . . Mom took a few things, we all
> took something, and we burned the rest. Soon as it
> was gone, I felt I'd broken a law. All that crap
> belonged to the race, not to me. Every scrap should

> be stored somewhere. You never know which one
> shard left unburned would tell the tale. (65–66)

Ironically, both Emerson and Thoreau wrote about the usefulness of this kind of blatant destruction of the past[7] which so of-
fends the sentimental Vita (whose attraction to the past helps
explain her attraction to the historian Niles). Thoreau was
especially specific; in *Walden*, he demanded that old possessions
be periodically submitted to a "purifying destruction" by fire
(75).[8] Emerson and Thoreau, however, were interested in this
type of purgation as a means of freeing themselves of the past in
order to live more fully in the present. Don, on the contrary,
rejects his past so that he might escape into the future.

In fact, Don is not only cutting himself off from his
Navaho roots, he is turning his back on the real needs of his
people in the present. Rather than remain in New Mexico and
provide the local Navahos with the medical assistance they need,
Don has opted to follow the "road" which leads to material
comfort and glory in the future. It is for this reason that Father
Doherty finds it necessary to oppose Don's planned departure
for California. From the age of five, the Father explains, Don had
believed that medicine was his "calling." It was to be his way of
being fully himself, his way of living according to "Spontaneity
or Instinct," but now when he can do most for his people, Don
rejects the life of a doctor for "clean surroundings, intellectual
problems, no patients, no pain, no filth, no ugliness. Only
success" (77). Although he is acutely aware of the damage done
to the Navahos on the local reservation as a result of their work
in uranium mines and because of the lack of proper nutrition
and health care, Don still refuses to stay and help them. In his
mind, "there's no time for one person in a hundred years to
begin to correct a millennium of genetic neglect" (52). Don thus
rationalizes his moral failure. Certainly, he might help Dr.
Lindermann find a cure for cancer, but in choosing to follow

---

[7]Emerson, "Self-Reliance" 82-84; Emerson, "Circles" 319-20;
and Thoreau 25-26, 72-76.

[8]Relevant in this context is R. W. B. Lewis's discussion of
Thoreau's "rituals of purification" (20-27).

Lindermann, Don has betrayed his present spiritual and moral possibilities in order to rush into a nebulous, if easy, future.

While Niles is preoccupied with the past and Don with the future, the two characters who seem most in harmony with Doherty are the forty-year-old Marion Clay and her young lover, the tennis star "Zappy." Marion, like Niles, has had some contact with art circles; however, as a Chicago gallery owner and the widow of a contemporary artist (who Niles, in his role as guardian of the past, once disparagingly called a "regionalist artist"), she seems to be free of the stale formulas that plague Niles. Indeed, Marion seems to understand how successful art remains a living "friend." She tells the others how excited she became while preparing for a retrospective of her husband's work. She had thought that such preparation would be "morbid," but instead she found that "it was like a big blowout with a lot of old friends" (66). Although she found contentment amidst her husband's paintings while preparing them for a show, Marion does not live in the past. On the contrary, she is attracted to a life fully committed to the present. It is probably for this reason that she was drawn to her deceased husband, whose complete dedication to his art was unaffected by past accomplishments or future hopes, and is now drawn to Zappy, whose dedication to his "calling" represents an equally great commitment to life in the present.

Ironically, it is, in fact, Zappy the young tennis player who most manifests Father Doherty's brand of self-reliance. Underlying a somewhat comic preoccupation with his well-being is a total commitment to tennis. Tennis is Zappy's link to the present; indeed, tennis is his life—a fact that he has known for some time. In a very revealing passage, Zappy remembers how at the age of eleven he was introduced to his "calling" by two older boys:

> . . . I hit that first ball and I said, "This is me. This is what I do. What I do is tennis." And once you know, then there's no way out. You've been showed something. Even if it's just tennis, you can't turn around and say you wasn't showed that.
>
> So I went to church and said a novena for those meatballs, 'cause they didn't know all the butterflies that was in my stomach, that they'd been my angels.

> But, man, on the way home, anybody had asked me
> what I did, right there I'd have said, "I play tennis."
> Didn't know love from lob, didn't matter. That's
> what I am. 'Cause once you know what you are, the
> rest is just work. (91)

For Zappy a fulfilled life in the present is synonymous with playing tennis. Certainly, none of his matches will have world historical significance; nevertheless, in living according to his "Instincts," his life is as spiritually fulfilled as he could wish—a fact to which his prayer of thanks attests. In dedicating himself to his "calling" without concern for past or future, Zappy like Father Doherty, who is totally committed to his "calling," has much in common with Emerson's "roses." Both simply "are what they are; they exist with God to-day. There is no time to them." They are, thus, "perfect in every moment of [their] existence."

It is Zappy, then, not the humanist Niles, nor the scientist Don, who most clearly approaches a spiritually fulfilled life. In allowing the otherwise unheroic Zappy this degree of enlightenment, Wilson—like Emerson—emphasizes the fact that spiritual and moral fulfillment is not the inheritance of wealth or education but the inheritance of the self-reliant individual, who, firmly anchored in the present, listens only to his/her own inner voice, the voice of "Spontaneity or Instinct." Throughout the play Doherty attempts to awaken Niles and, most especially, Don to this fact. To be sure, Doherty's efforts are the focus of the play's plot. During the "extended present moment" around which the play is structured, the Father, contradicting his own belief that "if you leave [people] alone they'll do what their heart knows is right" (71), continually prods Don's heart.

As the play comes to an end and the *"stentorian voice"* from the helicopter above announces that *"The road is now clear!"* (93), the play's characters prepare to continue with their lives. Of the characters who have found shelter in the mission, Marion and especially Zappy live most fully in the present. Consequently, when they depart, they merely receive Father Doherty's blessing and his prayer that Zappy might win his coming match in San Diego. For Niles and Vita the reopening of the road is not an immediate signal for departure. Niles, at Vita's request, will remain for the Father's evening mass—a symbolic gesture toward the development of a more balanced attitude. Rather than escape into research concerning the historical past or seek self-destructive punishment for personal failures in the recent past, Niles is seemingly being led by Vita[9] and the Father toward a new faith in the possibility of a spiritually fulfilled life in the present. For Niles, the immersion into the "extended present moment" around which the play is built has resulted in the beginning of a rebirth. In fact, as the Father suggests, Niles will probably soon return to his eastern college and begin genuinely to teach his students—that is, he will devote himself to his students in the present and not try to hide himself behind the study of the past.

While the play manifests a degree of resolution with respect to the destinies of Marion and Zappy, on the one hand, and Niles and Vita, on the other, the major plot conflict—that between the Father and Don—lacks the completeness of resolution which is a prerequisite to a fully cathartic experience. Although Father Doherty remains completely convinced of his interpretation of Don's responsibilities, he gives up the chase. With some prompting from Niles, the Father accepts the fact that he cannot impose his moral values on Don. Any choice that Don makes must be entirely his own; it must be a product of his own "Spontaneity or Instinct." The spiritual awakening that the Father hopes for cannot come from without but only from within. In Don's case, however, it does not come at all: as the play ends, he leaves the mission for Berkeley. Don fails to see the double nature of the present. His departure is an admission that the present, in this case the "extended present moment," is only a prologue to his future. In rejecting present responsibility for

---

[9]Vita, as her name suggests, represents a positive life force. Indeed, she is like the play's other woman character, Marion Clay, in that both display strongly developed life-affirming and nurturing elements of character. Both seem to function primarily as maternal supports for the males with whom they are associated: Vita cares for and tends to Niles as Marion cares for and tends to Zappy.

future success, the spiritual for the mundane, Don epitomizes the loss of grace referred to in the title "Angels Fall."

Don's departure is more than a disappointment for Doherty. It is symptomatic of what Wilson suggests to be the major failure of American culture: the tendency to espouse technological progress at the expense of human values. Like Emerson (who wrote: "Not in time is the race progressive. . . . The arts and inventions of each period are only its costume and do not invigorate men. The harm of the improved machinery may compensate its good" ["Self-Reliance" 86].), Wilson sees the worship of progress or, as Father Doherty calls it, "energy" (93) as more harmful than good. However, what was merely problematic in the nineteenth century is potentially catastrophic in the twentieth century. A sense of urgency underlies the Father's outburst near the end of the play. Upon hearing the announcement from the hovering helicopter that the roads are clear, the Father angrily responds: "The road is not clear! You're sick as cats! You've made the bomb your God and you're praying for the bomb to call in the number. Well, you'll get it if you don't watch out" (93). Wilson, speaking through the Father, seems to imply that the next nuclear incident may be the last.

Certainly, *Angels Fall* is meant as a warning to late twentieth-century Americans. Living with the moment to moment possibility of extinction, Wilson suggests that his contemporaries can save themselves from nuclear holocaust only by discovering and developing the inner moral strength that nineteenth-century American idealists like Emerson, Thoreau and Whitman had attributed to the democratic individual. Indeed, from an Emersonian perspective, the play's "locked-door" form, with its secluded and diverse characters, has a value credited in neither the reviews of the original New York productions nor in later critical assessments. Form and content harmonize as *Angels Fall*, representing a plea for an Emerson-like self-reliance, takes on a heightened moral significance. As the play ends, Father Doherty rings the mission bells, calling his congregation to a service. These bells are meant to have wider reverberations for an audience. The hope for a future rests with individuals who are willing to answer Doherty's call with a full awareness of their moral responsibilities and spiritual possibilities in the present.

REFERENCES

Barnett, Gene A. *Lanford Wilson*. Boston: G. K. Hall, 1987.

Brustein, Robert. "On Theatre: Thoughts at Half Season." *New Republic* Year-End Issue 1982: 26–27.

Busby, Mark. *Lanford Wilson* (Western Writers Series 81). Boise, ID: Boise State Univ., 1987.

Dewey, John. "Ralph Waldo Emerson." *Characters and Events: Popular Essays in Social and Political Philosophy*. Ed. Joseph Ratner. New York: Octagon, 1970. I, 69–77.

Emerson, Ralph Waldo. "History," "Self-Reliance," "Circles." *Essays: First Series, Vol. II of The Complete Works of Ralph Waldo Emerson*. Boston: Houghton Mifflin, 1903. 1–42, 43–90, 299–322.

Erben, Rudolf. "The Western Holdup Play: The Pilgrimage Continues." *Western American Literature* 23 (1989): 311–22.

Gill, Brendan. "Events Before Mass." *New Yorker* 31 January 1983: 101.

Haller, Scot. "The Dramatic Rise of Lanford Wilson." *Saturday Review* 8 (August 1981): 26–29.

Lewis, R. W. B. *The American Adam: Innocence, Tragedy, and Tradition in the Nineteenth Century*. Chicago: U of Chicago P, 1955.

Matthiessen, F. O. *American Renaissance: Art and Expression in the Age of Emerson and Whitman*. Oxford: Oxford UP, 1968.

Novick, Julius. "Affirmative Actions." *Village Voice* 26 October 1982: 103.

Rich, Frank. "Play: 'Angels Fall,' Lanford Wilson's Apocalypse." *New York Times* 18 October 1982: C15.

Savran, David, ed. *In Their Own Words*. New York: Theatre Communications Group, 1988.

Simon, John. "Ideals Lost—and Found." *New York* 7 February 1983: 58.

——. "Too Much Heart? Too Much Brain?" *New York* 1 November 1982: 81–82.

Thoreau, Henry David. *Walden*. Vol. II of *The Writings of Henry David Thoreau*. Boston: Houghton Mifflin, 1906.

Whitman, Walt. "Democratic Vistas," "Poetry To-Day in
America—Shakspere—The Future." *Prose Works 1892.* Ed.
Floyd Stovall. New York: New York UP, 1964. II, 361–426,
474–90.
Wilder, Thornton. *Three Plays.* New York: Bantam, 1958.
Wilson, Lanford. *Angels Fall.* New York: Hill and Wang, 1983.

Angels Fall: An American Melodrama of Beset Manhood

Susan Harris Smith

A reading of any modern American play must address two questions: by what definition is the play "modern" and by what definition is it "American?" Obviously, the definition of "modern" is a fairly recent one but the problem of determining the "American" qualities of a play has plagued literary studies for almost two centuries. The desire for indigenous American dramatic expression courses through American cultural history. Because playwrights, critics and literary historians often apologetically felt that the drama was a lesser form lagging behind the other art forms in asserting its natural distinctiveness, a special sense of urgency about the creation of a non-European, separate dramatic mode for America informed essays on the subject. Though the need for a native drama was repeatedly expressed, the specific nature of the new drama was dealt with, for the most part, in airy vagaries and useless generalities.

An anonymous essayist in the *American Quarterly Review* in 1827 represented both the tone and substance that preceded and have followed in similar documents: "By a national drama, we mean, not merely a class of dramatic productions written by Americans, but one appealing directly to the national feelings; founded upon domestic incidents—illustrating or satirizing domestic manners—and, above all, displaying a generous chivalry in the maintenance and vindication of those great and illustrious peculiarities of situation and character, by which we are distinguished from all other nations" (339). First, the author assumes that a "national feeling" already exists, not that it is the cultural work of drama to create it. Second, other than insisting upon a focus on "domestic incidents" and a "vindication" of America, his argument lacks particulars.

Nearly a hundred years later, Thomas Dickinson, wrestling with the same problem, was more prescriptive: "If we could drop everything that is meant by the term 'American' and retain the meaning of 'pioneer,' we should have lost nothing" (208). He concluded with a description of a formula for new American drama: "The motive may be the motive of the normal American village, expressed in the temper of the pioneer spirit. The cohering power of the play will lie in simple neighborliness, in crude hanging together; the temper of the play will be that laconic optimism, that sturdy imaginativeness that marked the first settlers" (219). "Laconic optimism" are the key words here, pointing to that understated but insistent belief that the "American way," however flawed, is superior to the alternative, an insistence that is the leitmotif of much American drama.

Recently, poststructuralism has decentered received notions of an "American character" and challenged the idea that American culture or any national culture is homogeneous. Critics of American drama, however, have been slow to let go of traditional approaches and continue to read American plays for their "Americanness." Perhaps this impulse derives from the marginalized placement of most American drama outside the canon but, whatever the cause, critics have a tendency to search for a "representative" voice in a playwright. That these voices have traditionally been white and male (O'Neill, Miller, Williams) and continue to be (Mamet, Shepard, Rabe) hardly comes as a surprise given that American culture is still suckling an outworn creed of masculine frontierism.

Lanford Wilson has been singled out as a playwright who has captured the voice of the American people and the spirit of the times (Schewey 18). Robert Asahina suggests that Wilson "represents a distinctly American tradition" (231). Hailing him as "America's poet of loss and endurance," Ross Wetzsteon designates Wilson as a populist, "the heir to Thornton Wilder" (43). Frank Rich has praised Wilson as "one of the few artists of our theatre who can truly make America sing" (C15). Daniel Marowski claims that Wilson's plays are performed "more often than those of almost any other dramatist currently working in the United States" (458). These accolades and assertions that Wilson speaks for a nation demand some examination. If, indeed, Lanford Wilson does sing America, whose song is it?

Though the critics generally concede that *Angels Fall* is not one of Lanford Wilson's best plays, they do find it to be representative of his empathetic, humanist impulses. Also, they feel that it embodies the recurring thematic strains that characterize most of Wilson's work. Wetzsteon sums it up as a sustaining national nostalgia: "rootlessness, change, and isolation may have replaced home, continuity, and connection, yet glimpses of that idyllic past can save us from despair" (44). Many reviewers also noted that the play is a "lifeboat" or "snowbound" play, a version of the "barroom" play, in which diverse characters are thrown together by circumstance to thrash out their lives. The characters' whining, obsessive self-regard suggests that the play could be defined also as a "diaper drama," a form symptomatic of much American drama.

Benedict Nightingale coined the term "diaper drama" when, while on sabbatical leave from the *New Statesman* during the 1983–84 season to cover the American theatrical scene, he observed the dominance of the parent/child struggle and the paucity of ideas in contemporary American drama. Martin Esslin has also addressed the problem in "'Dead! And Never Called Me Mother!': The Missing Dimension in American Drama." Neither critic denies the power of family-oriented drama but both question the extent to which American playwrights in particular employ the conceit. Given such examples as *Hedda Gabler*, *Long Day's Journey Into Night* and *Death of a Salesman*, they argue, it is possible to create a deeply felt and culturally significant drama arising from family situations. What is so largely missing in the current spate of American drama, Esslin argues, is a profound philosophical and spiritual dimension that would force audiences to think critically about wider issues such as "the nature of human relations, indeed, the position of human beings in this mysterious universe—the human condition—itself" (25).

While, on one hand, Lanford Wilson's *Angels Fall* is a diaper drama about an extended family, or, in Dickinson's term, "a village," on the other, it ostensibly provides the context for exploring issues outside the confines of domestic parameters. Set in a small Catholic mission in northwestern New Mexico during a uranium spill at a nearby mine, the play isolates disparate people in a frightening and potentially life-threatening circumstance. Wilson's group represents a cross-section of professional America in pairs: Niles, a professor of art history, and Vita, his wife, an illustrator of children's books; Zappy, a tennis pro, and Marion, his companion, a widowed art gallery owner; Don, half Navajo and a medical student, and Father Doherty, the parish priest. Each pair contains one male who is *in extremis* (Niles, Zappy and Don). In true melodramatic fashion, the exceptional circumstance of convergence and interaction acts as a catalyst that causes changes for the better in all their lives. Psychic tensions are heightened and played out to the full so that there are no secrets left and, on the individual level, at least, there is satisfactory closure.

For the duration of the threat, the characters become a mutually supportive "family," a collective focused on the shared objective of survival and, after some squabbling, relating to each other in nurturing ways. Momentarily, they are one against the depersonalized presence dramatized as authoritative voices speaking through bullhorns from helicopters circling overhead and denying egress from the church. However, their union quickly dissolves when the roads are open and, now healed, they resume their individual pursuits of happiness.

On first impression, it seems as if Wilson is creating a situation similar to a modern European one such as Genet's *The Balcony* in which a revolution is raging outside the brothel and, by extension, the theatre. If this were the case, the audience would be being charged to look beyond the paradigmatic story that has been dramatized to larger issues suggested by the play's widest context and would be alerted to the necessity to act and address problems of mutual concern. However, the critics have not read *Angels Fall* as a "modern" play in this sense but as an "American" play, as an allegory about the failure of the citizenry to fulfill the American promise. For these readers, *Angels Fall* is not *No Exit* and, if they are correct, the escape which Wilson allows, though simplistic, sentimental, didactic and schematic, is actually a healthy corrective to floundering in a nihilistic metaphysical *angst* or raging in an existential void.

Gene A. Barnett's evaluation of Wilson's stance is symptomatic of the critics' desire to appropriate him for an American humanist cause. "First of all," Barnett writes, "he is very 'American.'" Arguing that Wilson's upbringing as a small-town Baptist gave him a sense that "one has an obligation to live meaningfully," Barnett insists that Wilson is "proud of the American heritage and concerned with preserving it" and that he is "typically American in his urge toward experimentation and in his optimism" (149). For Barnett, *Angels Fall* is a "sealed-room play" and a "morality play" (125) that "skirts sentimentality in the rather easy answers his characters find at the crossroads" (132).

Barnett's assessment expands upon the well-established pattern that Henry I. Schvey has documented in "Images of the Past in the Plays of Lanford Wilson" and that Barry B. Witham develops in "Images of America: Wilson, Weller and Horowitz." For Schvey, Wilson's characters are largely misfits and outcasts with no definite place in society who are searching for a fugitive happiness. Schvey's survey ends with *Talley's Folly* and with the conclusion that all of Wilson's works "are concerned with the relationship between the individual and the past, and all of them (in contrast to Wilson's earlier works) use the stage setting metaphorically to suggest a special relationship between the characters, their past, and their hopes for the future" (240). Though he is concerned with only one of Wilson's plays, *5th of July*, Witham's argument similarly suggests the necessity of "a return to the past in order to confront the future" (225). Witham reads Wilson's message as having specifically nationalist implications, arguing that each character has to confront not only individual failure but also "their collective failure of not making America a better place to live" (225). All three critics, therefore, read Wilson as an American essentialist.

But to what extent is the world of Lanford Wilson's misfits in search of meaning peculiarly American as opposed to modern? Does *Angels Fall* fit into some existing pattern of

American literary themes that precludes inclusion in a larger discourse community? On one hand, it would appear not to fit the paradigm. After all, the tension in *Angels Fall* does not result from the popularized American myth of adolescent males running alone to the rural west for self-realization away from a female-dominated urban east. There is no yearning for "a world elsewhere" and no "errand into the wilderness." Furthermore, there is certainly no individual transcendence or spiritual redemption for the separated individual, no Adamic man alone freely redefining himself in an open wilderness. *Angels Fall* is not a Jeffersonian agrarian or Emersonian transcendental romance. In fact, the men eschew nature, possibly because there is no nature left to idealize, only land being pillaged for its mineral resources and in danger of total annihilation from nuclear disaster. Instead, the play argues for marital and/or maternal domesticity coupled with a commitment to social engagement in narrowly defined, urban, institutional and bureaucratic contexts.

Suspicious of monolithic claims about the uniqueness of the "American experience," a form of xenophobic provincialism and exceptionalism that separates it from a modern context and equally uneasy with the assertion that the male experience is the American experience, I would like to propose a more circumspect reading, one which resists the tidy packaging of the play as quintessentially American, at least in the terms offered by the male critics. To this end, I want to explore several related questions. First, how "American" is Lanford Wilson's *Angels Fall*? Historically, the American subject has been understood to be the nation itself and the place of the individual within it. Giles Gunn summarizes the fundamental components of the essential paradigm of the American experience as originally formulated by Perry Miller and revised by a number of critics including R. W. B. Lewis, Leo Marx and Leslie Fiedler: "a single, solitary self who is either characteristically transplanted from another culture (and hence unfinished), or essentially unformed and uncultivated (and hence innocent), falling, so to speak, into experience and encountering there that ideal 'Other' in response to which he must, at the minimum, redefine himself and, at the maximum, virtually recreate himself" (191).

Recently this generalization has been modified to acknowledge that the "American experience" is an exclusionary one embracing only white males. Nina Baym, in a consideration of American fiction, characterizes the search for "cultural essence" as "a melodrama of beset manhood," one in which the pure male self, divorced from adversarial, constricting and female society, lights out for the free territory on a romantic quest for "self-definition" (130–31). But even examined from this perspective, *Angels Fall* is not "American." The women have come with the men and are presented as necessary sustainers rather than inhibitors in the quest. The men confront no "Other" nor do they recreate themselves. Niles undergoes a repositioning of himself towards his work; he will return to campus as an unstructured, relativist heretic. Don leaves the reservation to pursue a career he has no doubts about and Zappy is unchanged. Also, there is little dialectical interplay between the self and the environment. Finally, the burdens of history, that is the white males' responsibilities for the Indians' situation and for the place of women in society, are evaded.

Late in *Angels Fall*, Father Doherty reads from the second epistle of Peter (2 Peter 3:11): "Seeing then that all these things shall be dissolved, what manner of persons ought ye to be in all holy conversation and godliness?" (89–90) The Biblical answer is that we should "look for new heavens and a new earth, wherein dwelleth righteousness" (2 Peter 3:13). However, critics such as Gerald Weales and Julius Novick were quick to read the play as providing an exclusively secular answer to the Biblical question: find and follow a vocation (Weales 690; Novick 103). For the three questing men, Niles, Zappy and Don, this means teaching, tennis and medical research. Does the world of work exist in a dialectical relation to the world of imminent catastrophe, a no longer "natural" world undone by relentless acquisitive, technological man, or is it presented simply as its dark underbelly, a futile retreat into a finite, material world? What are the relationships among the spiritual world of the church, the nuclear world of the mines and the secular world of work? Certainly, if Doherty's position is taken as the central argument of the play, secular salvation would appear to be the answer. This idea of an earthly, not to say materialistic, "calling" privileges a solipsistic view and valorizes individual work. In fact, work replaces religion.

It is, perhaps, this attitude towards work that makes *Angels Fall* an "American" play. Privileging work elevates it to the supreme activity in which man can be engaged. In his work, he will have his identity and, in having a work-defined identity, his life will be meaningful. This bourgeois, and I must add, educated-class, sanctification of work, raises it above mere economic necessity to the level of a moral imperative in which the self is fully realized ethically as well as psychologically. In an inversion of the Thoreauvian ethos, where they live will be the city and what they live for will be work. But is this a purely "American" phenomenon? After all, it is an attitude that is endemic to international modernism as much as it is characteristic of the American Puritan/capitalist ideology.

In his analysis of the role of work in modern society, *Man & Work: Literature and Culture in Industrial Society*, David Meakin locates the validation for the spiritualized status of work in the concurrence of capitalism, protestantism and modern psychological theories. Freud in *Civilization and Its Discontents*, Meakin recalls, made work a potential force for integrated self-realization as well as a link to the human community. Likewise, Jung argued that work, as a free act without infantile constraint, could constitute a liberation for the individual (Meakin 3–5). This idealistic view of work troubles Meakin because he finds it to be based on a nostalgia for a feudal society with reciprocal relationships and obligations to an organic community (162–80). As a Marxist, Meakin's ultimate concern is that such a romantic attitude towards work leads to exploitation by fascist ideologies and to the inculcation of passivity and apathy (197).

The problem of work in *Angels Fall*, obviously, has little to do with oppressed workers because the diseased Navajo miners and the Navajo maid, Maria, are part of the off-stage context of the play and not the focal point. The middle-class men in crisis, Niles, Zappy and Don, are all in skilled professions they entered out of desire, not need. What is at issue and what makes Meakin's concern pertinent is the romantic notion that work salvages the stressed soul and that self-fulfilling work is an ideal end in itself. Once free of their neurotic, infantile restraints,

Wilson implies, Niles and Zappy can be happy in their work and, finally free from Father Doherty's parental and moralizing stranglehold, Don will find peace. All will be engaged rewardingly in what Henry Adams called the "virtuous materialism" of capitalism. For the audience, this is a familiar world that conforms to a comfortable horizon of expectations; the myopic commitment to the self doesn't disrupt existing patterns, private or public.

Much modernist literature cries out against work as degrading, echoing Marxist theories of systematic dehumanizing and commodification of the worker. But there is also, as James Knapp points out, an equally powerful modernist voice stressing the liberating power of work. In *Literary Modernism and the Transformation of Work*, Knapp cites Antonio Gramsci's argument that work could mediate between the social and natural orders, free man from magic and superstition and provide a basis for a subsequent development of a historical, dialectical conception of the world which understands change (14). In *Angels Fall*, however, work wholly absorbs the characters' attention and absolves them of involvement with the natural world and limits change to modest adjustments in their behavior. Therefore, by Knapp's analysis, Wilson's commitment to work is confusing rather than liberating, retrogressive rather than progressively modern.

But what of the second part of the original equation, that the public or common good is the ultimate aim of the private man? With the ascendancy of what Robert N. Bellah *et alia* call "ontological individualism" in America, the community suffers a loss of commitment. In *Habits of the Heart: Individualism and Commitment in American Life*, they state their concern over what they perceive to be a conflict between "the therapeutic attitude grounded in a conception of authentic self-knowledge and an ethic that rests in absolute and moral obligations," that is, a separation between self and state (102). Of the action in the play, one might argue that at least those in the "helping professions," teaching and medicine, are answering their communal imperatives. Niles is returning to his university to be a heretic; presumably he will enable his students to resist received ideas and will enrich the academic community he originally fled. Don, because he will be doing research in cancer, will improve the medical community and, by extension, those suffering from cancer. Unlike Niles and Zappy who will return to their original communities, Don repositions himself by running away from his tribe. The specter of rampant disease on the reservation was too much for him; he was unable to take on "a millennium of genetic neglect" but he flees in an attitude of "abject humiliation" (52).

The real problem, though, is that this group, momentarily joined in the church because of a shared problem, disbands for individual realization and does not coalesce around the pressing issue that should unite them permanently, namely the threat of nuclear catastrophe. This strategy of self-absorption and flight, one which Christopher Lasch has called "the minimalist aesthetic," arises when the sense of personal responsibility has been overwhelmed; "political protest," he observes, "degenerates into a whine of self-pity" (77). From such a stance, private achievement, albeit in the service of others, and personal happiness displace political participation in a national issue. To return to Bellah *et alia*, such erosion of the republican tradition, that is, the fusion of self-interest with civic responsibility, threatens to undermine the coherence we have almost lost. Interesting, exciting and challenging work, they argue, must have a large moral and social context in order that American society can be reconstituted (286). Clearly, the resolution offered in *Angels Fall* is an escape not a confrontation; Niles, Don and Zappy will fight as individuals in small skirmishes, not as part of a collective in the big ecological and political battles.

As for a traditional spiritual dimension to the problem, only Vita is shown to be responsive. She, alone, positions herself in cosmic terms: "I hadn't seen stars before. It's the first time I'd had the feeling that the earth was a planet moving through a galaxy of stars" (61). This awareness of a world beyond herself doesn't take her very far, however. At the end of the play, she, again alone, takes part in a religious ritual. But how should her participation in the Mass with a handful of Navajos who "shuffle in," "mumble sincerely" and "shuffle out" be understood (63)? As the discovery of a "new heaven" or merely as a return to an old one?

If, as William Herman has argued, Wilson is a "clear-eyed moralist in depicting the ways in which America has failed" and that "his plays can be seen as attempts to redeem that failure" (199), what lost, traditional cultural values are reinstated at the end of *Angels Fall*? There is no denunciatory stance towards bourgeois values and scarcely a call to nineteenth-century hardy individualism. Little of the material past is being preserved; in fact, it is being destroyed and fragmented. Vita describes regretfully the way in which her family burned her father's war and western memorabilia. Marion, too, in carrying out her dead husband's wishes, broke up and dispersed his collection, the pieces of which will at least be housed in museums. Wilson's program for redeeming America is unclear.

The characterization of Don's native heritage poses another problem in reading *Angels Fall* as "American." Don is Maria's illegitimate son, a half Navajo, which is to say that he is descended from the tribe that in 1864 was force-marched from its homeland around Canyon de Chelly to a reservation on the arid Pecos bottom around the Bosque Redondo where the Navajo were given, in the American government's view, "the truths of Christianity" (Utley 84). The mission where Don grew up, therefore, from one perspective represents the consolidated forces of church and state against the Navajo. In short, Don's American heritage is quite different from Niles's and Zappy's. Furthermore, he had been romanticized as a Noble Savage, the "Brave with Arrow" in Ernie's painting (Wilson 42). It might be said that Wilson fetishizes Don. Wilson endows Don with greater stature than the other men because of his mature and realistic assessment of the overwhelming health problems facing his tribe. Also, Don is able to diagnose Niles's illness as physical rather than mental. In fact, in terms of self-regarding motives, Don really should not be grouped with Niles and Zappy; he knows from the start of the play who he is and what he wants to do. Father Doherty, on the other hand, is the dependent person in the relationship. In finally freeing himself from Father Doherty and leaving the reservation to do well-paying cancer research in the big city, Don is transformed into a Henry-Adams-style techno-philosopher, an active pragmatic individualist leaving the tribal Virgin for the test-tube Dynamo.

In *Angels Fall,* if work mediates cultural alienation, it constitutes a masculinist hegemony. Of all the critics writing on *Angels Fall,* only Gerald Weales notes the discrepancy between the way the women and men are treated. In a discussion of the way in which the play emphasizes the individual's right to make his own choices, Weales observes that "the two women characters fit oddly into this thematic scheme. The professor's wife is a children's book author who dismisses her own work, but the tennis player's sweetie is the widow of a painter and the owner of a gallery who sees herself as a Theo Van Gogh, a necessary connection between the artist and the world. Yet, within the play, she, like the professor's wife, functions as a lover-wife-mother" (690). And, of course, the off-stage Maria is Father Doherty's servant, her identity lying solely in her subservient and nurturing relationship with him.

In the transaction between salvation and work, the women are a necessary though marginalized factor in the equation. Though they are not wholly devalued or objectified, they are subordinated to the men as their support systems. This sentimentalized femininity is consistent with the subtextual Puritanism of the play. Linda K. Kerber has shown that the classic expression of Puritanism was the assumption that normal society rested on female deference. Puritanism tempered by a later Romanticism, she argues, led to a "distinctive American self, a self which could stand as a metaphor for America at large." But, she warns, "it must be understood that the new American myth was male" (175).

In one of the earliest analyses of woman's position in American culture, David Potter noted that American social generalizations were mostly in masculine terms and that, as a consequence, "the characteristics of American men are the characteristics of the American people," a notion reified by Frederick Jackson Turner's frontier hypothesis about the self-reliant male on a free land (280). More recently, Nina Baym has summed up the historical positioning of women as being outside the American experience. Although Baym is directing her criticism at fiction, her observations could as easily apply to the drama: "the matter of American experience is inherently male. . . . I would suggest that the theoretical model of a story which may become the vehicle of cultural essence is 'a melo-drama of beset manhood'" (130). It would appear that beset men are blubbering babies.

For the three women in *Angels Fall*, the future means con-tinuing to change diapers even though they may be less messy. Marion will mother Zappy, Vita will nurse Niles and Maria Tabaha will nurture Father Doherty. Furthermore, all these couplings presumably will continue to be emotionally fulfilling but non-procreative. True, Father Doherty mentions that Vita is young enough to have children, but this passing remark elicits no response either from her or from Niles. It would appear that the result of narrow, if liberated, professional vocationalism will be a secure, sterile insularity, a temporary and temporal hedge against the inevitable apocalypse.

It is tempting to resist the received critical opinions on *Angels Fall* as simply an "American" play glorifying a national and masculine determination to work and to push for a strong reading that would ironize the work ethic in the context of the inevitable ecological apocalypse. Such a reading would suggest that Wilson exhibits a European, existentialist stance, a we-can't-go-on, we-must-go-on attitude that positions futile optimism within a nihilistic frame, that makes of Father Doherty a touching Kierkegaardian clown. But there is little in the play itself or in Wilson's own comments on his work to validate such an interpretation. Wilson himself has said of *Burn This* that he is not concerned about "a monster sniffing at the window. It's about the monster within. And that's the territory I consider dangerous" (Freedman 64). The same would seem to apply to *Angels Fall*. But what of the monster without? Has Wilson provided an alternative paradigmatic model, what Wallace Stevens called "fresh spirituals?"

In *Angels Fall*, Lanford Wilson has created an aesthetic that circumscribes and orders life. The in-God's-house dispute ultimately does not challenge the characters' or the audience's complicity with the outside "worlds," neither the world outside the church within the frame of the play nor the world outside the theatre. The valorization of individual work in small communities pre-empts a responsive, resistant strike against technological intrusion and violation of the environment. The recuperation of the Protestant work ethic is meant to heal the disjunctive fissure in American life between the individual and the community and between man and woman, a solution that is marked by temporal relativism. It allows the characters and, by extension the audience, to say: "The only time that matters is my time, now." The play's conclusion promises that Don, Niles and Zappy become functional, efficient men, exerting maximum energy and not lolling about in a state of whining, neurasthenic apathy; they are restored to socially sanctioned, stable productivity.

Both characters and audience are contained in Wilson's soothing construct which offers an illusion of humanist freedom and growth. From a masculine perspective, individuals and couples will flourish. The collective spirit, never more than tenuously and temporarily focused on a shared concern about the imminent ecological disaster anyway, succumbs to selfish preservationist and escapist instincts. Though the play appears to be a vindication of the human capacity to prevail, in fact, technology triumphs. If their actions are, as Father Doherty says, "rehearsals for the end of the world" (88), they are futile gestures that shore up personal survival at the expense of the race. They refuse to see "that all this shall be dissolved" (95) and there is no suggestion that the audience should see things any differently.

Angels Fall is a retrogressive, white male fairy tale in which the women will keep the home fires burning, in which the educated Indian has been assimilated into the culture, in which the uneducated Indians remain on the reservation as workers under the church's care and in which work subsumes nagging spiritual doubts and sanctifies the individual pursuit of happiness. And it is these attributes that make it an "American" play. In these respects it does not represent much of an advance over the early prescription about vindicating American behavior. Certainly, the distinction between illustrating and satirizing "domestic manners" is problematic at best. Furthermore, *Angels Fall* inculcates national pride in the "crude hanging together" and "laconic optimism" that Dickinson prophesied would be the dramatic formula for the new society.

REFERENCES

"American Drama." *American Quarterly Review* 1 (1827): 338–43.

Asahina, Robert. *"Angels Fall."* *Hudson Review* 36 (1983): 231, 233, 235.

Barnett, Gene A. *Lanford Wilson*. Boston: G. K. Hall, 1987.

Baym, Nina. "Melodramas of Beset Manhood: How Theories of American Fiction Exclude Women Authors." *American Quarterly* 33 (1981): 123–39.

Bellah, Robert N., Richard Madsen, William M. Sullivan, Ann Swidler, and Steven M. Tipton. *Habits of the Heart: Individualism and Commitment in American Life*. Los Angeles: U of California P, 1985.

Dickinson, Thomas. *The Case of American Drama*. Boston: Houghton Mifflin, 1915.

Esslin, Martin. "'Dead! And Never Called me Mother!': The Missing Dimension in American Drama." *Studies in the Literary Imagination* 21.2 (1988): 23–33.

Freedman, Samuel G. "Lanford Wilson Comes Home." *New York Times* 30 August 1987, sec. 6, part 2: 29, 63–64.

Gunn, Giles. *The Interpretation of Otherness: Literature, Religion, and the American Imagination*. New York: Oxford UP, 1979.

Herman, William. *Understanding Contemporary American Drama*. Columbia: U of South Carolina P, 1987.

Jacobi, Martin J. "The Comic Vision of Lanford Wilson." *Studies in the Literary Imagination* 21 (Fall 1988): 119–34.

Kerber, Linda K. "Can a Woman Be an Individual? The Limits of Puritan Tradition in the Early Republic." *Texas Studies in Literature and Language* 25 (1983): 166–78.

Knapp, James. *Literary Modernism and the Transformation of Work*. Evanston, IL: Northwestern UP, 1988.

Lasch, Christopher. *The Minimal Self*. New York: W. W. Norton, 1984.

Marowski, Daniel G., ed. "Lanford Wilson." *Contemporary Literary Criticism*. Detroit: Gale, 1986. 458–66.

Meakin, David. *Man & Work: Literature and Culture in Industrial Society*. London: Methuen, 1976.

Novick, Julius. "Affirmative Actions." *Village Voice* 26 October 1982: 103.

Potter, David. "American Women and American Character." *History and American Society*. Ed. Don E. Fehrenbacher. New York: Oxford UP, 1973. 278–303.

Rich, Frank. "Play: 'Angels Fall,' Lanford Wilson's Apocalypse." *New York Times* 18 October 1982: C15.

Savran, David, ed. *In Their Own Words*. New York: Theatre Communications Group, 1988.

Schewey, Don. "I Hear America Talking." *Rolling Stone* 22 July 1982: 18.

Schvey, Henry I. "Images of the Past in the Plays of Lanford Wilson." *Essays in Contemporary American Drama*. Ed. Hedwig Bock and Albert Wertheim. Munich: Max Hüber Verlag, 1981. 225–40.

Utley, Robert M. *The Indian Frontier of the American West 1846–1890*. Albuquerque: U of New Mexico P, 1984.

Weales, Gerald. "*Angels Fall*: Epistle of Peter to New Mexico." *Commonweal* 17 December 1982: 690–91.

Wetzsteon, Ross. "The Most Populist Playwright." *New York* 8 November 1982: 40–41, 44–45.

Wilson, Lanford. *Angels Fall*. New York: Hill and Wang, 1983.

Witham, Barry B. "Images of America: Wilson, Weller, and Horowitz." *Theatre Journal* 34 (1982): 223–32.

From Provincial Yearnings
to Urban Danger:
Lanford Wilson's *Three Sisters*
and *Burn This*

Felicia Hardison Londré

> Man has been so preoccupied with wars, filling his
> life with campaigns and invasions and victories, and
> now that he doesn't have that diversion it's left an
> enormous emptiness in his life. Just now we have
> nothing to fill out that emptiness with, but he is
> searching, passionately, and of course, someday he'll
> find it. Oh, let it be soon. (*Three Sisters* 67)

Vershinin's line from Act Four of Lanford Wilson's translation of Chekhov's *Three Sisters* might serve as an analogy for
Wilson's own work in the 1980's. When the decade began, Wilson was "preoccupied with wars"—a projected cycle of five
plays to be collected under the umbrella title *The War in Lebanon*,
which would show the impact of the Civil War, World Wars I
and II and the Viet Nam conflict on succeeding generations of
the Talley family in the rural Missouri town of Lebanon. The first
two plays he completed, *5th of July* (1978; revised version, *Fifth of
July* [1982]) and *Talley's Folly* (1979 at Circle Repertory Theatre;
1980 on Broadway), were his most critically acclaimed works to
date. The third Talley play, *A Tale Told*, was poorly received in its

initial run at Circle Rep in 1981; revised and retitled *Talley & Son*
in 1985, it fared little better. The rest of the *War in Lebanon* cycle
was never written.

For five years, from his underappreciated *Angels Fall*
(1982) until *Burn This* (1987), there was no new original play by
Lanford Wilson. That hiatus in his creative flow was unusual for
a playwright who had seen thirty of his plays produced in New
York in the seventeen years from 1963 to 1980. After "filling his
life"—to use Vershinin's words—"with campaigns and invasions
and victories" (he had won the Pulitzer Prize with *Talley's Folly*),
Wilson was left with "an enormous emptiness in his life." With
Talley & Son and *Angels Fall*, he had met his self-imposed
challenge of conquering the well-made play form—experiment-
ing with Ibsen as a model rather than Chekhov—but, he recalled,
that effort "burned me out completely. I said I didn't want to
have another original thought in my head for a year . . . and I
didn't, for two" (Savran 315). Elsewhere he has stated: "My last
commercial theater venture did me in. I don't want to hear
anything about contracts and negotiations" (Klein 12). He
wondered what the well-made play experience would do to his
characteristic style and found that "once you know how a play is
supposed to be built, it's not easy to shake" (Savran 314).

It was then that Mark Lamos, artistic director of the
Hartford Stage Company, invited Wilson to provide a new
translation for that theatre's scheduled production of Chekhov's
Three Sisters. "That's the kind of thing I had been looking to do,"
Wilson recalled, "—something completely different, something
without the responsibility of saying something, or of coming up
with original characters, or a set that's interesting" (Frank). He
saw the commission as "a parenthesis" in his work, "a
restorative" (Klein 12), and it also gave Wilson the chance to
explore what he calls his "favorite play ever" (Klein 13).

"He is searching, passionately," Vershinin says, "and of
course, someday he'll find it." The translation project became a
part of Wilson's own search. He credits *Three Sisters* with helping
him to "throw over the well-made play" (Savran 315). It also
apparently rekindled his creative drive, and the result was *Burn
This*, a play about passion. Just as the passion between Vershinin
and Masha smoulders, unexpressed, until the town conflagration

in Act Three, so Wilson's plays had simmered with ordinary emotions of ordinary people until *Three Sisters* ignited the explosion of extraordinary emotions in *Burn This*. What happens between Pale and Anna in his play is, according to Wilson, "an enormous passion that has to be consummated somehow; passion like this is really the one in a lifetime, and they would forever regret not acting on it. It's a juggernaut that just knocks down everything in front of it" (Bennetts 220).

How did the juggernaut of *Burn This* issue from a Chekhovian play that is "often reduced to a static cliché in which characters mope, complain about living in the provinces, and long to go to Moscow?" (Klein 13) This essay will examine the significance of *Three Sisters* within Wilson's recent development.

The full-length plays in Wilson's canon fall into a pattern of alternation between an urban milieu and a midwestern or western setting. *Balm in Gilead* (1965) was an urban play, followed by the midwestern *Rimers of Eldritch* (1966). Next came the 1968 premieres of *Gingham Dog*, set in an apartment in New York's East Village, and *Lemon Sky*, set in California. The urban *Hot l Baltimore* (1973) was succeeded by the midwestern *Mound Builders* (1975). Then Wilson began his cycle of Missouri plays. "That became what I was supposed to be about," Wilson protested in a *New York Times* interview. "People thought I wrote historical plays about Missouri. And I've *always* been about what's happening now. The Talley plays were a trip I took back there. It took longer than I thought. But I always felt it was a side trip that took me away from the line of my work" (Freedman 63). The commercial success of that regional "side trip" must have been difficult to put behind him, an initiative requiring a greater effort of the will than the Prozorov sisters could muster to leave their provincial town and return to Moscow. According to Samuel G. Freedman, *Burn This* represents "Wilson's effort to travel from the Chekhovian Missouri of his most popular plays back into the urban danger zone" (29). *Three Sisters*, as we have seen, was the way station.

Wilson began his task by commissioning two translations, one by a Dartmouth professor of Russian, the other by a Russian native speaker. He listened repeatedly to a recording of a Moscow Art Theatre performance of the play in Russian, and he took a Berlitz course in Russian, three hours a day, five days a week, for two months. Those 100–plus hours "seemed like 100 years," he recalled (Klein 13). "I got into the habit of leaving my Russian teacher, walking blindly to Charlie's, and having two very slow martinis. After two, I sort of remembered who I was, where I was, and had forgotten those god-awful Russian conjugations and endings. I really enjoyed it" (Frank). "At first I just wanted to be able to read, to at least know the alphabet and some of the rules to look up words in the dictionary. But then it got very exciting and I'd say to myself, 'Hey, wait a minute. I know that sentence!' And I found out that Russian is gorgeous" (Syse, "Playwright turns translator" 43).

Refusing to cut a single line of his favorite author's work, Wilson declared: "I've stuck to the intention of every word as best I understand it. . . . What Chekhov has done is so seamless, it's a miracle. There's no reason why these foolish characters should generate such incredible empathy by the end. It's an endless repetition of chords—detail, detail, detail—and it's just flabbergasting" (Klein 13). A ready example of Wilson's ability to render Chekhov's seamless accretion of character details is old Ferapont's constant query, *Chevo?* (What?) in Russian. Other translators use "What's that?" (Elisaveta Fen), "Eh?" (Ronald Hingley) and "What is it?" (Eugene Bristow), but Wilson emphasizes Ferapont's deafness while giving the line a comic touch by rendering it, "Say what?" (10) And he builds upon this when, in Act Three, Ferapont twice responds, *Slushayu* (I'm listening) in Russian to Olga's instructions; other translators have him say "Very good, Madam" (Fen), "Very well, miss" (Hingley) and "Yes, ma'am" (Bristow), but Wilson remains closest to the original with his "I hear you" (42). Some larger Chekhovian chords also found their way into *Burn This*. Burton, for example, echoes Baron Tusenbach in his inability to fulfill his best impulses; at one point he says, "I decided I should experience work—I forget why" (70). Anna even says: "If I can't have a life at least I can work" (102).

Burn This comes closer than any other of his plays to fitting Wilson's description of what he admires in Chekhov: "There is no payoff. [His plays] have unexpected juxtapositions. Every time you think you know where he is going, he goes another way" (Syse, "Playwright turns translator" 45). The reviews of *Burn This* echo such observations. "The payoff of 'Burn This' is perilously slight," wrote Frank Rich. William A. Henry III commented on the play's unexpected directions: "*Burn This* starts out as a sly sketch of the way we live now, making fun equally of hip characters onstage and of the dead roommate's unseen blue-collar family. Then the show metamorphoses into a scary collision between those two cultures. Finally it becomes a romance between the elegant choreographer and the dead man's explosive, disturbing older brother—a sexually charged clash of classes reminiscent of *It Happened One Night* or, in its brutality and danger, of the misfit infatuation in *Requiem for a Heavyweight*. The final scene is a rapprochement so tentative that it is played entirely in the dark: these reluctant lovers are unable even to look at each other."

Wilson is also fascinated by Chekhov's use of language, observing that he "wrote very simply. And we are told he wrote very much the way people spoke, which was a breakthrough for that time. Of course, in those days people spoke a little better. Today our language in America has gone to hell in a handbasket" (Syse, "Playwright turns translator" 45). Thus, when Wilson follows Chekhov's example in writing the way people speak, he has to write language that has gone to hell in a handbasket. That aspect of *Burn This* is probably best summed up in Edith Oliver's comment: "The action runs almost three hours and could probably be shortened by at least one of them just by killing the obscenities."

Wilson's approach to translating *Three Sisters* was to try "to make it as ordinary as soap" (Abarbanel 17). He said, "I have tried not to use any phrases that were not used in America before 1900. The question I asked myself was—'If Chekhov had written this in America in English in 1900, what would it have been like?'" (Syse, "Playwright turns translator" 45) Wilson's success may be judged by comparing his rendering of Kulygin's Act Four anecdote with other translations. Elisaveta Fen's version is:

> A schoolmaster once wrote "nonsense" in Russian
> over a pupil's essay, and the pupil puzzled over it,

thinking it was a Latin word. Frightfully funny, you know! (314)

Ronald Hingley offers:

> A schoolmaster once wrote "bunkum" on a pupil's essay and the boy thought it was Latin and started declining it. Bunkum, bunkum, bunkum, bunki, bunkom bunko. Terribly funny that. (251)

Eugene K. Bristow's variation on Hingley is:

> One time in a seminary, a teacher wrote "hokum" on a student's essay, and the student was certain it was Latin and began declining: hoki, hoko, hoko, hokum, hokum . . . . Wonderfully funny. (146)

Finally, Lanford Wilson gets the most humor out of the line by keeping it closest to Chekhov's original Russian phrasing and vocabulary:

> Yes, well, at a seminary once the instructor wrote on a student's paper "Nonsense" and the student, thinking it was written in Latin, read it as "Consensus." Wonderfully amusing. (58)

According to Wilson, "What's been wrong with most translations is that they have been done by academic people who may write very accurately, but you can't speak them. They are just not stageworthy" (Syse, "Playwright turns translator" 43). "I've tried as much as I could to shake the translated sound out of it" (Abarbanel 17). The previously quoted line by Vershinin provides a good example of Wilson's technique:

> Man has been so preoccupied with wars, filling his life with campaigns and invasions and victories, and now that he doesn't have that diversion it's left an enormous emptiness in his life. Just now we have nothing to fill out that emptiness with, but he is searching, passionately, and of course, someday he'll find it. Oh, let it be soon. (67)

The dangling preposition, the switch in pronouns from *he* (man) to *we* and back to *he* and the pronoun without an antecedent (it) are the stuff of everyday speech, not of academic translation.

How does Wilson's translation work in production? Theatre critics are not usually prone to comment upon—or even notice—the quality of a translation. However, there is an abundance of critical comment on Wilson's *Three Sisters*. In his review of the Hartford Stage Company production, Mel Gussow wrote:

> The intention was not to re-evaluate or to transplant Chekhov but to blend him with a 20th-century Wilsonian sensibility. The result is both conversational and lyrical. To give one example: In Masha's first speech, she remembers the vitality of the town when her father was alive and then comments on her own malaise. In alternate translations, Masha says, "I'm in the doldrums today, not very cheerful," and "I'm depressed today." In Mr Wilson's version, she sighs and says, "I'm in a melancholy humor—unhappy me," and immediately we have a feeling of Masha's wistfulness, her sublime disappointment with herself and with life.

When the Steppenwolf Theater Ensemble of Chicago staged Wilson's translation in December 1984, Richard Christiansen of the *Chicago Tribune* commented:

> Lanford Wilson's new translation, sometimes too contemporary in its language, has the great, shining virtue of making the Chekhov original absolutely clear in its meaning. From the very beginning of the play, when the sisters talk of the passage of time and the death of their father, the themes of the illusory nature of existence and the elusive quality of happiness, which are at the play's center, come to the forefront.

Tom Valeo of the *Chicago Daily Herald* wrote of "flashes of insight" that emerged from

dialogue that is so realistic it's almost mundane at
times. Dreary dinner conversation suddenly yields
an unsettling debate about the inevitability of human misery, and amidst the confused chatter following a fire come words of such shocking cruelty
that they seem to reveal the nature of evil itself. . . .
The new translation by Pulitzer-winning playwright
Lanford Wilson also contributes to the immediacy of
the action on stage. By transforming the dialogue
into contemporary speech, Wilson shakes the
stuffiness out of the script and makes the characters
seem more plausible. But although he never strays
very far from conventional translations of the play,
Wilson's language is so agile it sometimes clashes
with the unrelenting despair voiced by Chekhov's
characters.

According to Jean Nathan of the *Lincoln Park Spectator*, director
Austin Pendleton and the Steppenwolf cast were helped by a
translation that

brings the play closer to the English-hearing ear
without ever descending to vulgar colloquialisms.
The rhythm of speech is broad, smooth; the syntax is
much improved over earlier, more turgid, stilted
versions.

Lisa Goff of *Crain's Chicago Business* appreciated it as an "idio-
matic, energetic version with American rhythms and speech
patterns. For the first time," she wrote, "I felt as if I might be
experiencing the dialogue the way a Russian-speaking audience
would."

It is difficult to say whether doing the translation influenced Wilson's use of language in *Burn This*, especially since
Wilson's style had been labelled Chekhovian long before he
worked on *Three Sisters*. C. Warren Robertson lists several critics
who had earlier noted the affinity: John Beaufort, Michael
Feingold, Erika Munk, Julius Novick and John Simon (535). In
any case, the Chekhovian resonances in *Burn This* are unmistakable, although most are more subtle than Larry's line: "My

arms are falling off, my head hurts, I'm exhausted. For the first time in my life I have sympathy for Olga in *Three Sisters*" (57). Anna later says, "I'm tired and sick, and I've got work to do" (84). In another passage, the sound of a *"distant bell"*—echoing Chekhov's penchant for music and sounds from unseen sources—initiates a dialogue sequence about bells that serves no purpose other than providing character bits for Larry and Burton (70). When Act II begins, Burton has been reading his latest script to Anna. Her response is: "Oh, I like it. It's so sad. God." "Sad?," Burton says, sounding rather like Chekhov when confronted with Stanislavski's interpretation of *The Cherry Orchard*: "I thought they were having fun." Anna replies: "Oh no, sure. But underneath all that, God, they're so lonely." Burton protests that his characters are "smaller than life," but Anna remarks that "They're very real. . . . And you have your space. Only it's distance between people rather than distance between places" (51).

In Act One, a gun is planted in Pale's possession, but it is never used; perhaps this is a subtle reference to Chekhov's overcoming the need for a last-act gunshot in *The Cherry Orchard*. Like Vershinin in *Three Sisters*, Pale has two children and a wife he cannot stand. Pale and Anna are both "sick of the age" they are "living in" (87). And it is certainly not without significance that the role of Anna in Wilson's play about a grand passion was created by Joan Allen, who had played Masha in the Steppenwolf production of *Three Sisters*. In fact, her farewell to Vershinin was cited by several reviewers as the emotional peak of the production. In Richard Christiansen's words: "There is the stunning, heart-wrenching moment near the close of the play when Joan Allen, as the moody, unhappily married Masha, must say goodbye to Vershinin (Joe Ponazecki, in a quiet, steady performance of great strength), the Army officer she loves. Walking in from a far side of the stage, Allen spots her man on the opposite side, literally flings herself on him and wraps herself around him. When her sister tries to pry her from him, Allen shudders and moans as if desperately wounded and throws herself to the ground, crying as if her heart will break." According to Glenna Syse, "her clawing farewell to her lover is a scene never to be forgotten" ("Steppenwolf's 'Sisters' a spell-binder").

One of the most haunting images in *Burn This* is Anna's experience of waking up early, when it was "not quite light," to an "intermittent soft flutter sound" and discovering that it was the walls "pulsating" with live butterflies pinned through each wing, "all beating their bodies against the walls—all around" her (21). Perhaps this was Wilson's subliminal transformation of the plight of the three sisters—too good, too educated, too beautiful for the environment from which they could not escape but only beat themselves hopelessly against the bounds of their provincial town. When Pale storms into Anna's loft in Act One, he reminds her: "I'm the one who saved you from the ferocious butterflies" (25). Metaphorically too, Pale liberates Anna from the familiar confines of the life she has been leading. In Wilson's play, as if to vindicate Masha and Vershinin, passion triumphs. One of the last lines is: "Why should love always be tragic?" (98)

Certainly, the similarities I have detected between *Three Sisters* and *Burn This* are tenuous. There is no clear indication that Lanford Wilson could not have written exactly the same play even if he had not first done the translation. However, there is no denying the fact that he had lain fallow for several years until the translation sparked his own creativity anew. Whether or not the texture of *Burn This* owes a debt to Chekhov, the fresh start in Wilson's career probably does. Lanford Wilson joins such important dramatists as Tom Stoppard, Michael Frayn, Christopher Fry, Lillian Hellman and Maria Irene Fornes in contributing their talents to enriching the English-language theatre with translations of plays by such continental masters as Václav Havel, Chekhov and Tolstoy, Jean Giradoux, Jean Anouilh and Federico Garciá Lorca. It is a noble task, and it is only fitting that blessings be showered in return upon the playwright-translator's own work.

REFERENCES

Abarbanel, Jonathan. "Tacos and Theatre Talk with Lanford Wilson and Austin Pendleton." *Lincoln Park Spectator* (Chicago) 11 December 1984: 17.

Bennetts, Leslie. "Lanford Wilson & Terrence McNally: On love, responsibility, and sexual obsession." *Vogue* 178, 2 (1988): 216, 220.

Chekhov, Anton. *Five Major Plays*. Tr. Ronald Hingley. New York: Bantam, 1982.

——. *Plays*. Tr. Eugene K. Bristow. New York: W. W. Norton, 1977.

——. *Plays*. Tr. Elisaveta Fen. Harmondsworth: Penguin, 1974.

——. *Three Sisters*. Tr. Lanford Wilson. New York: Dramatists Play Service, 1984.

Christiansen, Richard. "'Sisters' speaks with new clarity." *Chicago Tribune* 6 December 1984, sec. 3: 9.

Frank, Leah D. "Lanford Wilson's World is the Stage." *Chelsea Clinton News* (New York) 22 December 1983: 12.

Freedman, Samuel G. "Lanford Wilson Comes Home." *New York Times* 30 August 1987, sec. 6, part 2: 29, 63–64.

Goff, Lisa. "Theater." *Crain's Chicago Business* 17 December 1984.

Gussow, Mel. "Theater: Chekhov's 'Three Sisters' in Hartford." *New York Times* 6 April 1984: C18.

Henry, William A., III. "Skirmishing Along the Borders." *Time* 26 October 1987: 136.

Klein, Alvin. "Wilson's View of Chekhov." *New York Times* 25 March 1984, sec. 23: 12–13.

Nathan, Jean. "Chekhov's 'Three Sisters': Undertow of Passion and Despair." *Lincoln Park Spectator* (Chicago) 11 December 1984: 18.

Oliver, Edith. "The Theatre." *New Yorker* 26 October 1987: 130.

Rich, Frank. "The Stage: 'Burn This,' by Wilson." *New York Times* 15 October 1987: C23.

Robertson, C. Warren. "Lanford Wilson (13 April 1937–)." *American Playwrights Since 1945: A Guide to Scholarship, Criticism, and Performance*. Ed. Philip C. Kolin. New York: Greenwood, 1989. 528–39.

Savran, David, ed. *In Their Own Words*. New York: Theatre
    Communications Group, 1988.
Syse, Glenna. "Playwright turns translator." *Chicago Sun-Times* 4
    December 1984: 43, 45.
——. "Steppenwolf's 'Sisters' a spellbinder." *Chicago Sun-Times* 7
    December 1984.
Valeo, Tom. "'Sisters' makes audience fourth sibling of misery."
    The Daily Herald (Chicago) 8 December 1984.
Wilson, Lanford. *Burn This*. New York: Hill and Wang, 1987.

"The Monster Within" in Lanford Wilson's *Burn This*

Martin J. Jacobi

Lanford Wilson has said of *Burn This* (1987) that it is "not about a monster sniffing at the window. It's about the monster within. And that's the territory I consider dangerous" (Freedman 64). The "monster within," and characters' attempts to manage it, have been central components of Wilson's plays throughout his career. In some of the early plays the characters are unable to manage their monsters and so meet violent ends. In this category are, for example, Leslie Bright of *The Madness of Lady Bright* (1964), whose fear of old age and subsequent loss of his homosexual liaisons cause him to unravel mentally during the course of the play; Joe of *Balm in Gilead* (1965), who cannot decide what to do about his girlfriend, his livelihood and his life, and whose indecision causes his violent murder by the agents of Chuckles the gangster; and the characters of *Serenading Louie* (1970), whose inability to find meaning in their relationships and daily lives ultimately results in all their deaths. In later plays the protagonists have been able both to identify and to control—if not exorcise—their monsters. Ken Talley of *5th of July* (1978; revised version, *Fifth of July* [1982]) fears that the high school students he has agreed to teach will be revolted by his war injuries, and Niles Harris of *Angels Fall* (1983) fears returning to his university professorship since he feels he has nothing to say; through their own efforts and the help of friends and family, both Ken and Niles are able to confront their monsters and defeat them. In *Burn This*, the dangerous monster is the protagonist's fear of committing herself to anything or anyone, and her eventual management of it constitutes the play's dramatic development.[1]

The "monster within" can also be thought of as Wilson's own monster. The playwright has remarked that the title refers to a phrase a writer attaches to a particularly painful private letter (Freedman 29), and, adding credence to this thought, Kenneth Burke has argued that the motivation for art in part arises from an author's obsession with personal problems. An artist, Burke says in *The Philosophy of Literary Form*, "will naturally tend to write about that which most deeply engrosses him—and nothing more deeply engrosses a man than his *burdens*" (17). In writing about his problems, the artist tries to develop a strategy for alleviating their burden, either by adjusting his attitude and approach towards the problems, thereby removing the bad effects, or by presenting them in a way that induces the audience to accept his attitude, thereby socializing them. That is, the artist has both a cathartic intention—the release of the anxieties and suffering caused by pent-up problems—and a strategic intention—the resolution of these problems. Although these intentions may not be realized through the work of art, the attempt is, in this theory, a primary motivation for the creative activity.

Burke expands on this function of authorial catharsis by including a rhetorical function, similar to that served by proverbs. "Proverbs," he maintains, "are *strategies* for dealing with *situations*. In so far as situations are typical and recurrent in a given social structure, people develop names for them and strategies for handling them." Literary works, he continues, can be considered "proverbs writ large" (*Philosophy of Literary Form* 296–97): while particulars of an author's problem are of course unique, in its broad lineaments no problem is unique; due to humanity's common biological heritage and to a given social structure, the author's problem is a personal individuation of a pattern of experience shared to some degree by all humans (*Counter-Statement* 143). In fact a work of art is understood by the audience *because* they share this common ground with the

---

[1] For a fuller discussion of this progression, see Jacobi.

author. While a work of art is a strategy for encompassing a troublesome situation in the author's life, it is also "equipment for living" for the audience, its usefulness being determined by the extent to which the author states his problems and their solutions in terms understandable and persuasive to the audience (*Philosophy of Literary Form* 304). Therefore, in understanding what Wilson's plays are doing for him we can better understand what they can offer us.

In the following pages, I want to bring together under the aegis of Burke's critical theory the various strands I have introduced. First, I want to examine the play as the development of the protagonist's ability to manage her inner monster, to gain control of her life and so begin to enjoy it. I want then to examine the play for what it says about the playwright's personal strategies. The connection between these examinations comes by reading the protagonist's development as a metaphor for the development of artistic eloquence, certainly a topic important to Wilson or any other playwright. Besides this professional advice, *Burn This* also offers personal advice to its author, which I also want to consider. Finally, I want to extrapolate Wilson's personal strategy for its general utility as equipment for living for the audience.

The characters of *Burn This* are the protagonist, Anna, a dancer; Larry, an unattached homosexual who shares a loft apartment with her; Burton, a science fiction writer and Anna's pseudo-romantic interest; and Pale, a restaurant manager and the brother of Anna and Larry's other housemate, Robbie. Robbie, also a homosexual and Anna's professional partner, has just been killed with his lover in a boating accident, and as the play opens she has just returned from his funeral.

Anna, we find out, is a passive person who has isolated herself from other people and from her society. For instance, at one point Larry says, "She's had a very protected life. I mean, she's never had to even carry her own passport or plane tickets— she's not had to make her own way much" (94). Anna offers a qualification on this observation when she says, "I'm beginning to think that as an artist I have absolutely no life experience to draw from. Or else I'm just too chicken to let anyone see what I really am" (53). She also qualifies Larry's observation in this remark to Pale: "I have never had a personal life. I wasn't scared of it, I just had no place for it, it wasn't important" (86). However, she does answer affirmatively his question, "You gonna never leave your room, what?" (82) Because of Wilson's development of her character her qualifications ring hollow. In light of her dispassionate relationship with Burton and her general isolation from life, it is fairer to say that she has been "too chicken" to live her life and so has nothing on which she could draw for her art. Now, however, she is faced with a problem: the death of her dancing partner means that she cannot continue as she has been and must strike out on some new course. She considers giving up dancing to develop her interest in choreography.

Another course she considers is to accept Burton's proposal of marriage, even though she has no strong feeling for him nor he for her. Burton, who would be wealthy without a successful writing career, is able to get two hundred thousand dollars from movie producers for first drafts of his science fiction novels. He is polite and pleasant to Anna and Larry, and she intimates, after her return from the funeral, that she might finally accept his open offer of marriage. However, about five o'clock the next morning, before anything definite has been arranged, Pale appears at the apartment door to retrieve his brother's belongings. He is as passionate as Burton is reserved, and within the first fifteen minutes of his appearance he has berated New York City's drivers and the lack of parking, people's attempts to leave telephone messages with third parties and—in a lengthy, scatological and hilarious monologue—the insincerity of most apologies. Pale continues his highly charged verbal assault until he finally collapses on the couch, weeping for his brother; shortly afterward Anna, operating according to what she later calls "the bird-with-the-broken-wing syndrome," takes him into her bedroom.

Over the two and one-half months that follow the events just related, she becomes engaged in her new career as a chore-ographer, and as the second act opens she and Burton have just returned from a New Year's Eve party. Anna, Burton and Larry are talking when Pale arrives, very drunk, and almost immedi-ately picks a fight with Burton. Anna kicks out Burton even though, as she tells Larry, "I had almost decided if he proposed again I was going to accept him" (74). Of course, making Burton leave while Pale lies on the couch indicates that she had not decided at all. That night Anna and Pale make love again but the next morning she tells Pale that she wants their relationship to end. Pale's response is, "Why? You're afraid you might get interested. Have to feel somethin'" (85). Although she claims as her reason her relationship with Burton, Pale reminds her of her comment the night before that she hadn't slept with anyone since the time in October with him.

Anna fights her growing interest in Pale because she is afraid of the commitment which a full relationship would have. In the words of Saul Bellow's Henderson the Rain King, "suffering is about the only reliable burster of the spirit's sleep. There is a rumor of long standing that love also does it" (68). A life with Burton, in which neither person feels strongly about the other and so makes no demands upon the other, would cause her no suffering, whereas a life with Pale not only would force demands upon her but also threaten her with the suffering which is always possible to a person who is fully alive.

The play's last scene takes place a month later. When Burton wonders if Anna has been seeing Pale, Larry answers that it doesn't matter; he tells Burton that her dance, which is to have its premiere that evening but for which she has already received a commission, is about her relationship with Pale. Later that evening, when Anna returns to her apartment after a very well-received performance of her work, Pale is waiting for her; Larry had given him tickets to the dance and keys to the apartment, and then arranged that Anna return and find Pale there. Pale and Anna talk about the dance and decide, tentatively, that they should continue to see each other.

It seems clear that Anna's monster is not Pale, despite his insistent "sniffing" after her, but her own long-standing fear of commitment—to a profession, to people and ultimately to life. In fact, the repeated references to him as "burning," "on fire" and so forth suggest rather that he is the agent for purifying her— that, far from being the monster which paralyzes her, he is both the catalyst that helps her engage herself in her life and the inspiration for her art. She has changed from a passive, isolated and alienated woman to an active, involved and committed one; she has also changed from a performer, of limited success if not talent, to a successful creator. Anna's personal development and its relationship to her professional development suggest a strategy Wilson is developing for his own personal and professional life.

If *Burn This* were limited to the romantic story of a young woman finding love and a means for professional growth, it would be an unremarkable play. As it happens, the play can also be read as a meditation on the requirements for artistic growth and eloquence, requirements which have their analogues for personal growth and the art of living well.

In an essay called "The Poetic Process," Burke makes a differentiation between "emotional form" and "technical form" (*Counter-Statement* 51). The former consists of the subject matter of art—the selection of consistent details to express the artist's attitude—and the latter constitutes the structure which these details take, so that the artist's attitude will not be merely *expressed* but rather *communicated* to an audience. An overemphasis on either of these attributes causes problems: too much of the former "makes for the ideal of spontaneity and 'pure' emotion, and leads to barbarism in art"; too much of the latter "leads to virtuosity, or decoration." Artistic eloquence, Burke continues, combines these elements: "In that fluctuating region between pure emotion and pure decoration, humanity and craftsmanship, utterance and performance, lies the field of art, the evocation of emotion by mechanism, a norm which, like all norms, is a conflict become fusion" (55–56). I want to suggest that the characters in *Burn This* represent the elements of artistic development, with Pale the representative of pure emotion, Burton the representative of pure decoration, and Anna the representative of the "conflict become fusion."

From his first entrance into the play, Pale is easy to identify as the component of emotional form. Everything for him is emotional excess: he rants with nonstop frenzy about widely divergent concerns; he drinks heavily, curses excessively, works incessantly and importunes Anna insistently. On the other hand, he lacks any discernible structure in his life, any sense of order, a lack which is also represented in his fractured syntax. Further, he claims to be disinterested in the arts as a profession. He does profess to have composed "these tone poems, concertos and shit—huge big orchestrations, use like two orchestras"; while taking showers, he continues, "I get going some symphony, these like giant themes come to me, these like world-shaking changes in tempo and these great huge melodies, these incredible variations, man" (39). However, he does not know how to read music and has never written down these compositions; rather, they "come to him" and he expresses them. The next morning, while he is taking a shower, Larry asks Anna, "Any great tone poems come out of there yet?" and Anna responds, "Not a peep" (45). Pale expresses emotion, but he does not communicate it in any structured artistic way.

Burton, on the other hand, is depicted as the pure element of technical form and as emotionally inert.[2] Wilson describes him as *"very interested in his process"* (6), which can be taken to mean that he is interested in the craftsmanship involved in artistic creativity. However, while he may be an excellent craftsman, he lacks the necessities for eloquence. As audience, we are surprised at his lack of awareness of the artistic tradition, since knowledge of the tradition is a commonly accepted requirement for an artist. When he tells Larry about his interest in "passion, faith, myths, love, derring-do," Larry alludes to Wagner's *The Flying Dutchman*. Burton responds by saying "I don't know *The Flying* fuckin' *Dutchman*" (14–15). When he talks about his idea for his next project, we are reminded enough of Synge's *Riders to the Sea* that, given his ignorance of Wagner, we imagine yet another gap in his background.

A more important problem for Burton than this gap in his background is his lack of emotionally powerful subject matter. Burke observes that

---

[2]Burke has suggested that the "experimental tinkering with names . . . does suggest lines of inquiry" in the analysis of a work of art ("Fact, Inference, and Proof" 162; see also *A Rhetoric of Motives* 204, for Burke's pun analysis of Keats's "Ode on a Grecian Urn"). According to this approach, Burton represents Anna's "burden," insofar as he represents the inability to feel strong emotions.

> a man may, in undergoing stress, . . . accept its full
> impact, may let it pour down upon him, as though
> he were putting his face up into a thundershower. If
> he survives, the period of stress is not a period of
> blankness, but a period of great intricacy and sub-
> tlety which lives on in the memory and can be
> drawn upon. The artist's technique of articulation
> often enables him to admit what other men, by
> emotional subterfuge, deny. (*Counter-Statement* 76)

Instead of remaining open to experience, Burton employs
emotional subterfuges to avoid the stress of emotional involvement. When he realizes that he has lost Anna, his response is to
trigger what he calls "a protective mechanism sort of thing . . .
my immune system defending me" (93). His immune system, it
happens, has been protecting him from emotional involvement
for some time. In a telling anecdote, he relates to Larry and Anna
that, years before, when he was a messenger in the city, he had
been walking down a deserted street at night during a snowfall;
he had had to urinate and, unable to find anyplace open,
relieved himself in a doorway. As he was finishing, a man
walked up and propositioned him. "I just shook it off and turned
around and leaned against the wall and watched it snow while
he went down on me. I came, and he put it away and said 'thank
you,' if you believe it, and I said, 'Have a good life,' and went on
walking down to the Village. And I never thought about it
again" (63). Burton's recounting of his liaison fascinates Larry,
who claims that he will think about it for the rest of his own life.
Burton will not; indeed he hardly thought of it at the moment it
was transpiring. Furthermore, even though he was substantially
uninvolved at that time, he has only grown less so. As he tells
Larry, "I just haven't felt that open to the world since those
days" (95).

He has been so successful in closing himself to the world
that in his work mechanism has replaced inspiration. As he is
lecturing Anna and Larry about the evil of the movie industry,
Larry remarks that he likes movies. He proceeds to quote from
Lust in the Dust and Burton expresses surprise that Larry would
have bothered to memorize the lines. That Burton thinks he has

memorized them hints, I think, at his *modus operandi* for finding
subject matter for his own work. For a person who cannot feel,
cribbing from the powerful feelings of others is the only
alternative to a pure decoration. This is not to say that an artist
cannot reindividuate earlier works in the tradition, as, for
instance, many have done with Homer, but the artist is required
to make the work new by investing some of his own feeling. In
Larry's words: "Burton, you don't memorize. There are some
things so true that they enter your soul as you hear them" (17).

Burton's lack of emotional commitment extends to his dis-
interest in the use made of his science fiction stories. He sells
them to the movie industry, which he freely admits is incapable
of artistic excellence, nor does he care that the cinematic treat-
ments bear little resemblance to his writing; he even makes a
point not to watch the movie versions and so has not heard of
the ridiculous additions which Larry relates to him. Burton's
artistic prostitution is reinforced in an exchange with Larry, who
compliments him on "some beautiful writing." Burton responds:
"Beautiful writing? It's anathema to a movie. No, you can't get
involved with it. You'd kill yourself. You can't worry what
they're going to do to it. Start something else; take your two
hundred thou and split" (16).

Burton does realize the necessity for emotional content. At
one point he tells Anna that art should be made "as personal as
you can. Believe me, you can't imagine a feeling everyone hasn't
had. Make it personal, tell the truth, and then write 'Burn this' on
it" (60). However, since he cannot follow his own advice, we
should know that Wilson wants us to see him as flawed. To
drive this realization home, Wilson has Burton experience
trouble with his latest project, which he calls a "weird-ass love
story" (13). Since his project is much more grounded in standard
realism than are his science fiction stories, he finds that "[e]very
time I start to work on the love story, I swiftly segue into droid-
busting on Barsoom. . . . The space stuff's more fun. The other
one isn't fun" (55). Burton, it seems clear, is not Wilson's idea of

a successful writer, at least not a writer who could create, for instance, the "weird-ass love story" which is *Burn This*.[3]

Burton, then, establishes the extreme of technical form just as Pale has established the extreme of emotional form. With Anna, Wilson shows how the two extremes are fused in order to obtain artistic success. When the play opens, Anna is thirty-two, therefore nearing the end of her performance career, and in any event having just lost her dance partner. Robbie's death punctuates if not produces the death of her career. The death of this previous career is emphasized by her comments that she is "stiff as a board" and "completely out of touch with [her] body" (19). During the course of the play she removes the restrictions she had placed on her capacity for strong emotions and allows herself to experience them. As a result, she is able to develop both the raw material and the inspiration for artistic creativity. Pale personifies both these components: When Larry informs Burton that Anna had kicked Pale out of her life after the New Year's Eve encounter, Burton responds: "She threw him out? Boy, she is a piece of work, isn't she? And then goes off and makes a dance about him, great" (94).

Anna's artistic development is represented in the play by the two references to butterflies. The first, part of an incident that took place the night after the funeral, is an example of what Burke calls "watershed moments," the "'critical points' within the work . . . where some new quality enters. Sometimes these are obvious, even so obvious as to threaten the integrity of the work" (*Philosophy of Literary Form* 78). Anna had stayed overnight with Robbie's relatives and was sleeping in the room

---

[3]The draft which Burton has produced by the end of the play suggests the possibility that he is taking the same path Anna is on, that he has moved from pure technique, through the emotional pain of losing Anna, to the ability to write at least the draft of a "weird-ass love story." It should be noted, however, that he has only the negative loss, and no new experience, on which to base the art; in the context of my argument, it is difficult to say whether his draft might be any good. Furthermore, and more importantly, *Burn This* is not his play but Anna's, and the issue is relatively unimportant.

of one of his nephews. This young boy had been collecting butterflies during the day and had pinned them to his wall. The
butterflies, however, had not been killed by the alcohol the boy
used but only stunned, and Anna had awakened during the
night to an "intermittent soft flutter sound" and walls that
looked as if they were pulsating with life (21–22).

T. S. Eliot's J. Alfred Prufrock refers to himself as "pinned
and wriggling on the wall," and perhaps her fear of life is
analogous to the fear exhibited by Eliot's character. Further,
perhaps the butterflies are to be seen as the traditional literary
symbol for the soul; their awakening suggests that her suffering
for Robbie has burst her spirit's sleep, that she has died to her
old life and been born into a new one. And perhaps Pale's
unpinning of the butterflies from the wall suggests the role he is
to play in her change.

The second reference occurs early in the second act. Referring to her choreographic work, she remarks, "I almost feel as if
I've finally burst my chrysalis after thirty years of incubation"
(52). She has been incubating in that she has been developing the
skills—the "process" or "mechanics"—of dancing, but she has
not yet adequately developed from her "embryonic" state so that
she can put them to a fully creative use. Burton corrects her
biological metaphor, supplying "metamorphosis" as the
appropriate name for the process in which a chrysalis evolves
into a butterfly. Burton's correction emphasizes the qualitative
nature of the metamorphosis from dancer to choreographer.
Unquestionably, a performer brings an element of creativity to
her interpretation of a dance, just as, for example, a pianist does
in her interpretation of a musical piece. Nonetheless, the maker
of a work of art has done more than creatively interpret a work;
she has brought it into being. As Plato argues in the *Ion*, the
performer's inspiration is dependent upon the prior inspiration
of the poet. Socrates employs an analogy with a magnet to make
the point: "In like manner, the Muse first of all inspires men
herself; and from these inspired persons a chain of other persons
is suspended, who take the inspiration." This distinction is not
meant to demean professional dancers, but, rather, to link Anna
at the play's beginning professionally with Burton as good

craftsmen and agents of technical form, and to indicate the development in her professional life.

Residing on the outskirts of the central action of Anna's development is her housemate, Larry. He is, as has already been mentioned, knowledgeable about the emotional intensity required for good art and, as a successful layout designer in the advertising industry, he also possesses technical skill. Further, he is the impresario, as it were, of the play's concluding performance, in that he is the agent for bringing together Anna and Pale at the play's end; symbolically he has created if not art, then an artist. In charting Anna's artistic evolution through the play, it is tempting to say that she starts at the position exemplified by Burton and, through the agency of Pale, moves towards the position exemplified by Larry. Although it may be tempting to label Larry as Wilson's idea of the artist, it would be inaccurate.

Larry is aware of the necessity for emotional intensity, but he seeks out only vicarious thrills. For example, although Burton's liaison has generated no emotion in the author, it does in Larry; for another example, while he observes Anna's and Pale's suffering and works to bring them together, he experiences the enjoyment of the relationship only by talking to one of the individuals about the other. He is romantically unattached throughout the play, functioning as an observer of and commentator on the action of others, not as an agent for action. In fact, his strongest response does not even come from the actions of another person, but from the symbolic action of a movie, *Lust in the Dust*. Larry is not a bad person, in fact he has many positive qualities, but he does nothing important with his abilities. So, when Burton wonders what Anna is going to do with her life, he inadvertently yet accurately intimates that Larry is doing nothing with his (94). Rather than standing for the eloquent artist, then, he rather serves as a caution.

In part he is Wilson's caution to himself, on both personal and professional planes. It is not hard to imagine that anyone could be obsessed with the personal difficulties inherent in an openness to emotional experiences, and not hard to imagine that someone would want to retreat from such perceived dangers. Larry's retreat into physical and emotional isolation, therefore, might represent a monster within Wilson. Larry's sexual

nonconformity can be read as the dramatic indicator of his isolation, for certainly Wilson's previous plays are rife with social
outcasts whose alienation is represented by sexual means. One
thinks of the prostitutes and pimps of *Balm in Gilead* and *The Hot
l Baltimore*, and of the characters involved in incest in *Home Free!*
(1964), in voyeurism in *The Rimers of Eldritch* (1966), in misce-
genation in *The Gingham Dog* (1967) and in homosexuality in *The
Madness of Lady Bright* and *Fifth of July*. Such sexual nonconformity, as with Larry's homosexuality, provides dramatically
powerful reasons for a forced separation from mainstream
American society.

Regardless of why one is separated from society—and regardless of whether one's reasons are even seen by society as a
substantive cause for separation—the result of estrangement,
and especially the result of not trying to overcome whatever
causes the estrangement, is increasing isolation and perhaps
even insanity or death. Perhaps Wilson feels himself an outcast
from American society for some reason, perhaps even for some
reason more specific than the concern he voices for the country's
loss of its culture and sense of history (see Berkvist; Gussow,
"Lanford Wilson on Broadway"; Haller; Kakutani). He has said
to Ross Wetzsteon that he mourns the corruption of American
values and, more personally, that he has put the pain from his
childhood memories into his plays: "A friend of mine once told
me," he relates to Wetzsteon, "that in all my work I'm either
trying to put my family back together again or to create a new
one. I guess he was right" (43). He and his mother had been
deserted by his father (an event in his life dramatized in *Lemon
Sky* [1970]), and, for whatever reason, he has never married. And
perhaps his professional requirements that he observe,
contemplate and comment on the issues of others have made
him, as they have many writers, feel somehow separated from
his society.

Elsewhere I have argued that in the development of
Wilson's collected oeuvre the estranged characters evolve from
victims who are destroyed by their monsters to those who come
to manage them and so come to be perceived by both society and
the audience as positive (121). To overcome their monsters the
characters must decide to act, as Ken in *Fifth of July* decides to

take the job as high school teacher, as Niles in *Angels Fall* decides to turn away from his despair and as Anna decides to commit herself to her new career and to a relationship with Pale. Larry, for all his positive attributes and charm, remains at play's end still uncommitted to action, and still isolated.

Larry serves, I think, as a professional caution as well. Mel Gussow has said that "the secret to be burned" is that Larry "is destined to be a watcher on the sidelines, at most a voyeur, but not someone who realizes his own passions. In a sense, that charge becomes self-descriptive of the plight of the objective artist, the playwright, who is condemned to be an observer and not an actor" ("Lanford Wilson's Lonely World" 5). Frank Rich concurs, saying that "in a play in which no pair of lovers— whether homosexual or heterosexual—has ever lived together, Larry's voyeurism and disconnectedness seem to say more about the playwright's feelings on loss and longing than the showier romance at center stage" (23). Professionally, Wilson may be obsessed with the requirement of "putting his face up into a thundershower" of emotional experiences in order to have material for his art. The playwright, he knows, must be an observer and must also emphasize the symbolic action of his drama over the actions of everyday life, yet he must be careful not to remove himself from life—certainly not to the extent that Burton has distanced himself, and not even, at least not permanently, to the middle ground which Larry occupies.

Wilson's strategy for alleviating personal and professional problems is dramatized by Anna. Struggling with her fear of committing herself to a relationship with Pale, Anna works out her strategy in the form of an artistic creation; thus, when Burton asks if Anna is still seeing Pale, Larry says: "It doesn't matter if she's seen him. It doesn't matter. The dance she's done is Pale and Anna. No, he hasn't been over. No, she hasn't seen him; it doesn't matter" (92). It doesn't matter whether Anna is seeing Pale, Larry maintains, because she clearly exhibits through her art her obsession with him. Further, "it doesn't matter" because Burton still has no chance to get her back: although she may not be seeing Pale, she nonetheless has been able to figure out how to make the relationship work.

As Anna uses her dance to develop a strategy for her life, so Wilson uses *Burn This*. Not just the title but also the subject matter of the play refers to that particularly painful problem to which Wilson alluded in his interview with Samuel Freedman, and the dramatic development is his strategy for dealing with it. If he has felt threatened by his own monster of isolation and passivity, then this play is surely a way of managing the threat. The play assuages any fear that an emphasis on his craft may limit his ability to engage others socially and physically as well as just symbolically. With Anna rather than Larry as the consummate artist, the strategy is to maintain human contact *through* his art and to balance emotional and technical form. With this strategy, Wilson has the means for remaining one of the leading dramatists on the current American scene.

Of course, a play limited to the management of an author's private monsters is not art but psychological therapy. Art communicates and, in Burke's theory, has an educative as well as therapeutic function: A strategy for dealing with an authorial obsession is adaptable by an audience, in part because an author's problem is comparable to problems which all people, either explicitly or potentially, also have. Burke says: "The various kinds of moods, feelings, emotions, perceptions, sensations, and attitudes discussed in manuals of psychology and exemplified in works of art, we consider universal experiences . . . because all men, under certain conditions, and when not in mental or physical collapse, are capable of experiencing them" (*Counter-Statement* 149). Along the same lines Burton says, apropos of Anna's effort to create a dance: "Make it as personal as you can. Believe me, you can't imagine a feeling everyone hasn't had" (60).

Burton himself is irresponsible in this regard. When he mentions his difficulty writing the "weird-ass love story," he complains that it "isn't fun." He wants to avoid both the emotional complexity and the work required to produce art which can please as well as instruct both its author and its audience. Born of a wealthy family, he has never had to work, and he exhibits no awareness of moral responsibility; his approach to writing has been that it should be fun and games.

Wilson, unlike this character, is fully aware of the artistic responsibility of education. He has told Robert Berkvist that he feels it important that his plays involve cultural questions such as "what are we losing and what is it doing to us?" (3), and in a conversation with Michiko Kakutani he remarks that he sees his plays as "Baptist sermons" that ask why people behave the way they do and that provide answers for what should be done about it (6). In fact, he has intimated that he has a "calling" to provide these sermons. In a discussion with Trish Dace, he tells of a time in Chicago when "I was writing stories. I tried dialogue, and before I'd gotten through the first page I knew I was a playwright" (3). This epiphany is echoed in *Angels Fall* when a character recounts the first time he played tennis: "I hit that first ball and I said, 'This is me. This is what I do. What I do is tennis.' And once you know, then there's no way out" (91). The tennis player's remarks are in the context of an attempt by another character, Father Doherty, to get Niles Harris to return to his profession as a professor of art history. Teaching, Doherty says, is "one of those professions, I've always thought, one is called to. As an artist is called, or as a priest is called, or as a doctor is called" (90). Wilson provides lessons both specific to artists and generalized for use by the majority of the audience.[4]

Burn This teaches the artist to be a careful and honest observer but also an actor. It teaches the artist to confront personal monsters, develop a strategy to keep them in control if not exorcise them and use the conflict as the raw material for art. It teaches the artist the importance of developing a strategy to fuse emotional and technical form. That is, what Wilson provides as a strategy for his own professional concerns he thereby, insofar as all artists share these concerns, provides as a strategy for them.

---

[4]Wilson has told Scot Haller, "My subject in school was art history. And through that I learned what we have done, what our heritage was, and what we are doing to it" (26). As Anna represents one aspect of the playwright's personality and concerns, Niles represents another, and an argument could also be made that while he is concerned about having something to say to an audience, his plays are attempts to tame *that* monster.

Since most members of the audience will not be professional artists, Wilson's lessons must be adaptable for general purposes. As metaphorical lessons on the "art of living," the play teaches us to be aware of the universal human tendencies towards self-imposed isolation, towards passivity, towards a sense of alienation, that arise out of a fear of the complexities inevitably created by emotional engagement; it teaches us that, left unaddressed, these tendencies can become a monster that will destroy us. It teaches us that we must instead be open to emotional experience and that we must be honest and careful observers of people and events; that we must be active agents in the business of our community; and that we must develop a structure so that the experiences, and our fears, are manageable.

In sum, *Burn This* teaches us that the development of art or the maintenance of the artful life is not easy. The fullness of these difficulties is intimated in the distinction between Anna's personal and professional development. Personally, she moves from a dispassionate relationship with Burton to an emotionally powerful relationship with Pale; professionally, however, she begins with an over-emphasis on technical form (the Burton principle) and adds emotional form (the Pale principle), thereby developing the ability to create the fusion of art. That is, while personally she ends with Pale, professionally she goes beyond him. If the professional and personal planes are indeed connected, as I have been arguing, we can imagine that the romantic relationship has serious problems unless Pale can progress as well. Otherwise, he is doomed to being merely the catalyst for awakening Anna to future and fuller emotional engagements.

Anna's last words in the play, referring to their relationship, are, "I don't want this . . . Oh, Lord, I didn't want this . . ."; Pale's last words, and the last words of the play, are "I know. I don't want it, either. I didn't expect nothin' like this. I'm gonna cry all over your hair" (99). Gussow says of the conclusion that "it would be precipitous to think of that as a happy ending. There is no guarantee of durability in this relationship" ("Lanford Wilson's Lonely World" 5). Of course there are no guarantees as regards Anna's professional or personal life. She does not know, she says to Larry, if the butterflies Pale unpinned from the wall lived or died; analogously she does not know if she will be able to maintain the high quality of her artistic creativity, and, likewise, no one knows if her relationship with Pale will live or die.

Wilson does not present as his lesson the lie of sentimental romanticism, but although it is precipitous to predict successes for Anna, neither does he mean us to take the play's ending as sad. She has so far succeeded in her new career and there is something positive in her relationship with Pale; the shift in verb tense in Anna's last lines suggests as much. She may well be saying not that she doesn't want this relationship but that at one time she didn't want it. Furthermore, the ending does suggest that Pale can become the sort of person who can sustain a relationship with Anna and that Anna and Pale are "moving" together. In the closing stage directions, they begin at opposite ends of a couch; Pale *"reaches his hand toward her; she reaches toward him. They touch."* He then moves to her end of the couch and she lies against his chest (99).

Perhaps Anna's next dance will be a flop, and perhaps in a year or so she and Pale will no longer be seeing each other. Yet, for the psychological and rhetorical intentions of *Burn This*, these possibilities are not issues. What is at issue is that Anna has taken the step to be an artist and have a relationship. Wilson's lesson to himself and to his audience, finally, is not that nothing is durable, but, rather, "nothing ventured, nothing gained."

REFERENCES

Bellow, Saul. *Henderson the Rain King*. New York: Viking, 1973.

Bennetts, Leslie. "Marshall Mason Explores a New Stage." *New York Times* 11 October 1987, sec. 2: 3, 14.

Berkvist, Robert. "Lanford Wilson—Can He Score on Broadway?" *New York Times* 17 February 1980, sec. 2: 1, 33.

Burke, Kenneth. *Counter-Statement*. New York, 1931; rpt. Berkeley: U of California P, 1968.

——. "Fact, Inference, and Proof in the Analysis of Literary Symbolism." *Terms for Order*. Ed. Stanley Edgar Hyman. Bloomington: Indiana UP, 1964. 145–72.

——. *The Philosophy of Literary Form: Studies in Symbolic Action*. Baton Rouge, 1941; rpt. Berkeley: U of California P, 1973.

——. *A Rhetoric of Motives*. New York, 1950; rpt. Berkeley: U of California P, 1969.

Dace, Trish. "Plainsongs and Fancies." *Soho Weekly News* 5 November 1980: 20.

Freedman, Samuel. "Lanford Wilson Comes Home." *New York Times* 30 August 1987, sec. 6, part 2: 29, 63–64.

Gussow, Mel. "Lanford Wilson on Broadway." *Horizon* 23 (May 1980): 30–37.

——. "Lanford Wilson's Lonely World of Displaced Persons." *New York Times* 25 October 1987, sec. 2: 5.

Haller, Scot. "The Dramatic Rise of Lanford Wilson." *Saturday Review* 8 (August 1981): 26–29.

Jacobi, Martin. "The Comic Vision of Lanford Wilson." *Studies in the Literary Imagination* 21 (Fall 1988): 119–34.

Kakutani, Michiko. "I Write the World as I See It Around Me." *New York Times* 8 July 1984, sec 2: 4, 6.

Rich, Frank. "Stage: 'Burn This,' by Wilson." *New York Times* 15 October 1987: C23.

Wetzsteon, Ross. "The Most Populous Playwright." *New York* 8 November 1982: 40–41, 44–45.

Wilson, Lanford. *Angels Fall*. New York: Hill and Wang, 1983.

——. *Burn This*. New York: Hill and Wang, 1987.

Heathcliff in Manhattan:
Fire and Ice in Lanford Wilson's
Burn This

Henry I. Schvey

"My love for Linton is like the foliage in the woods.
Time will change it, I'm well aware, as winter
changes the trees. My love for Heathcliff resembles
the eternal rocks beneath—a source of little visible
delight, but necessary."
                    —Emily Brontë, *Wuthering Heights* (122)

In an essay on the plays of Lanford Wilson written in 1979,
just prior to his receiving the Pulitzer Prize for *Talley's Folly*, I
observed that despite the absence of sustained critical attention,
his work seemed to be moving away from a tendency toward
sentimentalized characterization and in the direction of a
willingness to pare his dramatic world down to its barest
essentials (240). However, instead of writing his best work, for
five years of the decade of the 1980's Wilson worked on the third
part of his trilogy of the Talley family, *Talley & Son* (1985), a
work which achieved neither the critical nor commercial success
of the first two parts, *5th of July* (1978) and *Talley's Folly* (1980).
The result has been that Wilson's reputation as one of America's
leading playwrights slipped, and what began as an interesting
detour—the examination of a single, southern Missouri family at
different historical periods and from different perspectives—

suddenly began to loom as the sole focus and possible dead end to Wilson's career. Even when he emerged from the world of the Talleys, resultant works such as *Angels Fall* (1983) or a translation of Chekhov's *The Three Sisters* (1984) somehow seemed too highly derivative of other work.

One commonly held critical perspective was that Wilson's solipsistic exploration of his own rural past in Lebanon, Missouri, led not to rejuvenation of his creative energies, but to repeated mining of increasingly familiar material. Thus, the collection of outcast and unfulfilled characters in *Angels Fall*, set in an isolated adobe mission in northern New Mexico, closely resemble a similar assortment of characters languishing uncertainly in the Talley place in *5th of July*, or for that matter, the outcasts inhabiting *The Hot l Baltimore* (1973). Not only did Wilson's casts of characters begin to look suspiciously interchangeable, the quasi-apocalyptic mood of *Angels Fall* ("The only good thing that can come from . . . these rehearsals for the end of the world, is that it makes us get our act together" [88]), was all too reminiscent of similar thematic material in earlier plays like *The Mound Builders* (1976), where the focus was on the rediscovery of an apparently lost Cahokian Indian civilization ("The species crawls up out of the warm ocean for a few million years and crawls back to it again to die" [88]), or even *The Hot l Baltimore*, where the setting of a once grand hotel inhabited by prostitutes and derelicts on the verge of demolition acts as a metaphor for the need for vitality and hope in a world where no hope exists. Thus, the prostitute April calls for more music at the end of the play, screaming, "Come on, they're gonna tear up the dance floor in a minute; the bulldozers are barking at the door. Turn it up, Bill, or I'll break your arm. Turn it up!" (145)

The new decade which began with a Pulitzer Prize and seemed ready to provide the possibility of further significant consolidation of his mounting reputation as one of our finest dramatists, led instead to what the *New York Times* describes as the "common opinion of Wilson as a lyric poet of safe material, a master of the well-made play at a time when the well-made play was devalued currency" (Freedman 63). Wilson himself has alluded to the impasse that his career was at, remarking about the Talley plays that "[they] were a trip I took back there. It took longer than I thought. But I always felt it was a side trip that took me away from the line of my work" (Freedman 63).

Whether the Talley trilogy is in fact an extended departure from the true direction of Wilson's work is highly debatable, since the plays share many characteristics with his earlier plays, both thematically and stylistically. However, they do divagate from the more obviously risk-taking sort of writing with which Wilson began his career, such as the one-act *The Madness of Lady Bright* (1964), essentially an extended monologue by a *"screaming, preening"* drag queen of forty who is *"rapidly losing a long-kept 'beauty'"* (74), or the raw, urban cadences of *Balm in Gilead* (1965), a play which was originally produced by Ellen Stewart at the Café La Mama and, for all its immaturities in plotting and dramatic structure, establishes the world of Wilson's outcast characters perhaps more precisely than any other of his plays. Set in an all-night coffee shop on Upper Broadway, the action consists of numerous simultaneous conversations which overlap and, eventually, interlock. In the opening stage directions Wilson notes that "Everything seems to move in a circle." The characters, despite their differences, "constitute a whole, revolving around some common center. They are the riffraff, the bums, the petty thieves, the scum, the lost, the desperate, the dispossessed, the cool" (3).

Interestingly, this early work was collaboratively revived by the Circle Repertory Company and the Steppenwolf Theater Ensemble of Chicago, and the revival, directed by John Malkovich in 1984, may have contributed to the revival of Wilson's career as well. Malkovich's production, which was performed at a lightning pace, concealed the play's obvious flaws in plotting and revealed instead the explosive intensity of its dialogue and characterizations. The result was that Wilson's quintessential play about the 1960's suddenly was transformed (with the help of contemporary music by Bruce Springsteen, Tom Waits and Ricky Lee Jones) into an extremely successful play for the 1980's.

Wilson's reaction to the remarkable revivals of *Balm in Gilead* (and, in 1985, *Lemon Sky*), plays which might have been merely considered pieces of juvenilia, is most revealing: "[They] excited me. I was impressed—no that isn't the word. I was delighted that the plays were as good as they were, that they were solid work" (Freedman 64). Noting that "I wasn't daunted," the playwright set out to achieve a possible synthesis between the raw urban energy of *Balm in Gilead*, and the greater experience, depth of characterization and linguistic subtlety which inform his later work:

> I wanted to have the sophistication, the maturity, whatever, of being 50. . . . I wanted to write characters who can speak the English language. But I also wanted that youthful vitality, that excitement. And trying to get those two into the same play was the challenge. (Freedman 64)

The result of this fusion is *Burn This* (1987), which in the words of Wilson's longtime director Marshall Mason "is a return to some of the early energy of Lanford's writing, and to his unruly sense of structure" (Bennetts 3). Like the earlier *Talley's Folly*, *Burn This* is "a no-holds-barred romantic love story" (*Talley's Folly* 4); but unlike the earlier play, it is not set in a quaintly picturesque gazebo in southern Missouri, but in a bare dancer's loft in lower Manhattan. Whereas the romantic setting of *Talley's Folly* "isn't bare, it isn't burned out, it's run-down, and the difference is all the difference. And valentines need frou-frou" (*Talley's Folly* 4). Anna's studio loft in *Burn This* is "*the sort of place that you would kill for or wouldn't be caught dead in*" (5). It is "*sparsely furnished. There is an exercise barre on one mirrored wall and a dining area. There are pipes on the ceiling, and an old sprinkler system is still intact. There is new oak flooring; the walls are white; the only picture is a large framed dance poster. A fire escape runs across the entire upstage*" (5).

Set in mid-October coldness when "*The sky has the least color left*" (5), it is significant that Anna inaccurately describes the season as "the middle of winter" (29) since this is her state of mind for most of the play. Having just experienced the accidental death by drowning of her closest friend, the dancer/choreographer Robbie, the prevailing mood of the play's opening is cold and death-driven. Anna and her surviving roommate Larry have just returned to New York from the small town where Robbie's funeral was held, a world where his homosexual

lifestyle was never acknowledged and where his career as a
dancer went unmourned. Confessing that "I didn't even have a
damn minute to say goodbye," Anna's mind reflects the cold
sterility of her bare white studio, and bereft of her partner and
closest friend, she is increasingly attuned to the ticking "sound of
the biological clock" (55) and the awareness that "I'm sick of the
age I'm living in" (87). The arrival of her boyfriend Burton, a
wealthy screenwriter of lavish but empty films (and costumed in
the New York production with a "sportswear wardrobe that has
Bourgeois Jerk plastered all over it" [Rich]), does little to relieve
the prevailing mood of gloom. Appropriately in terms of his
relationship to Anna, Burton has just returned from vacationing
in Canada where it is "Cold. Snowy. Exhausting" (8).

Into this world arrives Pale (played in the original version
by the same John Malkovich who directed *Balm in Gilead* with
such intensity at the Circle Rep), with a long, flowing Byronic
hairpiece and an opening speech which seems completely
foreign to the world of Lanford Wilson, owing more to the street-
wise gutter-speak of David Mamet's small-time grifters than to
the sophisticated and urbane world of dancers into which he has
plunged:

> Goddamn this fuckin' place, how can anybody live
> this shit city? I'm not doin' it, I'm not drivin' my car
> this goddamn sewer, every fuckin' time. Who are
> these assholes? Some bug-eyed, fat-lipped half
> nigger, all right; some of my best friends, thinks he
> owns this fuckin' *space*. The city's got this *space*
> specially reserved for his private use. Twenty-five
> fuckin' minutes I'm driving around this garbage
> street; I pull up this space, I look back, this fuckin'
> baby-shit green Trans Am's on my ass going *beep-
> beep*. I get out, this fucker says that's my *space*. I
> showed him the fuckin' tire iron; I told the fucker,
> You want this space, you're gonna wake up tomor-
> row, find you slept in your fuckin' car. This ain't
> your space, you treasure your pop-up headlights,
> Ho-Jo. Am I right? That shit? There's no talkin' to
> shit like that. (25)

Although by profession the manager of a successful restaurant, Pale describes himself as "a water-deliverer. For fires. I put out fires. I'm a relief pitcher, like Sparky Lyle. . . . Anybody needs relieving. I'm a roving fireman. Very healthy occupation. I'm puttin' out somebody else's fire, I'm puttin' out my own. *Quid pro*—something; symbiosis" (33–34). However, Pale's self-description is only partially accurate. In fact he is less "water-deliverer" than fire starter, since the "relief pitcher" cannot be called in until there is a fire to be extinguished. In the frigid world inhabited by Anna, there is no fire, no passion; as she says of herself, "I have never had a personal life. I wasn't scared of it, I just had no place for it, it wasn't important" (86). Like Sally in *Talley's Folly* who needs to understand from Matt Friedman that "People are eggs" and that they "Gotta be hatched or boiled or beat up into something like a lot of other eggs. Then you're cookin'" (35), Anna needs to be brought back to life by Pale, a man who confesses, "I got like a toaster oven I carry around with me in my belly someplace. I don't use heat. I sleep the windows open, no covers, I fuckin' hate things over me. Ray'll tell you: Here comes that dumb fuck Pale with a radiator up his ass" (29).

As one might expect of a play bearing the title "Burn This," Wilson is highly sensitive to fire symbolism here, and it would not be inappropriate to suggest that Pale is used to ignite the dormant feelings in Anna, just as her arctic white studio contains what Tennessee Williams in *The Glass Menagerie* termed "an accidental touch of poetic truth" in the fire escape which runs across the entire upstage. Like Catherine in *Wuthering Heights*, who sacrifices the safety of a relationship with her aristocratic Linton for the danger and excitement of the Byronic anti-hero Heathcliff, Anna opts to discard the wealthy and predictable Burton with whom she "see[s] things very similarly, and share[s] a great deal" (86) in favor of Pale, who packs a gun, has Mafia connections in all probability and terrifies her: "I said I don't like you. I don't want to know you. I don't want to see you again. There is no reason for you to come here. I have nothing for you. I don't like you and I'm frightened of you" (86).

In *Wuthering Heights*, Linton's home, Thrushcross Grange, is associated with safety, wealth and domestic tranquility ("a splendid place carpeted with crimson, and crimson-covered chairs and tables, and a pure white ceiling bordered by gold, a shower of glass drops hanging in silver chains from the centre, and shimmering with little soft tapers" [89]), in contrast to the demonic world of Wuthering Heights which, like Heathcliff himself, is associated with "the radiance of an immense fire, compounded of coal, peat, and wood" (52). As Catherine observes in contrasting her two suitors to her servant Nellie Dean, Heathcliff is "more like myself than I am. Whatever our souls are made of, his and mine are the same, and Linton's is as different as a moonbeam from lightning, or frost from fire" (121).

Offering a heat and passion that is completely absent in the lives of the other three characters, Pale's raw energy warms Anna into renewed life and the possibility of creativity at the end of the play, just like the V.S.O.P. brandy from which he derives his name is capable of providing renewed vigor for frozen bodies in distress. Although Larry notes while lighting a match to a cigarette that "You are hazardous to people's health, Pale" (80), it is precisely the sort of hazard which Anna needs to overcome death, both in terms of Robbie's loss and her own spiritual death-in-life.

Throughout the work, repeated reference is made to the lack of passion or fire in contemporary urban America, yet it is precisely this heat for which all of the characters are searching. Larry, Anna's surviving homosexual roommate, works in an advertising agency where "The only thing everyone believes in is the automobile" (24). However, his comic response to Pale's arrival is to invoke images of heat and sexual desire in his quotation from the camp Western starring Divine, *Lust in the Dust*: "Where did you come from? What do you want? It's me, isn't it? You've always wanted me. You want to have your filthy way with me in the hot desert sun. Ravage me like I've never been ravaged before" (28).

Analogously, Burton, Anna's boyfriend, while vacationing in the snowy wilds of northern Canada, describes his longing to write about "some humongous mega-passion, something felt much deeper than we know" (13). However, even as he describes this Lawrencian vision, the stage direction noting that he is "*Getting juice from the fridge*" (13) serves ironically to underscore Burton's connection with the world of frozen climes, rather than the "passions, faith, myths, love, derring-do, for godsake. Heroes and heroines" (14) which obsess him. Like Larry, who observes "there are some things so true that they enter your soul as you hear them," Burton longs to write something genuine and personal—"Make it personal, tell the truth, and then write 'Burn this' on it" (60); while Anna complains, "I'm sick of the age I'm living in. I don't like feeling ripped off and scared. . . . I'm being pillaged and I'm being raped. And I don't like it" (87–88).

If the world of contemporary America is described as cold and sterile, Pale is conceived as its antithesis. Brutally honest and feeling beneath a vulgar and violent exterior, he is intended as a larger-than-life presence, a force of nature:

> I like the ocean. That hurricane. I like those gigantic, citywide fires—like Passaic, wherever; fuckin' Jersey's burnin' down three times a week. Good riddance. Avalanches! Whole villages wiped out. Somethin' that can—like—amaze you. (38)

Similarly, the world of Wuthering Heights is repeatedly associated with storm as well as fire: "About midnight, while we still sat up, the storm came rattling over the heights in full fury. There was a violent wind, as well as thunder, and either one or the other split a tree off at the corner of the building; a huge bough fell across the roof, and knocked down a portion of the east chimney-stack, sending a clatter of stones and soot into the kitchen fire" (125).

Pale, despite his assurance that "I never felt nothin' for nobody" (84), is, like Heathcliff, fiercely emotional despite his violent exterior. Like Heathcliff, who is driven to acts of vengeance and cruelty by his love for Catherine, Pale's cruelty is counter-balanced by his guilt and by his grief for his departed brother, as well as by the obsessiveness of his craving and love for Anna.

Although street smart and fully cognizant of how the world operates with a currency of deception—"Lies happen like every ten seconds. Half the people you see on the street don't mean a thing they're doin'. Hug up some bitch, don't mean nothin' to them. . . . My brother Sammy, older'n me, kissed his bride, said he wanted to bite the lips off her. People ain't easy"

(83)—in his relationship with Anna, he is able to direct her towards a truth deeper than she is capable of facing: "You don't think I'm dangerous; you think you're afraid of me is what you think. . . . Why? (*Pause*) You're afraid you might get interested. Have to feel somethin'" (85).

For Lanford Wilson, "this play is not about a monster sniffing at the window. It's about the monster within. And that's the territory I consider dangerous" (Freedman 64). Daring to confront this monster within, and inviting Pale to burn his way into her body and spirit, Anna is purified, both of her despair over Robbie's death, and of her own spiritual malaise. The dance she choreographs at the end of the play is of course an expression of the necessary union between herself and Pale and it is the passion which, ironically, Burton foreshadows earlier in the play when he expresses frustration over the meagerness of his characters' breadth: "I want something larger than life. Those people are smaller than life" (51).

In describing the "hash" John Malkovich made of Lanford Wilson's play, interrupting "the good work the other players have been doing," Walter Kerr assumed that Malkovich's fury, which "comes on like a nor'easter with the wind at its tail, a hurricane howl of a storm that has no quiet eye to it," somehow works against the playwright's intentions: "If only Mr. Wilson and his director, Marshall W. Mason, could go back into rehearsal, determined to make the misfit fit the other pieces of the play" (21). In fact, Malkovich's deliberately outsized portrayal is precisely what the playwright wanted, and the success of the play is entirely predicated on the audience's being capable (as Anna finally is) of accepting the implications and the necessity of Pale's union with Anna.

Ultimately, *Burn This* is not intended as the work of psychological realism that Kerr assumed it was. Rather, as in Brontë's novel, realism and romance are inextricably intertwined, allowing for the playwright's daring collision between the world of elemental force ("the eternal rocks beneath") with the weary, fragile and effete world of the Soho art scene. By doing so, the playwright deliberately risked critical censure for his apparent confusion of these two realms. In fact, this "confusion" explains the tremendous power of the play. With

Burn This, Lanford Wilson dared in mid-career to return to the dangerous and "unruly" sensibility of his earlier work, and emerged a fresher, more exciting playwright for having braved his own "monster within."

REFERENCES

Bennetts, Leslie. "Marshall Mason Explores a New Stage." *New York Times* 11 October 1987, sec. 2: 3, 14.

Brontë, Emily. *Wuthering Heights*. Harmondsworth: Penguin, 1973.

Freedman, Samuel G. "Lanford Wilson Comes Home." *New York Times* 30 August 1987, sec 6, part 2: 29, 63–64.

Kerr, Walter. "When Best-Laid Plans Go Awry." *New York Times* 15 November 1987, sec 2: 5, 21.

Rich, Frank. "Stage: 'Burn This,' by Wilson." *New York Times* 15 October 1987: C23.

Schvey, Henry I. "Images of the Past in the Plays of Lanford Wilson." *Essays on Contemporary American Drama*. Ed. Hedwig Bock and Albert Wertheim. Munich: Max Hüber Verlag, 1981. 225–40.

Wilson, Lanford. *Angels Fall*. New York: Hill and Wang, 1983.

———. *Balm in Gilead and Other Plays*. New York: Hill and Wang, 1965.

———. *Burn This*. New York: Hill and Wang, 1987.

———. *The Hot l Baltimore*. New York: Hill and Wang, 1973.

———. "The Madness of Lady Bright." *The Rimers of Eldritch and Other Plays*. New York: Hill and Wang, 1967. 73–91.

———. *The Mound Builders*. New York: Hill and Wang, 1976.

———. *Talley's Folly*. New York: Hill and Wang, 1979.

Lanford Wilson's *Liebestod*: Character, Archetype and Myth in *Burn This*

Daniel J. Watermeier

Like his earlier *Talley's Folly* (1979), Wilson's *Burn This* (1987) is essentially a romantic comedy, concerned with how and why an unlikely pair "fall in love." Wilson, through Matt Friedman, the protagonist of *Talley's Folly*, describes that play as a waltz, "one-two-three, one-two-three, a no-holds-barred romantic story." Contemporary critics have called it "an easy comfortable love story with a happy ending" (Barnett 122) or "a simple, innocent, and deliberately old-fashioned romance" (Schvey 238). *Burn This*, however, might be described as a "knock-down, drag-out" love story, ironic, difficult and un-comfortable, with an ending which at best is only tentatively happy. Wilson himself has described the romantic passion at the core of *Burn This* as "a juggernaut that just knocks down ev-erything in front of it" (Bennetts 220). It moves not to the steady, melodic strains of an old-fashioned Missouri waltz, but to the compellingly dynamic, but often discordant rhythms of contemporary jazz or rock.[1] While *Talley's Folly* is set somewhat nostalgically in a recent past—1944—*Burn This* is located firmly, even fiercely, in the present. Wilson, however, through various verbal and scenic allusions associates his present-day lovers with several legendary "fatal lovers," principally, but not exclusively, Teutonic in origin and Romantic in temperament. Contrapuntally, he plays the immediate present against a distant, mythic past and realistically drawn characters against archetypes. In contrast to the simpler *Talley's Folly*, *Burn This* is a much more sophisticated and complex exploration of the nature of passionate love, or more accurately of eros, its relationship to death, to renewal and creativity, and perhaps its significance in our own time.

The plot of *Burn This* centers on Anna, a modern dancer and aspiring choreographer. In the first scene, we discover that she has just returned from the funeral of her best friend Robbie, also a dancer and choreographer, who was killed in a boating accident with his lover, Dominic. Anna had shared her huge Manhattan loft apartment, the setting for the action, with Robbie and Larry, a former dancer, now a graphic designer, who is also gay. Anna is clearly bereft at the loss of Robbie, who was not only her roommate and friend, but also her model and mentor as an artist. Anna is consoled by Larry and by her boyfriend, Burton, a successful screenwriter.

The dramatic conflict erupts in the second scene. A month has passed since the funeral. At five o'clock in the morning, Robbie's older brother Pale—a nickname taken from his favorite drink, Very Special Old Pale Cognac—literally barges into the loft to collect Robbie's "things." His behavior is, for the most part, outrageously loutish and his language vilely obscene, but Anna discerns that Pale—whose real name is Jimmy—is mainly

---

[1] The considerable incidental music for the New York production of *Burn This* was taken from an album by the jazz composer/pianist Peter Kater. The album is entitled *Two Hearts* (PDK Records 1986). The title instrumental and other selections such as "Search," "Spirit," "Joani's Song," "Departures," "Arrivals" and "Emergence" did effectively complement the dramatic action and mood.

acting out his own feelings of loss and anger. Although initially
put off she gradually becomes empathetic. When Pale finally
breaks down weeping, Anna comforts him and then takes him to
her bed, succumbing to what she later describes to Larry as "the
bird-with-the-broken-wing syndrome" (47).[2]

In the opening scene of Act Two, which takes place three
months later on New Year's Eve, after a violent confrontation
between Pale and Burton, Anna rejects Burton and once again
she and Pale go to bed together. On the morning after, however,
Anna tells Pale that she's afraid of becoming emotionally involved with him, that indeed she's frightened of him, and she
asks him to leave. Pale does so without protest, but with his
departure Anna reveals her ambivalence. When Larry observes,
"If you didn't want him to go, you sure fooled me. It's okay,
doll," she replies tearfully, "It's not okay, doll, it fucking sucks."
Anna resolves to lose herself in work. "If I can't have a life," she
says, "at least I can work" (88).[3]

The final two scenes take place a month later on the
afternoon and evening of the opening of a new dance piece that
Anna has choreographed. In the first scene, Burton arrives at the
apartment presumably to see Anna, whom he hasn't seen since
New Year's Eve, but finds only Larry. Burton tells Larry that he's
finished the film script that he's been working on for several
months. Larry, in turn, describes the dance that Anna has
choreographed in the interim. It's about Pale and Anna, he says,
and it's set in the loft, with "a synthesized kind of city noise,

---

[2]Unless otherwise indicated, references are to the version
of *Burn This* published by Hill and Wang in 1987. For this essay, I
did have access to a typescript version used in the New York
production. There are some relatively minor, but still significant,
differences between the two versions. When pertinent, I have
cited such differences below.

[3]This line seems to have been an addition to the published
Hill and Wang edition of the play. It does not appear in the typescript version that was used for the New York production. It also
obviously echoes Sonya's lines at the end of *Uncle Vanya*.
Wilson's admiration for and indebtedness to Chekhov is well-
documented. *Burn This* contains several Chekhovian echoes.

with a foghorn and gulls" as the musical accompaniments. "It's kind of epic," says Larry. "Well, for twelve minutes" (92). Realizing that he's lost Anna, Burton ruefully wishes Larry "Have a good life" and exits (95).

The final scene takes place "after midnight" and after the premiere of the dance. Anna enters her dark apartment only to find Pale there waiting for her. In the ensuing dialogue, Pale and Anna discover that Larry had arranged for Pale to see the dance and then contrived to bring them together alone in the apartment. As Pale observes, they've both been set up. Larry, indeed, gave Pale the following note: "Pale, doll. Here's a ticket for the program tonight and my keys. We're going to the cast party and won't be home until three. I don't know how you're doing, but Anna is in pretty bad shape. This isn't opera, this is life, why should love always be tragic? Burn this" (98). Although both Pale and Anna half-heartedly protest that they don't want a relationship, they also concede, as Pale says, that they "never felt nothin' like this." In the final moments of the play, Anna folds Larry's note into a tent, puts it into an ashtray and lights a match to it. As it burns, the lovers embrace in the enveloping darkness while the curtain rings down.

Wilson introduces the mythic context for his contemporary love story in a seemingly casual, almost off-handed manner. In the opening scene Burton struggles to describe his recent adventure in northern Canada where, inspired by the "very barren, very lonely" landscape where "you feel like you're all alone, or you're one with the . . . something," he got an idea for a new movie—"kind of a weird-ass love story" (12–13). He alludes to the wives of whalers waiting for their husbands to return from the sea. He says that his movie would be about "their _heart,_ or the men out there on the sea, their _heart._ Where's that love, or what is it, that power that allows those people to sustain that feeling? Through loss, through death. Is it less than the feelings we have? So they can humanly _cope_? Or is it more? I think they felt things in a much more profound way. There's some humongous mega-passion, something felt much deeper than we know. I don't know." Anna says, "I love it when you get an idea. You're so confused and enthusiastic" (13). Burton spurred on by her comment says that his idea is in his mind "just all fragmented" and mentions that while on his expedition he "had this book of Nordic tales, totally foreign from our stupid urban microcosm, all that crap." He goes on to say that he's "looking for passions, faith, myths, love, derring-do, ... Heroes and heroines." Larry pipes in: "Senta throwing herself into the sea." But Burton doesn't know, as he says, the story of *"The Flying fuckin' Dutchman"* (13–15). Larry summarizes it for him:

> LARRY: . . . The Dutchman's this sailor who is like condemned to perdition unless he finds a girl who'll really love him. But he can come ashore only about once every seven years to look for her.
> BURTON: Why?
> LARRY: You don't ask why in Wagner. So he goes to Norway and Senta falls in love with him, but she has this boyfriend hanging around and the Dutchman gets uptight and sails off again. And Senta throws herself into the . . . fjord.
> BURTON: To prove she loved him.
> LARRY: To save him from perdition, to break the spell. The sea starts boiling, the Dutchman's ship sinks, all hell breaks loose.
> ANNA: Big finish.
> BURTON: I like the sea boiling, but I'm not that much of an opera queen. (15)

Although none of the principals realize it either at the moment or even later, this passage ironically presages their lives in the subsequent action of *Burn This*, as well as Burton's movie script and Anna's dance. Indeed, it even echoes a similar moment in Act Two of Wagner's *The Flying Dutchman* in which Erik, the hunter who is Senta's suitor, relates his dream—which tragically comes true—of Senta's sailing off with a pale seaman dressed in black Spanish costume. *Burn This* is thus loosely structured as a play within a play (or opera) within another "play"—i.e., Burton's movie—and even within another "play"— i.e., Anna's dance—all taking their inspiration most directly from "The Flying Dutchman" legend: art reflecting life reflecting art. In this context, Anna is a contemporary Senta who saves the Dutchman (Pale) and herself from "perdition," while rejecting

her suitor Burton/Erik. Larry, who ironically refers to himself at
one point as an opera "Lady-in Waiting" rather than an "opera
queen," functions to a degree like the housekeeper/confidante
Mary in Wagner's opera. Wilson omits an analogue to Senta's
father Daland, but then Robbie does function as a surrogate,
psychological father-figure to complete the analogy. In any case,
Wilson does not pursue the parallels in depth. He is less
interested in re-telling *The Flying Dutchman* in contemporary
terms than in using it to help establish a general, collective
mythic framework for his present-day characters and their
conflicts.

The character of Pale, for example, is, on one level, an ab-
sorbing fusion of Romantic hero and modern anti-hero. Wilson
describes him as *"well built, and can be good-looking, but is certainly
sexy"* (25). He is vain about his looks, his hair and his flashy
expensive clothes. He's constantly admiring himself in the full-
length mirror that is an integral part of the scenery. Like a typical
Romantic hero, Pale is egocentric, emotionally explosive and
contemptuous of others, both individuals and society at large. In
his opening scene, he strides energetically about the stage,
scornfully railing at "city garbage and shit" (30), at Anna's
"empty fuckin' warehouse" loft (32), at homosexuals, at women,
including Anna herself and most of all at the "giganticness of
unconcern" (35). As he remarks in one of his calmer moments:
"People aren't human, you ever notice that?" (31)

He reveals that he hates physical restrictions and is im-
pervious to cold. He burns with passionate intensity: "I got like a
toaster oven I carry around with me in my belly someplace. I
don't use heat. I sleep the windows open, no covers, I fuckin'
hate things over me" (29). When Anna asks him what he does, he
answers cryptically, "I deliver. Water. I'm a water deliverer. For
fires. I put out fires. I'm a relief pitcher. Like Sparky Lyle. . . . I'm
a roving fireman. Very healthy occupation. I'm puttin' out
somebody else's fire, I'm puttin' out my own. *Quid pro*—
something; symbiosis. Or sometimes you just let it burn" (33–
34).[4] When asked what he likes, he says, "I like the ocean. That

---

[4]"The stirring up of conflict is a Luciferian virtue in the
true sense of the word. Conflict engenders fire, the fire of effects

hurricane. . . . I like those gigantic, citywide fires—like Passaic, wherever; fuckin' Jersey's burnin' down three times a week. Good riddance. Avalanches! Whole villages wiped out. Somethin' that can—like—amaze you" (38). He also confesses to composing whole romantic symphonies in the shower—*à la* Vivaldi, Puccini or Shostakovich—not "Hall & Oates" but "these tone poems, concertos and shit—huge big orchestrations, use like two orchestras. . . . these like giant themes come to me, these like world-shaking changes in tempo and these great huge melodies, these incredible variations, man. Get like the whole fuckin' war in it" (39).[5]

Like one of his shower symphonies, there are "incredible variations" in Pale's personality and behavior. His manic depressive "mood swings" catapult up and nose dive down. At one moment, he is vilifying homosexuality and the next he is stifling a sob crying, "My heart's killing me. My throat's hurtin', burnin', man" (39). His observations about "yuppie" pretentiousness and a widespread lack of concern in contemporary society for humanity and the environment, ring true. He exhibits a certain charm when, dressed in one of Anna's robes, he brews a pot of tea—straight orange pekoe, not *chichi* Earl Grey or Red Zinger. He has a knowledge of food and wine, and if pressed, he can cook *haute cuisine*. He can be gentle and considerate and he has firm, if idiosyncratic, standards of conduct and taste. But he is also a brawling drunkard and drug abuser, not a metaphorical roving fireman, but only the lonely workaholic manager of an Italian restaurant in Montclair, New Jersey.

---

and emotions, and like every other fire it has two aspects, that of combustion and that of creating light. On the one hand, emotion is the alchemical fire whose warmth brings everything into existence and whose heat burns all superfluities to ashes (*Omnes superfluitates combusit*). But on the other hand, emotion is the moment when steel meets flint and a spark is struck forth, for emotion is the source of consciousness. There is no change from darkness to light or from inertia to movement without emotion" (Jung, *Four Archetypes* 30–31).

[5]As Peter L. Thorslev has observed, the Byronic hero "often loves music or poetry" (8).

About his estranged wife who walked out on him, and now lives in Coral Gables, Florida, with their two children—a boy and a girl—this "man of feeling" in the Romantic mold says he "never felt nothin' for her. . . . I never felt nothin' for nobody" (84). He is filled not so much with romantic *angst* and *weltschmerz*, as self-loathing and self-pity—i.e., ego-suffering.[6] Pale seems larger-than-life, super human and, like all great heroes (like great actors, too, playing great heroes), he engages, as Michael Goldman has so perceptively observed, "a double impulse of attraction and repulsion" (13).

Moreover, behind his compelling surface anger, arrogance and contempt, and his narcissistic awareness of his own visceral responses, he has no real grasp of the deep psychic trauma that has created his present emotional turmoil. He is constantly examining himself in the mirror, but sees nothing beyond his surface reflection; full of "sound and fury," he is totally self-absorbed rather than self-reflective.

---

[6]For a description of the Romantic hero pertinent to Pale's character see Lilian R. Furst's essay "The Romantic Hero, or is he an Anti-Hero?" Furst observes that the Romantic hero's state of mind is best defined by the term *Ichschmerz* (ego-suffering) rather than *Weltschmerz* or *mal du siècle*. She writes: "For the roots of his affliction are neither in his grief for the world, as *Weltschmerz* would seem to imply, nor in conditions specific to his time, although these contribute to his discontent. The ultimate source of his malady resides in that solipsistic self-absorption that entraps him in a vicious circle. The proud awareness of himself as an exceptional being leads to a cultivation of his differentness and to an incessant brooding on his state. Eventually he reaches a depth of self-involution where his introverted sense of self completely distorts his perception of outer reality so that he sinks even further into himself" (42). According to Furst, the Romantic hero, because of *Ichschmerz*, also often exerts "a disruptive, indeed destructive force," in his relationships with others and he is frequently self-destructive as well. He is "irked by a society he rejects with vehemence, but he makes little or no positive effort at reform" (50). Instead of acting, he evades.

Like the Dutchman, Pale is lost, aimlessly wandering about a dark urban ocean, grief stricken and alienated. Robbie's death has sharpened his dissatisfactions with his life and heightened his existential aloneness. He even clumsily suggests at one point that his present state "has made me not as, you know—whatever—as I usually am" (26). At thirty-six, as he says, he's "fucked." Instinctively, he's looking for a safe harbor, a refuge from life's storms, "a girl who'll really love him" (15).

Towards the end of Act One, scene two, for example, emotionally spent and forgetting his aversion to heat and physical restriction, according to the stage direction, *"He has crawled onto the sofa and completely covered himself with an afghan, head and all"* (41), like a child hiding from the dark or a thunderstorm, a symbolic return to the security of the womb. Comforted by Anna, who, indeed, treats him as a mother would an ill child, feeling his forehead for temperature and getting him a soothing drink, Pale finds himself becoming sexually aroused by the proximity of her hair and breasts. "Aww, man," he says, "I'm so fucked. My gut aches. My balls are hurtin', they're gonna take stitches on my heart; I'm fuckin' *grievin'* here and you're givin' me a hard-on" (43). The moment, with its Oedipal echoes and suggestions of the complex relationship between *eros* and *thanatos*, is simultaneously comic and psychologically illuminating. Pale seems to need a mother/lover to take care of him, while Anna also seems to need a son/lover to take care of. In another context, Pale correctly describes such relationships: "*Quid pro*—something; symbiosis" (34).

Indeed, on another level, Pale is not so much a "bad man" as a "bad boy"—a *puer aeternus*. Less the fierce, romantic hero than the mischievous, sometimes even perverse, eternal boy-god Eros, perpetually flying about, indiscriminately setting hearts on fire with his torches or his poisoned barbed arrows—although Pale packs a gun rather than a bow—inspiring love, but never in love himself—at least not until his encounter with Psyche. Like Cupid in Apuleius's story, Pale also visits his Psyche only at night and Anna describes him as an "interesting" lover. Like Cupid, he even has a wound—a hurt hand. Pale's extravagantly excessive use of the word "fuck" may also be deliberate on Wilson's part. As the comedian George Carlin reminded us a decade or so ago, "fuck," after all, means "love." It's a slyly appropriate expletive for a modern day Eros.

Anna's character suggests a synthesis of mythic mother archetype, Romantic heroine and modern liberated woman—a mixture of feminine strength and beauty, but also vulnerability. She is described, for example, as *"very beautiful, tall and strong"* (5). There are implications, moreover, that she also has a certain "heroic" strength of character. She has pursued her career as a dancer and has lived an independent, even unorthodox, life—free of the usual restrictions of an ordinary job, marriage or parentage. Although apparently asked by Burton on more than one occasion, she has rejected marrying him. Even before Robbie died, she had decided to turn from dancing to choreography. Burton admires her for this decision. "I'm not as intrepid as Anna," he says, "quitting dance, trying to break into choreography." But Anna responds: "Oh yeah, at this late date. By myself" (18). At thirty-two, with Robbie's death "robbing" her of creative and psychological support, she feels more alone, less secure and, like Pale, more conscious of her limitations and her own mortality.

The death of Robbie, traumatic in itself, was made even more so by his funeral, which she describes as "a total nightmare." Indeed, both Larry and Anna describe the event in the images of a gothic romance or horror story. Robbie was laid out in a "great baroque maroon-and-gold casket with these ormolu geegaws all over it—angels and swags" (9). Robbie's hometown, a blue-collar, factory town, presumably in New Jersey, is described as a "combat zone" (10). His large, Catholic, "ethnic" (Italian?) family descended on Anna "like a plague of grasshoppers" (10). At the cemetery, everyone was "sobbing and beating their breasts." Anna says: "I got the distinct feeling that I was expected to throw myself across that hideous casket," like, as Burton adds, "the bereaved widow" (11). At the "wake" following the burial, the "place was mobbed. . . . everybody eating and drinking and talking" (20). Anna, who was raised in the upper middle-class Chicago suburb of Highland Park, seems to view their funeral behavior like that of some neolithic tribe. She is most upset by the fact that his family had never seen Robbie dance, nor did they seem to know that he was gay.

(Later, however, Pale says, "They know, they just don't know" [40]—i.e., they pretended not to know.):

> ANNA: I'm just so annoyed with myself, because all I can feel is anger. I was angry with Robbie and Dom for doing something that stupid; now I'm angry with his family. . . . They didn't even know him. . . . I didn't even have a damn minute to say goodbye. (24)

To make matters worse, when she misses the bus "back to civilization," she spends the night in "Robbie's little nephew's room in the attic." Pinned around the walls of this room are dozens of butterfly specimens that he's collected during the day. That night, Anna is awakened by "this intermittent soft flutter sound." The butterflies, she discovers, were not dead, but only drugged and, now revived, they're alive, "beating their bodies against the walls" (21). Panicked she races out of the room, naked except for a sheet wrapped around her (another allusion to Psyche?). Finally a "glowering older brother" (22), who later turns out to have been Pale, rescues her, and then unpins and frees the butterflies.

Pursuing the Cupid-Psyche allusion further, this incident may have special psychological and symbolic significance for, in Greek, *psyche* can mean both "soul" and "butterfly." Anna's intense, hysterical reaction to the pinned butterflies may be less to the physical event itself, than to a heightened subconscious recognition that her "soul" and Robbie's are "pinned butterflies."[7] In the usual multiple meanings of such recognitions, the "pinned butterflies" may also represent her feelings of anger, guilt and loss about Robbie. Angry with Robbie, she has symbolically pinned him to the wall wanting to hurt him as he has hurt her by his careless, untimely death, but she also feels guilty—horrified—about these feelings. Both his life and art and hers, furthermore, will remain "pinned"—i.e., unfulfilled,

---

[7] As Jung noted, symbols "do not occur solely in dreams. They appear in all kinds of psychic manifestations. There are symbolic thoughts and feelings, symbolic acts and situations" (*Man and His Symbols* 41).

unrealized—until she, with Pale/Eros's help, transfers her necessarily repressed, unrequited, unreciprocated love for Robbie to another. Indeed, even before Pale introduces himself to Anna, she recognizes him as Robbie's "double."[8]

In Act Two, Anna indirectly alludes to herself as a butterfly, telling Burton: "I almost feel as if I've finally burst my chrysalis after thirty years of incubation. That's the wrong word." Burton supplies the right word: "Metamorphosis" (52).[9] In a line, subsequently deleted from the published Hill and Wang version, Anna reports that Fred, the dance company director for whom she's creating a new dance, urged her to "just free your mind and let your body take flight."

Like a chrysalis, Anna has lived in a "cocoon." Larry says, "She's had a very protected life. . . . she's not had to make her

---

[8]Jung's essay "The Song of the Moth" seems particularly relevant to Wilson's imagery. In this essay Jung analyzes at great length a poetic image of a moth striving towards the sun, a symbol, according to him, of "intensity and power. . . . The phenomenon of psychic energy . . . the libido." Pale clearly represents a kind of psychic energy for which or for whom Anna "passionately longs." Such "passionate longing" for Jung had two sides: "It is the power which beautifies everything, but in a different set of circumstances, is quite likely to destroy everything. Hence a violent desire is either accompanied by anxiety at the start, or is remorselessly pursued by it. All passion is a challenge to fate, and what it does cannot be undone. Fear of fate is a very understandable phenomenon, for it is incalculable, immeasurable, full of unknown dangers. The perpetual hesitation of the neurotic to launch out into life is readily explained by his desire to stand aside so as not to get involved in the dangerous struggle for existence. But anyone who refuses to experience life must stifle his desire to live—in other words, he must commit partial suicide. This explains the death-fantasies that usually accompany the renunciation of desire." The case of Larry in this context is also instructive. (See *Symbols of Transformation* 79-117, especially 85-86, 109-10.)

[9]This word does not appear in the typescript version. There the sentence reads: "Yeah, but it sounds provocative."

own way much" (94). Anna says about herself when she's
struggling to create her dance: "I'm beginning to think that as an
artist I have absolutely no life experience to draw from" (53).
And at another point she wonders "what could I know about the
world living in Highland Park?" (11) She admired Robbie
because he "grew up in such different circumstances," less
secure, less protected than she, but he had the impulses, "all that
drive" she calls it, of the true artist (11). It is precisely this same
"drive" and his "differentness" that attracts Anna to Pale. As
Robbie's "double," and in a way that Robbie could never be, Pale
is Anna's "wish-fulfillment," her shadow self, her *animus* as she's
Pale's *anima*.

    At thirty-two, Anna is also beginning to feel a biological
pressure. Responding to Burton's suggestion that they "have
kids or something," she says, "That's something I haven't
thought about much. Or every time I did, I pushed it out of my
mind. But now—I don't know. I think my body chemistry is
changing, or maybe I just have time to think of things like that
now. I can feel a kind of anxiety or panic creeping up on me. The
sound of the biological clock or something" (54–55). Her mother
keeps a scrapbook of Anna's career, but "all she wants is grandchildren" (11). Her initial theme for her dance is "mother love"
which she concedes she knows "nothing about—yet" (53). She
has been absorbed in work, not in life. As she confesses to Pale,
"I have never had a personal life. I wasn't scared of it, I just had
no place for it, it wasn't important" (86). But life and art, love
and creativity are inextricably entangled.

    If Pale needs a safe harbor, a refuge from life's storms, a
love object, Anna, like Senta or Psyche, needs a rescuer, a dai-
mon-lover, a catalyst who will unpin, unstick or unglue her
deepest creative impulses as both a woman and artist, who will
challenge her, complete her, let her take flight, save her from a
humdrum, noncreative life. Burton is *"tall, athletic, . . . good
looking"* (6) and "rich as Croesus" (16), but he obviously doesn't
excite Anna artistically or biologically. Anna recognizes this. Her
attachment to Burton lacks passion. It is safe, conventional,
cerebral. She says, "we see things very similarly, and share a
great deal, and I like being with him. I, at least, would like to
give us the time to see if we're as compatible as we seem to be"

(86). When she finally creates a dance, it's not about "mother love," or *agape*, it's about *eros*—"Pale and Anna."

Burton, for that matter, is not passionately in love with Anna. He confesses to Larry that he's "feeling angry," more about losing to Pale than losing Anna, or, in fact, just about losing:

> BURTON: I have this problem I'm trying to cope with here. I was a rich kid, you know. . . . And I've never really . . . I've never lost anything before. Or, I've never lost. Before. . . . See what gets to me is, I keep feeling angry. You know, I could tear the shithead apart. . . . I could. But, you know, that doesn't mean anything. What's bothering me is, I keep feeling "Fuck *her*," you know?—and then I know that that's not really what I'm feeling—that's just a protective mechanism sort of thing that I've always used so I wouldn't lose. You know? 'Cause I've never lost. And I don't really feel "Fuck her" at all. That's just my immune system defending me. (93)

Larry drily responds, "It's a handy thing to have."

Burton describes his family as "rich, self-satisfied, alcoholically comatose, boring" (52), but he could also be describing himself. He wants desperately to create a movie that is truthful, epic, passionate and personal. He urges Anna about her dance: "Make it as personal as you can. Believe me, you can't imagine a feeling everyone hasn't had. Make it personal, tell the truth, and then write 'Burn this' on it" (60).[10] But there is a "hollowness of heart" in Burton. Even when he finally drafts a screenplay that's different from his usual sci-fi work, an urban love story, which Anna describes as "real" and "a giant leap into the unknown" (60), Burton "doesn't trust it" (60). He wrote it, he says, because he was "bored" and describes it as "nothing" (60). He vainly tries to fill his "hollow heart" with experiences—wilderness

---

[10]These lines are somewhat different from the version used in the New York production. There Burton says, "A writer shouldn't consider he's done his job unless he wants to write 'burn this' at the bottom of the page."

trekking, akido, sky-diving. He asks Larry in Act One, "Tell me what I need" (16), and in Act Two, Larry suggests that it's love. Burton, however, has rejected love for money like Wagner's *Ring of the Niebelung* giants, Fafner and Fasolt, whom he suggests with his *"big feet and big hands"* (6). His youthful dreams of becoming a serious writer and his willingness to take risks have dried up. As he tells Larry, "I just haven't felt that open to the world since those days" (95). He has become, as he says once about himself, "insensitive and stupid" (18)—a rich, but oafish giant, closed to love. He can fantasize epic fragments, but he can only realize banal "droid-busting on Barsoom" (55) sci-fi thrillers.

In terms of the plot, Larry functions as an effective foil to and manipulator of the principal characters, but as a dramatic character, he is not very clearly or distinctly developed. Wilson describes him as *"twenty-seven, medium everything, very bright, gay"* (7). He is observant, practical and realistic with a sharp, sardonic, sometimes racy sense of humor. As he notes, however, it's "a protective sense of humor" (56) which masks a deep bitterness and despondency. He says that he's "always willing to drape the joint in crepe" (8). He clearly despises his advertising job. "It sucks the big one" (8), as he says. Why he quit dancing is never clearly explained. He implies some regret. Perhaps he needed the security invariably not offered by a career as a dancer. He says, "I'm not really that improvisational. I like having a rough copy to work from, at least. Something to go by" (87).

He has no love interest, not even any "old friends." He is nostalgic for the lost "innocence and freedom of yesterday" (63). For Larry, life offers only two choices: you can be "ripped off and scared" or "pillaged and raped" (87). Like Burton, Larry has accepted the latter choice, but in so doing he has "lost heart." He can help Pale and Anna embrace love and life, but, as he says, his own arms have "fallen off" (55). Larry does hint at an erotic attraction to Burton. Indeed, Burton may represent Larry's shadow *persona* or shadow-lover. Burton, moreover, while heterosexual, confesses that he had a homosexual erotic experience as a younger man: "It was very nice, and I never thought about it. And it didn't mean anything, but I've never been sorry it happened or any of that crap" (63). Indeed his assertion twice that he "never thought about it" (63) hints that he has. Burton has chosen to reject or repress this aspect of his personality. The separation of Larry and Burton at the end of Act Two, scene three, is fraught with distance and sadness.

Together Larry and Burton stand as a contrasting, antithetical dyad to the dyad of Anna and Pale. Both Larry and Burton suffer from a loss of soul, of heart, a diminution of personality. There is a distance between them, and between them and Anna and Pale. Anna and Pale, however, by "falling in love" expand their personalities, open themselves to risk, to anxiety and suffering, but also to joy and creativity. They close the gap, diminish the differences and the distances between each other; and in so doing, they resolve old, stagnant internal conflicts, even while creating new, but potentially energizing, conflicts.

Anna's funeral experiences are not the only black comedic references to "gothic nightmares." In the opening scene, Burton, for example, who never saw his last, very successful sci-fi thriller, called *Far Voyager* (another veiled reference to *The Flying Dutchman*), is surprised to learn from Larry that the "Pit and the Pendulum scene" in the movie was "saved by forty midgets" (17). The script apparently was rewritten by the producer, Signer (a Nordic-sounding name suggesting Wagner's dwarf-King Alberich), who also inserted a "cave with the Vampire Queen— hanging upside down" (18) and probably added the midgets because, according to Burton, he's "short" and "gets off on little people" (18). Once after Signer had read one of his first drafts all he asked with "a crushed look" was "What happened to the tiny Australian Bushman?" (16) As Burton bitterly concludes, there are "no good movies" and when by chance, "once in five years," a good movie happens, "it's like this total aberration, a freak of nature like the Grand Canyon," which the producers then remake and "fuck it up the way it's supposed to be." Movies are "produced by whores, written by whores, directed by [whores]" (17).

Larry responds: "Burton, you don't have to tell me about whores, you're talking to someone who works in advertising" (17). Larry goes on to rail against the "stupidity" of the Chrysler Corporation for whom he's designing a Christmas card that you can or not hang on your Christmas tree or Hanukkah bush that says Season's Greetings! Traditional Christmas symbols with their religious associations rooted in Teutonic myth—snow, evergreens, holly, pines, mistletoe, bells, Santa Claus, reindeer—were rejected because they would offend some group. The "only thing everyone believes in is the automobile" (24). It doesn't offend anyone. In Act Two, scene one, Larry returning to the apartment after a trip to Detroit, his hometown—"the South's revenge" (57) he calls it—and after circling the airport for almost two hours, disparages New Year's Eve as a festive, celebratory holiday. His fellow passengers were zombies: "Everyone was going to a party. Nobody made it. Midnight came and went, nobody said a word. We just glared at each other" (56). Larry himself complains that his head hurts, that he's exhausted, that his "arms are falling off" (56)—he repeats this three times—and that going home causes him to lose his "protective sense of humor" (56). He hoped the plane "would crash and burn" (56). He rejects Anna's suggestion to go to a party. "Have you ever been to a gay New Year's Eve party?" he asks. "The suicide rate is higher than all of Scandinavia" (57). In his own suicidal mood, he complains about his "baby-machine" sisters and women in general who a decade ago were "exciting entities" but now "they're all turning into cows" (57).

The imagery suggests that generally the world "outside" of the pristine apartment has become an anti-human, alienating, animalistic, gothic nightmare, ruled by insensitive, greedy brutes, dwarf-kings who, like Signer, are without, as Larry says, "a modicum of taste" (24), and who ultimately destroy beauty and belief. The ideals of family, of community, of art, the celebration of the community's joy in itself, as Wagner wrote, and of love—i.e., *eros*—the wellspring of family, community and art, have been corrupted. Imaginative creators—artists—have become "whores," while biological creators—women—are "baby machines," "cows," or as Anna imagines, "a brood sow" (57). In such a world, love is cheaply romanticized or reduced to a visceral thrill. Larry on two separate occasions re-enacts a moment from one of his favorite movies, the campy sex-farce *Lust in the Dust*. At another point, a snippet from Billy Rose's "I'd Rather Be Blue" is sung first by Pale, then by Anna and reprised by Larry:

"I'd rather be blue
Thinking of you,
I'd rather be blue over you.
Than be happy with somebody called Burton." (49)

It is contrasted with a torchy rock lyric, also first sung by Pale and then again reprised by Larry:

"At night I wake up with the sheets soaking wet
There's a freight train runnin'
Through the middle of my head . . .
And you, you cool my desire.
Oh . . . oh . . . oh . . . I'm on fire . . ." (76)[11]

Eros, although it may encompass both, is neither lust nor sentimental romance.

At one point Larry observes, "There's a doomsday factor in our genes somewhere. Through the entire history of the species it's been the same story—the wrong people reproduce" (58). The action of *Burn This*, however, implies that Anna and Pale are the "right people." At the finale, they both, despite mental misgivings, surrender to their feelings. Pale is more subdued, his "wildness" has been tamed. He reveals that he has quit his job and is tending bar, working just eight hours a day. He also admits that Anna's dance was "real good" and he recognizes that it was "me and you up there" (96–97) and also Robbie. Anna also says that she "did it for Robbie" and "In my mind Robbie did it" (96). Anna and Pale are beginning to accommodate each other and with and through each other the death and loss of Robbie. Past, present and future—as myth and life—begin to converge.

The burning of the note suggests a parody, not of the ending of *The Flying Dutchman*, but of *Götterdämmerung*, in which Brunnhilde flings the firebrand on Siegfried's funeral pyre crying, "Siegfried! Siegfried! See! Brunnhilde greets you as wife!" All Anna can say is "I don't want this," while Pale sobs, as he did at the end of Act One, "I'm gonna cry all over your hair"

---

[11]This lyric was presumably written by Wilson with music by Peter Kater.

(99). In contrast to the epic Wagnerian conflagration, however, the tiny ashtray fire is hardly a "big finish." Wilson seems to imply that we are still seized by romantic impulses or longings, by epic passions; but that in the context of our times, such impulses are played out—in both life and art—on a much smaller scale and with much less confidence in their "rightness."

At the beginning of Act Two, Burton says disparagingly about the characters in his own developing screenplay that they're "smaller than life" and he wants "larger than life" (51). He asks, "Where's the pain? Where's the joy? Where's the ebullience?" Anna answers, "It's there. Everything doesn't have to be epic" (52). Burton counters: "Yes! Yes! Not in treatment, but at least in feeling . . ." (52). Like the mythic or legendary lovers on whom they are based and who they are intended to evoke, Pale and Anna do suffer the passion of love's anguish and love's joy. Their "feelings" are epic, even if they are less than heroic-sized.

Through love, furthermore, Pale and Anna like mythic lovers transcend their self-absorption. Although at one critical juncture Anna resists self-denial and Pale avoids self-affirmation because he thought Anna didn't like him—"'Cause I didn't want you to do something you didn't like," he says (98)—eventually, with Larry's help, they both surrender to the irresistible and inevitable. At the finale, "I" becomes, however tentatively, "we." Selfish *eros* changes to selfless *amor*; the mysterious forces of destiny or of will are manifested. In Wilson, no less than in Wagner, "you don't ask why."[12]

---

[12]See John Peter's discussion of "Wagner the Dramatist." Peter discusses Wagner's operas in the context of Schopenhauer's *The World as Will and Idea* (55–98). He describes *The Flying Dutchman* as "a portrayal of the Will in action, unappeasable, obsessional and extinguishing itself by a form of spontaneous combustion" (66). The action of *Tristan and Isolde*, he writes, "consists in the incurable yearning and final annihilation of the Will which takes physical form ('objectifies itself') in the two lovers and is enacted by them. In this sense it is fatuous to ask what 'really' happens in Act Two: we witness the Will taking

What the mythologist Joseph Campbell wrote about Joyce's *Ulysses* is no less applicable to *Burn This*. On the surface, *Ulysses* seems to be a narrative of the "casual, chance, fragmentary events of an apparently undistinguished life"; but when reflected in what Campbell calls, after Schopenhauer, the "conic mirror" of Joyce's art, it "discloses the form and dimension of a classic epic of destiny" (195). Wilson's treatment, also like Joyce's *Ulysses*, may be essentially comic, but it is no less real, no less mythic, no less accurate a representation of life than epic romances. Comedy, moreover, often contains tragic potentialities. Comedy springs from wish-fulfillment and drives toward a reconciliation of difference. It celebrates romantic and artistic imagination. These are fragile commodities, however. A threatening, dark, alienating world surrounds the flickering, ashtray fire.

REFERENCES

Barnett, Gene A. *Lanford Wilson*. Boston: G. K. Hall, 1987.
Bennetts, Leslie. "Lanford Wilson & Terrence McNally: On love, responsibility, and sexual obsession." *Vogue* 178, 2 (1988): 216, 220.
Campbell, Joseph. *The Masks of God: Creative Mythology*. New York: Penguin, 1968.
Furst, Lilian R. *The Contours of European Romanticism*. Lincoln: U of Nebraska P, 1979.
Goldman, Michael. *The Actor's Freedom: Toward a Theory of Drama*. New York: Viking, 1975.
Jung, C. G. *Four Archetypes*. Princeton, NJ: Princeton UP, 1969
———. *Symbols of Transformation*. 2nd ed. Princeton, NJ: Princeton UP, 1967.
———. ed. *Man and His Symbols*. New York: Dell, 1964.

shape as two people and enacting itself as love" (69). Both descriptions might also be applied to the action of *Burn This*.

Peter, John. *Vladimir's Carrot: Modern Drama and the Modern Imagination.* Chicago: U of Chicago P, 1987.

Schvey, Henry I. "Images of the Past in the Plays of Lanford Wilson." *Essays on Contemporary American Drama.* Ed. Hedwig Bock and Albert Wertheim. Munich: Max Hüber Verlag, 1981. 225–40.

Thorslev, Peter L. *The Byronic Hero: Types and Prototypes.* Minneapolis: U of Minnesota P, 1962.

Wilson, Lanford. *Burn This.* New York: Hill and Wang, 1987.

"Hell Is Watching Your Script Done Badly": An Interview with Lanford Wilson

Jackson R. Bryer

This interview was conducted on 3 February 1990, in New York at the office of the Circle Repertory Company. It was transcribed by Drew Eisenhauer.

Jackson R. Bryer: The first thing I wanted to ask you about is whether the six years that you spent in Chicago before you came to New York—which are always part of the biographical résumé—were really of any significance?

Lanford Wilson: It was the first time that I was on my own; that was interesting. I got my first apartment, I got the nickname Lance because the Spanish kids in the building couldn't say Lanford. They said Lanz: L-a-n-z. I worked, usually at advertising agencies and places like that. I was writing stories then. I started writing stories, I guess, in San Diego (that was in school) and continued on my own after that—sort of not realizing that I was continuing to write on my own. I think I was trying to make money, foolishly. I thought I was going to be a painter; I think I was trying to make money by writing stories. And then working at the advertising agency I discovered I was a playwright by trying to write a play. One of the stories—I thought, that would be better as a play!—and it turned out that I was a playwright. Then I went to school at the Downtown Center of the University of Chicago just to see what a playwright did. I met a lot of people who have since been in the plays, of course, a packet of them. I don't know, I think there was probably an important hardening off period after school. I realized that I was going to have to come to New York because there was no theatre activity then in Chicago at all, just zilch. As a matter of fact, the only live theatre was Second City, so I wrote an entire evening for Second City and of course didn't have the nerve to show it to them. But people in New York didn't mean anything to me at all so I immediately took it when I got to New York to the Upstairs at the Downstairs. I sat there and did the entire evening for the guy who turned out to be the head of the place—I can't remember his name. He offered me an acting job and I said I couldn't possibly take it—I came to New York with two actors and they'd kill me! Also it wasn't what I wanted.

Bryer: Could you have ever come directly to New York from California or Missouri? Was Chicago a transitional period?

Wilson: Yes, a transitional period and it gave me a chance to be on my own and wander around and go to the bars and sort of live a life.

Bryer: And process what you had experienced in California?

Wilson: Undoubtedly, and experience a great deal more. First city, first big city. San Diego was not a city; I saw the suburb where we lived and the downtown where I worked. I never saw any city part of it.

Bryer: Why did you go to Chicago rather than to some other big city?

Wilson: I had a friend who lived there, a friend from Ozark High School. I went there to visit him for two weeks and stayed six years. Chicago is a big city but it's easy for a mid-westerner to understand.

Bryer: Do you think that there was any effect on the nature of the plays, particularly the early plays, by virtue of the fact that you were a visual artist originally?

Wilson: I think so. I don't know quite what it is but I think so. I've often said that I only write plays so I can do posters for them. And that's true; it keeps me from thinking about the play while I'm doodling on the poster. I think probably the Surprise Box in *Home Free!* comes directly from fiddling around with package design and then, later, graphic design. It might just be that studying drawing taught me to see, to observe.

Bryer: You always say that the overlapping and the montage effect you got from reading plays; so that was not a visual kind of thing?

Wilson: No, I came to New York saying I wanted theatre to be a three-ring circus.

Bryer: Do you think that idea of a three-ring circus was intensified by the collaborative nature of the early work at Caffe Cino?

Wilson: No, I think I sort of lost it a little bit. *Balm in Gilead*, for instance, has that three-ring circus feel about it. From then on it gets less and less apparent, I believe, probably because *Balm in Gilead* was still influenced somewhat by *The Hostage*, which was the most important thing I'd seen in Chicago.

Bryer: But you don't think that the sort of ensemble nature of that play, for example, was intensified by the fact that you were writing for a group of people of which you were part?

Wilson: Oh, I didn't write that play for a group of people.

Bryer: You just wrote it out of the experience in that coffee shop?

Wilson: Whatever someone said in that coffee shop. No, I thought I was writing a book that couldn't ever be done as a play, a play to be read—if I ever showed it to anyone.

Bryer: Yes, you've said that actually it went against everything that Caffe Cino was because there were just so few people around. This was the most unlikely play to write.

Wilson: Right, it was a rebellion against the limitations, finally breaking out of a two-character or three-character form.

Bryer: You've usually been associated in some way with a particular company, especially Circle Rep. Would you say in general that the nature of the theatrical enterprise you were involved with was an influence on the kinds of plays you wrote?

Wilson: I think probably it was. I think Marshall Mason probably had a very strong influence, being Actors Studio, Moscow Art Theatre and Stanislavsky-oriented—that kind of acting, which I hadn't read much about or examined much. After meeting Marshall, I read all of those books and those writers and was probably very strongly influenced by that philosophy of acting or that method of acting, and I was trying to write for that kind of actor.

Bryer: Do you mean more of an emphasis on getting beneath the surface of the character?

Wilson: Yes, and being sure that there is a subtext and all of that. There always was in my work; that's why he was drawn to it. All of that was always there, but I think I might have been a little more absurd, I believe, if it hadn't been for Marshall and the group of actors that I started working with.

Bryer: You could say that some of the later plays are more tightly focused on individual people—their psychology and problems—so you could transfer what you're saying to that kind of schema too. The early plays are much more ensemble pieces, but as you say the individual was always there.

Wilson: The style of the early plays was always based on an ensemble acting that I had seen which was so brilliant in Joan Littlewood's production of *The Hostage*. The ensemble acting had been so strong and such a revelation to me when I saw it that I was writing for that—for sometime before I met Marshall. It just happened to click, in that he was interested in, and all of his training had been in, that approach to theatre.

Bryer: Do you think that meeting Marshall Mason and the whole Stanislavsky business made you look at characters more closely when you were writing them?

Wilson: I don't really know. I just said that it did. And then I believe that by *Serenading Louie* I was trying to focus on fewer people and to write them deeper. I think that was just a reaction to the multi-character collage-type play of *Rimers* and *Balm in Gilead* and some of the one-acts. I think it was just a way to focus on fewer characters and write them. When I started being printed I realized that printing does a terrible thing to you: You say, oh God, this is committed to print forever like this! I kept looking at *Rimers* and saying, I never did develop Josh; there's so much more to write about Josh and I don't know if in those ten lines or twenty lines I've got any indication of what I know about Josh, etc, etc. And all of the rest of them, there's just so much more to say about them; if I had more time on one character I could say a great deal more about them, or I could examine them deeper. So I was feeling that without the influence from Circle Rep, but one just fed the other very neatly. Also, Marshall was not necessarily just working in realism; I'm thinking of *Coffee Grounds Among the Tea Leaves* and some of the Strindberg plays we did. We weren't just realistic (we still aren't). We were perceived as that but that means nothing. I think the strongest influence was the way Marshall and his actors approached character. It made me want to write for that approach.

Bryer: When he reviewed *Hot l Baltimore*, Harold Clurman, referring to the difficulties of assembling a company like Circle Rep, said, "the actors must be chosen from among people who share kindred ideals, training and emotional or intellectual background." Do you think that's true?

Wilson: Oh, absolutely.

Bryer: How did you do that?

Wilson: It was attrition. We started out with so many people, and people would come, and since they weren't being paid it was only "Does this interest you?" If they didn't get what they were interested in they would go to the Open Theatre, to Wooster; they would go into classical theatre, they would go somewhere else. So only the people who said, yes, this I under-stand, this is the way I was trained, or this is the way I want to be trained, this is what I wanted to do—only those people stayed around to work with us. So they weren't chosen, they chose themselves. Marshall always said anyone is in the company who stays here. Anyone who hangs around, that's all you have to do. You have to stay here and be available to us and you're in the company. If you don't stay you're not in the company. People who did not stay were Spalding Gray, Doric Wilson who's out in San Francisco now, David Starkweather and actors who were just interested in something quite different from what we were doing.

Bryer: Describe a bit the process of developing your scripts with Circle Rep. How finished a script do you bring to the first reading? How much change generally occurs during the rehearsal process? From whom do those changes come—from the director, from the actors, from stage technicians, from all of the above?

Wilson: I finish a first draft and the actors read it with the rest of the company as audience. Based on what I hear, if the audience is confused, I usually clarify and do a second draft; that's what we go into rehearsal with. In rehearsal, I do some cutting, for length and for clarity, and some rewriting—but probably not more than five percent of the lines change in rehearsal. The play is always unfinished; it's published anyway.

Bryer: The advantages of writing your plays for a specific company are obvious, but you're now going through a period when your plays are being done in revivals; they're being done in lots of other situations. Most of the time when you've talked about those revivals—even productions outside of the normal regional theatre movement—you've been very generous towards them. But how do you deal with the fact that once it gets away from Circle Rep it's in other hands? It's being done by other actors, particularly in cases like *Burn This* and *Hot l Baltimore* where you wrote it for a specific group of actors. Can you let go that easily?

Wilson: Well, Broadway, and all of the commercial theatre, are so ephemeral. The original Broadway production that we did is so ephemeral that it teaches you to let go fairly quickly, when you start working on the understudy rehearsals and the replacements after four to six months if you're running that long. You start replacing people.

Bryer: You get outside the Circle Rep company almost immediately in a situation like that?

Wilson: Oh, no, we try to stay within the Circle Rep company as much as possible.

Bryer: So those are still Circle Rep actors as long as you're in New York?

Wilson: They're still Circle Rep actors, but not the person I wrote it for or not the person who went through that month-long rehearsal process, where you really begin to understand the play. I didn't write *Burn This* for Joan Allen. We just lucked out finding Joan. I wrote it for Nancy Snyder and still what I treasure is the first reading of the play that Nancy Snyder did. I loved Joan's work and we really lucked out finding her, so since she's the one who worked on it, that's all I see now; but I still can go back to Nancy's first reading. She was very fat and eight months pregnant and all wrong for the part at the time!

Bryer: You have to close your eyes to see it.

Wilson: Yes, just listen.

Bryer: What happens then when you go to East St. Louis to see a revival?

Wilson: Usually you're horrified, but you don't say that to the local paper.

Bryer: But you loved the *Balm in Gilead* revival, didn't you?

Wilson: It was fantastic, but you see the thrill is finding actors who are capable of doing the part somewhere else, in their own way completely, bringing an entirely different thing to it and not drowning under the words but really being able to do the part. That's thrilling! In the Second Stage revival of *Serenading Louie* with Dianne Wiest as Gabby, she did a moment completely different from the way it was written. She's saying, all those people in their Loden coats or whatever. I don't know exactly what the line is before that, but anyway she says, "Forgive me, . . . I don't want to see it." Dianne on whatever those lines were blew up, she just lost it completely. She just screamed this anger, which of course was this pent up anger at the way her husband had reacted and the lack of respect he had for her and her friends in the car, and the general frustration of her life with him right now. All of that was pent up and she just screamed this criticism of the students, realized she had made a total ass of herself, and took the "Forgive me" as an apology for, "I have no idea what happened to me," and had to work her way out of it. Well, it was just electrifying and it's just not in the play; it's in the subtext down there. It's not a moment; it became the moment in that production, and then everyone had to deal with "she's on the verge of losing it" for the rest of that scene and it colored the scene enormously and very beautifully.

Bryer: With a situation like that you wouldn't say to yourself, "that's not what I meant?"

Wilson: Oh, it can be completely antithetical to what we're dealing with, but she just let a substrata burst up through the surface and covered it immediately and it was brilliant. That subtext is certainly there.

Bryer: In another situation an actress could do something like that and you'd say that it was completely unwarranted?

Wilson: Yes, she would pick the wrong substrata. But all of the layers of everything she was feeling just burst through the surface all of a sudden, and then she had to deal with it. It was glorious! But yes, very often you have actors who are just on the wrong track altogether and they may bring a color which is very legitimate to that character but bring it forward much too soon, and where I have no use for it at that point, or much too late, or not get around to it at all. But when you're dealing with a genius like Dianne Wiest, they're going to surprise you, and they're going to be fine, because for one thing they understand the rhythm of the part; they understand the music of the play, they understand the depth of the character and the problem that the character is in and whatever they do is going to be thrilling. She could have turned a cartwheel and you would have said, yes,

yes, the character would do that at that point! But with someone who works in a completely different way or is just plain not good, it can be awful; it can be terrible. I saw a college production of *Burn This* and Pale's anger and frustration and pain (I think he's one of the most severely walking wounded that I've written) . . . this child just did not know that pain; he had no concept of it and so his performance was on the level of a tantrum. It was on the level of "you're not letting me go to the movies tonight. I have to stay home and do my homework." Pale became incomprehensible.

Bryer: But isn't that an example of a person just not having lived long enough at the age of nineteen?

Wilson: Well, yes, but a lot of people are seventy years old and haven't lived long enough.

Bryer: But certainly it would be rare for a nineteen year old to be able to express that.

Wilson: Very rare, but the guy who did Larry in the same production was brilliant, with all of the pain that you want in Pale—and it's just a bonus if you have it in Larry, because Larry covers it so well. All of the pain was there in Larry, every bit of it, but that particular actor obviously knew. There are also those people, and sometimes they become actors, who are born seventy years old.

Bryer: When you go back and see revivals now do you ever say to yourself, I'd really like to change something, I'd really like to do something different? Or do you figure the plays are of the time they were written and you don't have to do something to them? Have you changed anything in a revival?

Wilson: Oh yes, I change things all the time. You write a very difficult scene and they miss it altogether and you say to yourself, "I could have made that much simpler. I mean, I didn't want to, I wanted it to be the way that it was, but how did I ever expect anyone who didn't have the scene explained to them to understand?"

Bryer: Isn't that also possibly a consequence of the Circle Rep-Marshall Mason association, too, where you and he are so much in tune that he understands what you're doing and then you put the play out?

Wilson: Well, getting it right is certainly a result of that.

Bryer: But if you send it out to a director in East Oshkosh and they do the same scene . . .?

Wilson: And get nowhere and don't come close to it and they have no idea what the scene is about? It's just a risk you take. I think by the time we get finished with it I get it the way I want it and I just regret that I made it so complicated. But there's no other way it could be. You're not painting a painting when you're writing a play, you're painting an entire year's worth of paintings—an entire exhibition. You're working with the overall theme of the play, with the music of the piece, with the elegance of the design, with the depth of character and the characters' interactions creating the theme and song and design. You're working on subtleties that can't possibly be discerned in one viewing of the play or in one reading of it. When you see a production that misses what you've done completely, you're sorry—but there was no other way you could have written the play to make it less than it is.

Another odd thing is away from New York very often humor in the characters is missed altogether. When we did *Fifth of July* on Broadway, we had some people come backstage just jumping up and down saying this is so thrilling we just did this in college, and no one laughed at our production; we didn't do it funny like this. Of course here is Lanford spinning in his grave because I can't imagine . . . and thanking God I hadn't seen that production! But the angels all get back at you because I was subjected to *Burn This* where the only laugh was Larry. Fortunately he knew what he was doing, but the other actors really did not know there was a grain of humor in those other three characters. And the simplest thing, the simplest "I can't deal with that" throwaway line, was deeply felt. It was abominable. This is what Hell is. Hell is watching your script done badly. But other people with other experiences will do it correctly, and beautifully I'm sure. I pray.

Bryer: So when do you decide that it's your fault rather than the production?

Wilson: I suppose if you see something enough times where people just do not understand it. What have I changed because I just got sick of seeing it done badly? There've been occasional lines where I've said, "Oh to hell with it. It's never going to be done right, to hell with it! Cut it completely, take it out!" It's like poetry that you get wrong, just one word can absolutely kill you. In *Lemon Sky* there is a line right in the first beat of the play, within the first two pages. Every single time they do it the wrong way, every damn time. When this wonderful television show came up, by God it was wrong again. I forgot to tell them how to do it, and there it was—wrong again. It's just never going to be done right. It makes you understand how people see plays. They're trying to figure one thing out, they miss the whole next beat; then they're lost in the play and angry and frustrated and hate the play. It's a stupid play that doesn't make sense. You see it all the time.

Bryer: You have described in other interviews how various New York plays you saw when you first came to New York really made an impact on you, like Ionesco's *The Lesson*. Are you still amazed or struck by contemporary theatre, by plays that you've seen recently?

Wilson: Oh yes, even just timing, just tiny, tiny things. From tiny things to enormous things. In *Knock Knock*, Jules Feiffer introduces a monologue more brilliantly then any I have ever seen; it's just the most brilliant introduction of a monologue that I have ever seen in my life. A guy tells a story, and he does it by starting this game. Joan asks him how he came to be living in this house in the woods. He says, "Chicken Teriyaki." She says, "What?" He says, "I'll give you the answer, you give me the question. The answer is Chicken Teriyaki." She says, "I don't know what you're talking about." And he says, "The question is: 'Who's the oldest living Kamikaze pilot?'" And then he has another answer, and she says, "I don't know" and it's another joke; it's very funny. And then there's another answer, another question, and another, and then he says, "I was walking in the woods and I started going farther and farther and one day I came upon this house and Joe was living here." He's telling this story; he's answering the question that she asked a long time ago, and you're expecting it to be a joke and you're halfway through the monologue before you say, "He's telling his life story!" It's just the most wonderful realization in the world because you're just sitting there and you're way, way into it before you realize he's talking about himself!

I tried to do that in *Talley's Folly* and, as I told Jules, just fucked it completely. It came out very nicely but I sure didn't do what I'd set out to do. I wanted to repeat that process exactly and just steal that moment from him. I didn't, I did something else because I couldn't do it as well as he had. Probably all of the jokes that Matt tells that are actually jokes came from that question and answer in *Knock Knock*. Matt has about three jokes and then he starts telling his story, but it's not nearly as wonderful. As I say, it comes out fine, it comes out excellently, and I knew it came out excellently, but it's not what Jules did, it's not what I wanted to do. But I was playing fun games in writing *Talley's Folly*. When I was sort of in the middle of writing the ice-skating-on-the-floor moment I said, "This is a Sam Shepard moment, this is not a Lanford Wilson moment. If there had never been a Sam Shepard I don't think I ever could have done this." Sally breaks it off, and Matt says, "Don't let go! We're coming to the end of the pond." I went, that is just so silly, that's a Sam Shepard moment. So when I realized that, I said, OK, what I have to do is acknowledge that, and I wrote about a three-line take-off of Sam Shepard. So there's "The trees are looming up in front of me. They're coming right at me." and so on. All of that is Sam Shepard, Sam Shepard's style.

Bryer: Once you realized you'd done it, you had to acknowledge it?

Wilson: I had to acknowledge it and I wanted to sort of sign it: This is Sam Shepard, this is not me. It was just fun to parody him—really imitate him more than parody him—for two or three lines.

Bryer: In 1980, you told Mel Gussow that you would prefer to be Pinter, Wilde, Coward, Shepard or Shaw, rather than Lanford Wilson, "because they are so much themselves." Do you still feel that way? If not, why not? If so, why?

Wilson: I say a lot; you shouldn't listen to me! In an interview yesterday someone asked me suddenly, "Have you ever wanted to be some other playwright other than Lanford Wilson?" And I answered, shocked, "God, no!" And that's true. What I meant by that remark to Mel was that sometimes when I begin a project, I look over the first few pages and say, this is going to be another goddamned Lanford Wilson play! It's just that I'm amazed that I always recognize my signature, my way of writing, my backing into a situation or a character, or a sentence. I don't think of myself as having a style but, of course, I do. I'm surprised to discover it because it's unconscious; I'm not aware of it as I write and I'm always surprised to find it when I read something I've done. But one does get sick of one's own voice. I asked Pinter if he was annoyed that everything always came out Pinteresque and he said, "Oh God, yes! I reread the first page of a play, and think, it's going to be another goddamned Pinter play!" It's like being unhappy with the look of your ears; you're not fond of them, but they're always there.

Bryer: Are there any more Talley plays to come? You once planned five; what about the play about Whistler Talley?

Wilson: I think of the Talley plays as one long play and it's not finished yet.

Bryer: One of the essays in this *Wilson Casebook* talks about the female characters in the plays and says, "Generally speaking, if Lanford Wilson's male characters represent a cross-section of American manhood, the country is in trouble. In his major plays, it is Wilson's women who are more effective both as characters and as functioning people."

Wilson: Effective?

Bryer: Yes. The women are "almost always . . . the voice of hope and regeneration." "Wilson's men die or are wounded, and the women remain memorable. The men are the narrators, Alan, Matt and Timmy, for example—but the strong characters are the women, like April and Girl in *Hot l* or Lottie and Sally in *Talley's Folly* and *Tally & Son*."

Wilson: When people analyze my work, it always amazes me. I always say, "God, is that true?" Because when they're analyzing, they're analyzing not something that you do consciously, but something you do unconsciously more often. What can I tell you? I had a lousy father and a terrific mother and so it may have very strongly influenced the way I see people. Also I have a feeling my aunt was stronger than my uncle and a few other things. I have no objection to that; it makes me want to immediately reverse it and write something somehow the other way. The next play I write I'll change the names around.

Bryer: Just so you won't dwell on this, there's another essay in the book which says exactly the opposite! It's a feminist reading of *Angels Fall* and it says, "*Angels Fall* is a retrogressive, white male fairy tale in which the women will keep the home fires burning, in which the educated Indian has been assimilated into the culture, in which the uneducated Indians remain on the reservation as workers under the church's care and in which work subsumes nagging spiritual doubts and sanctifies the individual pursuit of happiness." This critic sees *Angels Fall* as a very male chauvinist play, which of course belies the other person who's saying that the female characters are the strongest characters. Do you think that the women in *Angels Fall* are more subservient than they are in the other plays?

Wilson: I don't think that Marion is subservient for a moment. And I think Vita has her hands full. She's a little testy from time to time. I don't think that she necessarily opted for the nurse position, nor have they had that relationship, nor is she particularly happy with it, and I think she lets him know it. I think they have a very healthy relationship. It's coming apart right now, and she is taking the position of wife for this trip. That kind of cliché interpretation of the married positions is certainly not the way their lives have been, I don't believe, and not the way that it will be in the future. I think that's indicated very clearly in the play. Marion, I think, is a very strong character. It happens that we're talking in the play about the death of an artist, or the death of art maybe, but certainly the death of an artist—the artist was a man—and how all of these people relate to him, from his critic to his wife to the new young man who's usurping his position, and his best friend, the priest. I'm really annoyed at what she said about the Indian; what is that with the Indian again? That's really appalling!

Bryer: "The educated Indian has been assimilated into the culture . . . the uneducated Indians remain on the reservation as workers under the church's care."

Wilson: "The educated Indian has been assimilated into the culture!" He is *dying* to be assimilated into the culture. It's ripping him to shreds because he's being so tempted. He's very wrong, of course, and I think I make the point very strongly that he's wrong. He only leaves because that's what people do, they leave their mentors, they do not stay with them, they leave them. He's found a new mentor, so he's left his father image and that's what people do. It's not necessarily best, but if he had stayed, would he then have been what she says about the uneducated Indian? Would he have been the good little boy? The priest wants him to rebel, but he doesn't; if he would have stayed he would have raised hell with the Church as the priest tells Niles to do with the college. This is a priest who wants people to rebel against authority. The Church, in this instance, can give you the strength to rebel even against the Church. No, no, no, it's all just too simplistic!

Bryer: There are actually two essays about *Angels Fall* in the book. One is that essay, which also makes the point that technology prevails in the play, rather than the human capacity to prevail, but the second essay is about the relationship between *Angels Fall* and Emerson. It says, "*Angels Fall* is meant as a warning to late twentieth-century Americans. Living with the moment to moment possibility of extinction, Wilson suggests that his contemporaries can save themselves from nuclear holocaust only by discovering and developing the inner moral strength nineteenth-century American idealists like Emerson,

Thoreau and Whitman had attributed to the democratic individual." The play is "a plea for an Emerson-like self-reliance."

Wilson: Well, I think I'm often "pleaing" for an "Emerson-like self-reliance." I don't apologize for that. When you say that technology prevails, the last moment of that play is: The son figure, crying, leaves the father figure; the father figure accepts that, goes out and rings the bell for the people to come in for their prayer. He is only interested in the individual, and in moral courage and strength. That's all he's asked for from God, and that's all he's trying to bestow. He's tried very hard to bestow it on this boy and failed. That doesn't mean that he doesn't have the rest of the flock to deal with. ("Flock" is my Baptist upbringing coming through there!) The ringing of that bell is the strongest moment in the play for me and there's nothing technologically advanced about that bell. And, of course, technology is absolutely screwing the land totally blind—as the priest says—and all the people in it. When Father Doherty rings that bell, I see it as an alarm that says, "Do not *you* fail as Don has."

Bryer: One of the other essays in the book is about the translation of *Three Sisters* and how that got you from *Angels Fall* to *Burn This*. A lot of other people have pointed out Chekhovian elements in the plays, but did the experience of dealing directly with Chekhov have any specific effect that you can recall?

Wilson: I did it deliberately to help shake me out of the sort of four-square planned play, the schematic play, that I felt *Angels Fall* was slightly. I tried to write *Angels Fall* as well as I could but it's still a locked-door play. No, I wrote *Burn This* blind, not wanting to know where it went or what was happening. I knew I was going to do that when I was writing *Angels Fall*. I knew I wasn't going to do another thing that could possibly be formulated, so, of course, a good half of the criticism is "*Burn This* is a formulated play."

Bryer: I wasn't necessarily speaking about *Burn This* because I knew you already had *Burn This* in mind before you even started the Chekhov translation. I mean working as directly with

Chekhov as you did in that translation, whether you saw things about Chekhov you'd never thought about before?

Wilson: Oh, I've adored Chekhov. I've adored him desperately, and at the same time he's just shamelessly vaudevillian sometimes, and beautifully so. When the scenes, the vaudevillian scenes, aren't done correctly, when they aren't done for comedy, they fall so flat on their face it's ridiculous. You can't work on Chekhov and not learn from him.

Bryer: Let's talk a little bit about *Burn This* because there are several essays in the book about it. I'm sure you're familiar with the criticism of *Burn This* which took the tack that Malkovich as Pale, as one critic said, has "got himself so far out on a limb, in terms of the acting style, that he's not only unrelated to the other characters in the play but he's unrelated to the actors themselves." You've said you had Malkovich in mind when you wrote Pale, but I know people who saw it without Malkovich and said that they liked the play better because there was less emphasis on watching Malkovich play Pale.

Wilson: People have said that to me. Since I know the play, I was able to separate them. I was never seeing Malkovich for the first time except for the first reading which was pretty much what you saw. So I never really had that experience. I can't say what it was like seeing the play for the first time. I have a feeling that what they were doing was seeing the play for the second time. I had people come back to see Malkovich and say, "Oh, my God, I had no idea that those other characters were so interesting." So it was just the shock of seeing Malkovich; if you saw it another time *with* Malkovich, I think you'd discover that there was a play around that performance. They were just as good as he was, just in their very own way. And they were on stage with him and he was on stage with them. I was never jolted out of the play watching John; it was just one of four brilliant performances.

Bryer: There's an essay in the book that relates *Burn This* and its portrait of Anna as an artist to your role as a playwright and sees the play as your working out of the role of the artist. It sees Anna standing poised between Burton and Pale; the dance she ends up choreographing is a resolution of her artistic problem. It says,

"The play can . . . be read as a meditation on the requirements for artistic growth and eloquence . . . the characters in *Burn This* represent the elements of artistic development, with Pale the representative of pure emotion, Burton the representative of pure decoration." In this interpretation Anna becomes the representative of the conflict between those two which she fuses in some ways in order to produce her dance. Does that sound interesting?

Wilson: Yes, that sounds very interesting and not at all untrue. The fun thing was having Burton go through the same process. And it was much easier than Anna because Anna was doing it in a different way. But Burton, who is sort of experiencing loss for the first time, has just as interesting a trip, I think. There's a thing just slightly beyond that no one has ever gotten; it's a question that I can't answer but I think I ask it. So much of art is sublimation, not all of it, God knows, but there's an element of sublimation in art I suppose, or so we're told. And if that's true, she's experienced it, and what will having Pale do to the art? It's just such an interesting question to me. I wonder if she'll be able to work with him now. I really don't know. It's real interesting. That's the opposite of what I'm really saying in the play, of course. What I'm really saying is that she does have to find this balance between, as you say, the purely decorative and purely emotional, and *her* work has been I think truly decorative as well. She doesn't know what else there is, but she finds that out.

Bryer: What I like about that essay is that it takes the emphasis away from the relationship between them as just a relationship and sees it in emblematic terms.

Wilson: That's exactly what I was talking about.

Bryer: All those people who found the relationship unlikely; of course it's unlikely and that's the whole point of it. As you said in another interview, it's a relationship built on all the things a relationship shouldn't be built on.

Wilson: There's no point in writing about a relationship that's probable. But at the same time it was exactly what she needed for her work.

Bryer: Yes, and, like all good plays, it ends and you have no idea where it's going to go.

Wilson: Not a clue, not a clue. And there are so many possibilities. When I was writing the work, when I knew that Larry was writing that note to get Pale to come to the concert and to get him to come to see Anna, I knew there was a possibility that he was in some way trying to destroy the relationship, or trying to destroy Anna in some way, because it was destroying his relationship with Anna. It's not necessarily the most healthy thing in the world for Anna to have Pale back in her life again. She's frustrated and miserable and angry and crazy but she's working.

Bryer: But it's more complicated than that because you can say the reason she's working is because Pale was in her life.

Wilson: Exactly! It's just all so much fun! I just adored it!

Bryer: You could also say that there is a part of Larry that wants to destroy this relationship.

Wilson: Especially his relationship with her, and doesn't give a damn if he destroys her in the process. So it's not just a simple caring gesture. It is, of course; but underneath it's more complicated than that.

Bryer: Yes, that's one of the things I liked about the play; it's incomplete.

Wilson: Yes. I think what some people objected to is that it appears to be complete. If they're happy with that, then they just weren't thinking, they weren't looking. They weren't seeing things correctly. "Oh, that's real neat, they lived happily ever after, but I don't believe it." Well, neither do I! Have they lived happily up to this point? Why should they live happily ever after? Anyway, I think the play is wonderfully interesting. I'm glad there are essays about it in there. I loved working on that play. I think it's much more interesting than a lot of the things I've done.

Bryer: In previous interviews, you have always chosen *The Mound Builders* as your favorite among your plays. Is that still so, or has *Burn This* replaced it—and, if so, why?

Wilson: Call it a tie.

Bryer: What are you doing now?

Wilson: I'm not, I'm not. I'm bumming around trying to think of something. There's a play about a painter somewhere. There's a play about an astronomer somewhere, and a few others; but it's not straight enough in my mind. If I get anything down, it runs into a wall. I think the people that I'm interested in are driven by their desire to have one thing and nothing else is important and they have it. In other words, they're compulsively working on astrophysics, they're compulsively working on art. Everyone of them has had that one thing. You throw up any conflict that doesn't have to do with their work and it doesn't affect them. Any conflict with their work is just situational. That's not interesting drama. Their wife leaves them, so what? Their kids don't love them anymore? Get away, who cares? It doesn't affect them. So I haven't found the right approach to that person; they allow no drama, they allow no conflict in their life.

Bryer: So you're still working essentially from character?

Wilson: Oh yes, but I don't know where. I don't know where this guy is going to lead me. He's led me half way into an astrophysicist play that rammed completely into a brick wall, because only a situation would threaten him. Only something that I consider artificial would threaten him and that's not interesting. And with the artist the same damn thing. Only being maimed or losing his sight could affect him; that's not interesting at all. I don't know how I'm going to trip this out. I really have no idea of what kind of play is going to come from that; probably it won't. I think this is something that has been cooking for a long, long time. The artist has been cooking for a very long time, since before *Burn This*. There are so many private devils, oh, so many private devils, that these people have and probably I'm just not ready to deal with those private devils yet. And also they're different from Niles's private devils but similar in some way. So I think I have to get past Niles's problem into theirs and the similarity keeps getting in my way. I was rewriting Niles as one of the artists and it's not Niles at all.

But still I see this guy with those glasses that peanut butter used to come in, those stemmed glasses that look like candy bowls. I see him with one of those filled with ice and vodka in his house, and this is a guy who says, "I don't sleep, I never sleep. I haven't slept." And we have seen him in the afternoon and we have seen him very late at night go out to eat with friends in the neighborhood and he comes back and someone is still there and they talk to him. All the while, there's ice and vodka. He talks to them about whatever their problem is or whatever his problem is or whatever until they're dropping. This is a much older man—sixty at least, he's probably sixty-five— and they go off exhausted near dawn. He fills up his drink with vodka, goes into another part of the room, sets down the vodka, turns on the light, and there is this gigantic canvas he is working on and he begins to work. He's exhausted everyone in sight and this is him! And that image has just haunted me for about four years now, and what it's telling me I don't know. Well, I know exactly what it's telling me, but I don't know how to approach it from the beginning. I don't know where it starts. I don't care where it goes but I don't know where it starts. Maybe that's where it goes. Maybe that's the end and that's why it's no fun to work on. If you know the end, it's certainly no fun; I can't work from there. But that's haunted me for a long, long, long, long while—the rare indomitable artist.

A "Shared Vision" of "the Human Scale of Life on Stage": An Interview with Marshall W. Mason

Jackson R. Bryer

This interview was conducted on 21 and 23 April 1990, in Independence, Kansas, at the William Inge Festival. It was transcribed by Drew Eisenhauer.

Jackson R. Bryer: Could you tell me about your background and how you got started in theatre?

Marshall W. Mason: I was born in Amarillo, Texas, and I lived my first six years there. My mother and father divorced when I was four. In the middle of my second grade year, my mother remarried and moved to New Orleans and they left me off with my maternal grandparents, in the small town of Luling, between Austin and San Antonio. Luling had a population of about four thousand people and so I had a real small-town childhood. When I reached high school, I decided to go back to Amarillo and live with my father because I knew the educational opportunities would be much better there. From the time I can first remember doing anything I was putting on shows. My first theatre experience was at the beginning of the second grade. The Baptist church was casting a Christmas play, showing how Christmas is celebrated around the world and the center of the play was a clown, who would come to life and say, "Oh, what is Christmas like?" and then we got to see this scene of what

Christmas was like in Mexico, and so forth. I got the part which was the lead. I remember it very clearly now—putting on the makeup and how excited we all were!

Bryer: How old were you?

Mason: I was seven I guess. Then a year or so later Halloween came up and I wrote a play and put it on in my class. I still have the program for that play! And every Saturday I would go to the movies. I'd go see the Saturday serial—Spiderwoman and stuff like that. When I was about eight years old, I saw *Pinky* with Jeanne Crain and Ethel Waters and it struck me so much to the core that I just wept. I said, somebody is responsible for making this movie better than any movie I've ever seen. So I sat through it for a second time until the credits came by, and they ended with "Directed by Elia Kazan." I said, that's why this picture's better—the director! For years I went around telling my school chums, "Elia Kazan is my favorite director." He was the only director I knew, and I didn't even know what a director really was! So Elia Kazan was my early childhood hero. I did not know that I wanted to be a director. I had no plans to be a director. I wanted to be an actor; I wrote plays and I directed them as well, but the reason was because I wanted to act. My drama teacher, Mrs. Whitworth, was very good. In addition to theatre I also played the tuba. I loved music, and I loved football. I think that's a great combination, and so from sixth grade on all the way through college, I marched at the football games!

Bryer: You played the tuba all the way through college?

Mason: Yes, all the way through college. Haven't touched one since!

Bryer: Did you have any other extracurricular activity?

Mason: Debate, which is a big deal in Texas, and I was a very good debater. When I said I wanted to be an actor, my family said that I had to have something to fall back on, so I had a secondary idea which was I would be a teacher. I won the state contest for Mr. Future Teacher of America for giving a little speech, so I got a scholarship to the University of Texas. I was planning to go there and major in theatre and minor in education. Then in the winter of my senior year I was playing in my front yard one Sunday afternoon. It makes you wonder about fate and things like that; I was never in my front yard. I never stayed home, but for some reason this Sunday afternoon I was home and for some reason I was out in the front yard when my friend Gary Tessler drove by, happened to see me and stopped. He asked where was I going to school, and I said I was going to the University of Texas, where I'd been planning to go all my life. And he said, "I'm going to Northwestern. You know it's the best theatre school in the world." So the next day I went in to school and asked my advisor, "Can you tell me anything about Northwestern University?" and he said, "Sure. I've got some catalogues here. Take one." So I took them home and read them. It read like a fairy tale to me; it just sounded so wonderful. It was already April by the time I got my application in, and the deadline was February. But I thought, "What the hell, I'll try." Not only did I get in but I got a full scholarship that paid for all my tuition and half my room and board!

When I got to Northwestern the big deal there was working with Alvina Krause, a very great teacher. I've learned almost everything I know from Miss Krause. In my first year I was in *Cherry Orchard* for Miss Krause; I played the stationmaster, who has no written lines. We worked on that play for four months and I really got into the character. Every summer Miss Krause took her best students away to Eagles Mere, Pennsylvania, to a playhouse there she'd been running for years. Only her very best students went. It wasn't like summer stock because we did great plays, but to go there you had to apply individually and ask her to go. At the end of sophomore year, I asked her to go to Eagles Mere and Miss Krause said no. At that point I realized that probably I was not going to be the world's greatest actor. I trusted her opinion and I felt very strongly that if I could not be the very best at what I was doing I did not want to be in the theatre. I had seen too much theatre that I really hated—poor performances, poor direction, poor plays.

Bryer: When you were growing up in Texas did you have much experience of live theatre?

Mason: We had a little theatre but most of my exposure was in school.

Bryer: But no experience with professional theatre? There weren't any road shows that came through?

Mason: No. I saw my first live professional stage play in Chicago, as a freshman at Northwestern; it was Cyril Ritchard in Gore Vidal's *Visit to a Small Planet*. It wasn't a very good play, and I don't remember anything especially about it.

Bryer: I interrupted you. You were in your sophomore year and you weren't going to be a great actor.

Mason: I decided if I couldn't be the best then I wouldn't stay in it at all. When Jim Goussef, Miss Krause's graduate assistant, heard that I was planning to transfer to law, he gave a party, invited me and proceeded to get me very drunk on Rhine wine. I remember a drunken conversation in which he said, "You cannot transfer out of the theatre. The theatre needs people like you, you believe in it so much." I said, "If I can't make a positive contribution to it, I certainly don't want to be one of the people dragging the theatre down, which is what I see all the time." He said, "Well, what about writing?" I said, "I try to write but I don't have anything really to say." He said, "What about directing?" and I said, "Well, there *is* a play that I would really like to direct, because there's no part for me in it. It's a play I really feel very strongly about—*Cat on a Hot Tin Roof*." He said, "I have a proposition for you. Why don't you stay at Northwestern this summer. We'll be doing the summer festival. I'm directing one of the plays and I'll make sure you have a really good part. You'll have the experience of doing rep, you'll be able to act all summer and then if you decide after that you still don't want to stay in the theatre, fine." And I said "Well, OK." So I spent the summer at Northwestern. It was a great summer; there's nothing in this world like playing rep. The fall came, Miss Krause came back to school, and she was in charge of the workshop productions, so I went in and said I wanted to direct a workshop production of *Cat on a Hot Tin Roof*. She had seen the Kazan production in New York and I guess she really thought it was relatively obscene. She

said, "Why do you want to do that *ugly* play?" And I said,
"Because I really think it speaks the truth." So she said, "OK,"
and I directed *Cat*.

Plays like *Under the Yum Yum Tree* were the things then on
Broadway and I was disgusted by the entire thing, having been
raised on Chekhov and Ibsen and other great plays. Most of the
directors I had worked for even in school would tell me all the
gestures to do and I felt totally boxed in. So I started directing as
an absolute rebel against all kinds of staging or any kind of
imposition from the director. My work with the actors was always in terms of "He's coming towards you. You've got to go
somewhere; go to the window." And I'd do this while they were
acting; I would work on creating the circumstances. I never
physically blocked the play; there was never any "move three
steps to the right" kind of thing, it was always totally from the
actor's need. It was never intellectual at all.

Bryer: You didn't walk into the rehearsal and know what you
were going to do until you saw the way the actors were moving
on the stage?

Mason: That continues to be my method. I still don't know what
else to do. My staging comes totally from impulses I see in the
actors.

Bryer: Do you think that's because you were an actor?

Mason: I hope so. I'm a very careful choreographer now, extremely careful, more careful than probably George Abbott ever
thought of being. I'm very careful about movement; it's all extremely well-defined in my mind. One move definitely is better
than another move, but my method of discovering those moves
still comes totally from the actors. My essential method has not
changed from when I started, but my emphasis has changed a
lot. To get back to *Cat*, it was just the first two acts; I cut it dras-
tically, so it ran about an hour and fifteen minutes. I have to
admit it's a production I've never surpassed; it was awfully
good. After the one performance, Miss Krause stood up and did
a critique as she always did, and she was very, very rough, to
put it mildly. John Simon has nothing on Miss Krause! She went

through the other two plays on the bill, ripping them to shreds, and then she came to *Cat* and her first line was, "I suppose you all noticed the superlative direction." Everybody stood and applauded and she went on to be extravagant in her praise of the whole thing.

It was a tremendous experience and the crazy thing was, of course, that after this everybody immediately said, "Oh, you're a director," and started treating me as a director. I hadn't done this to become a director; I had just directed this one play, to satisfy this guy who said, "The theatre needs people like you; you should try directing." I never had any doubt I could direct *Cat on a Hot Tin Roof*. I knew that play as though I had written it. It was very special to me, very personal, and I had no idea if I could ever direct any other play! The following spring, 1960, I directed a second production in workshop because I wanted to see if this would go away. I chose a play that I had an intellectual passion for, but it wasn't born in my heart as *Cat* was. It was Euripides's *The Trojan Women*, a virulent anti-war play. In the interim, I had seen a film called *The Young Lions* that changed my life, because I went in there as a young macho Texan and walked out a pacifist, feeling that war is never right. Brando's performance really reached me in a way that great art can. You'll find throughout any telling of my life that it's not plays that have affected me; it's films.

Bryer: Do you think that was because your original exposure was to films?

Mason: I don't know. Could be. I've had many great experiences with theatre, but the ones that have changed my life have been films. I feel that maybe film is the contemporary medium for expression, not just in terms of reaching a large number of people but also because there's something that makes viewing a film an intensely private act. With a play there is a *public* awareness; I don't lose myself as totally in the theatre as I do with a film.

Bryer: Have you ever directed a movie?

Mason: No. That's what I'm trying to do now.

Bryer: Is that something you've always wanted to do?

Mason: How long is always? My first director was Elia Kazan in a very strong film. It became a sort of lifetime ideal.

Bryer: But you could have gone to Hollywood long before now. So you have made some conscious choices, haven't you?

Mason: Yes, I did make some conscious choices. After I directed *Trojan Women* (it was extremely successful), Miss Krause took me to Eagles Mere after my junior year—where I played Malvolio in *Twelfth Night* and directed *Mary Stuart*, the first full-length play I did for her. I came back for my senior year and I became the first undergraduate ever to direct a major production at Northwestern; they had always been faculty-directed. Then, after another summer at Eagles Mere where I did *Cyrano* and *The Doctor's Dilemma*, I went to New York. I arrived in New York on September 1, 1961, and I had friends from Northwestern who were working down at the Caffe Cino. There was an actress there I knew named Jane Lowry; she'd played Varya in *The Cherry Orchard* at Northwestern and she was appearing in a little play at the Cino. It happened, as I subsequently learned, to be the second play they'd ever done, so I was really there at the beginning. I went down to the Village and went to the Caffe Cino and saw Doric Wilson's *Now She Dances*, a play about Salome as Oscar Wilde would have written it if he had written it like *The Importance of Being Ernest*. Jane played a very Oscar Wilde maid!

Bryer: You had come to New York as a director?

Mason: I had come to New York intending to pursue a career as a director. I had won the award twice at Northwestern as best director, and I had directed seven plays when I arrived in New York. I started hanging around Caffe Cino and met Joe Cino who was the owner. Eventually Joe asked, do you want to direct something, and I said sure. So I did my first play in New York, *The Rue Garden* by my Northwestern friend Claris Nelson. It was the first off-off-Broadway production to be reviewed. For some reason, Michael Smith of *The Village Voice* wandered into the

Caffe Cino that night and saw *The Rue Garden* and gave it a very
positive review. That early success was then followed in
sequence by other plays that Claris wrote. By the time I had done
my third production at the Cino I was full of myself. I decided
the only way I was going to "make it" in the professional theatre
was to produce my own plays. So I formed a production
company named Northwestern Productions with Claris and Rob
Thirkield. I was roommates with Rob in college and he was the
first rich person I'd ever really met. We formed Northwestern
Productions, and from the beginning I was really the producer as
well.

There were nine partners in Northwestern Productions (all
from Northwestern) and we decided to produce two plays and
tie them together. The first was Ibsen's *Little Eyolf* and the second
was Shaw's *Arms and the Man*. I was to direct the first one and I
had a dreadful experience. Everything that could go wrong did,
but we opened in April of 1964 to a rave from Howard Taubman
of the *New York Times* who said about me that "the play was
directed with a skill commensurate with that of the playwright."
Which for Ibsen ain't bad! A nice place to start on your New
York career with a review like that. Unfortunately, Walter Kerr
in the *Herald Tribune* said, "The characters become lost in their
own living room striding about like so many stuffed bears
taught to intone lines." Ironically, my directing technique always
arose from within the actors, and I never thought about actually
physically blocking people. At this point I realized that the
problem was not that the actors were over-blocked or taught to
intone lines or told anything external. On the contrary, they were
left to go at their own free will. In college, where people are very
idealistic, the actors were all serving the play, and so they moved
appropriately for what their characters were doing. Suddenly,
here we were in an off-Broadway commercial arena and the
actors tended to go down center front.

Bryer: You really let the actors take over too much?

Mason: It looked as if they were over-directed; the problem was
that they were under-directed. Though we had good reviews
(none as good as the *Times*), we didn't run very long. But we
went right on to our second production. I thought it was terrific;

the audiences came and they loved it, but the critics just slaughtered it. So we had one semi-success and one absolute flop and the money was gone. The two productions were over and I was back to the Caffe Cino after a year. In the interim, there had been a new arrival—Lanford Wilson. I read in *The Village Voice* a review of a play called *So Long at the Fair* and Michael Smith was absolutely ranting and raving about this new play at the Caffe Cino that was so exciting that he could not reveal the ending. I went down to the Cino and saw the final performance. The play (which does not exist anymore; we've lost it) concerned a young man from the South who had come to New York and a young woman who came over to his apartment to seduce him. He had his girlfriend back home, and he didn't know how to deal with this brash urban young lady who pursued him all over the place. He accidentally suffocates her on a hide-a-bed. She's trying to get him into bed and he finally strangles her with a pillow. She has meanwhile told her father that she's going to be at this number. The telephone starts ringing; he doesn't know what to do, and he folds her up in the hide-a-bed—a real *coup de théâtre*! It's that double sense that happens in the theatre; you know she can't really be dead, but in the play she's dead and he folds her up inside the God-damned thing, puts the pillows on it and sits down on it—and the telephone rings and the lights go out! And you're left going, "You can't do that!" It was just amazing, a wonderful play. However, the thing that impressed me most was an actor named Michael Warren Powell who played the boy in it and was really extraordinary.

Subsequently, I went back a little bit later and saw *Home Free!*, which Michael also starred in. I loved *Home Free!* This was before the Ferris wheel came into the play; it was an earlier version with a gyroscope. It started with a spotlight on the gyroscope. I came back again and I saw *The Madness of Lady Bright* with Neil Flanagan; he had directed *Home Free!* and now he was playing in *Lady Bright*. Then they did a revival of *Home Free!* and I came back to see that. In the revival Lanford had rewritten the play completely. In the first version of the play we did not know that they were brother and sister until the last moment. You were sucked into a very private world, a magical world that these two perfect people had created around them, and suddenly at the end you discovered that it was incest. It was a tremendous experience! In the rewritten version, the first thing you learn is that they are brother and sister. It was a very good production. The Ferris wheel had come in and there were all kinds of good rewrites but, to me, learning right up front they were brother and sister robbed the play of its whole emotional power. I saw it and I liked it; it was very very good and Michael again was fabulous. Then they did a revival of *The Madness of Lady Bright* and I saw that for the second time. The first production of *Home Free!* was absolutely fabulous. It was very mythic and wonderful. The second production had dirty laundry all over the apartment. It was very ugly, and very very gritty and unwashed and the opposite of a magical world that these two people had created. I had loved the magic of it. Not since Tennessee Williams had there been a writer like this. The first play, *So Long at the Fair,* was good, but what had struck me about it was Michael's performance. What struck me about *Home Free!* the minute I saw it was the *writing.* After I had seen the sweaty revival of *Home Free!,* Joe Cino said, "Well, what did you say to Lance?" I said, "I've never met Lance." He said, "You haven't met Lanford?" and I said, "No." He said, "Sit down, I'll bring him out." So he brought Lanford over and sat him down.

Bryer: This was about three or four months after you'd seen the first play? You didn't meet him until you had seen four or five productions of his work?

Mason: I had seen five productions before I actually met Lanford. Cino introduced us. Lanford was extremely thin and he had incredibly intense blue eyes that seemed to stand out about a foot and a half in front of his face. They were startling; they burst on the air. He was a frightening person to encounter—demonic. It was really his physical appearance that gave this impression although I'm sure the inner energy and talent were part of it as well. I was thin, but he was skinny—that's the way I looked at it. A very pointy nose and longish hair that he constantly played with and constantly would have to pull back over his brow, and those incredibly intense blue eyes—aggressive, rapacious eyes. I was frightened by him. He came over and very diffidently said, "You've seen my plays. I've heard you're a director." And I said, "Yes." He said, "Did you see the revision of *Home Free!*?" I said, "Yes, I did." And he said, "Haven't I really improved that play? Didn't I really make it good?" I said, "I think you ruined it." He said, "What do you mean?" and I told him what I thought. So my relationship with Lanford did not get off to a good start; the first thing he heard from me was that I thought he was totally fucked up and was going entirely in the wrong direction! He was quite convinced he was going in the right direction and so there was not a lot of shared wonderfulness.

Bryer: Did you argue about it at the time?

Mason: No, it was just sort of, "Well then, fuck you!"

Bryer: In other words, just complete withdrawal.

Mason: Yes. At this first meeting with Lanford we did not really communicate; we did not get along, nothing really happened, nothing really worked. It was arrogance running into arrogance. At that time I was twenty-four, and I was a terrible insomniac. I wanted to be awake all the time; sleeping was a waste of time and I didn't want to lose any time. I was a very driven person. One night in October of 1964 I was wandering around the Village unable to sleep, just trying to relax, trying to tire myself out to go to sleep. About two o'clock in the morning I ran into Lanford Wilson on the street, and we recognized each other from the Cino and he said, "Where are you going?" and I said, "I'm not able to sleep so I'm going to walk around until I'm tired." It was a cool night so we dropped into Whelan's Drug Store on Eighth Street and Greenwich Avenue and we went in and had a hot chocolate. Lanford started telling me about this play that he had written. And I said, "It sounds wonderful, I'd like to read it." He said, "Well, what are you doing now?" and I said, "That's true, I'm not doing anything." And he said, "Why don't you come on back to the hotel with me and read the play." So I followed him back to the Broadway Central Hotel and I sat on a day bed and read right through this play that he gave me that had some fifty-six characters in it. It was remarkable.

With my classical background the only thing I could compare it to was *The Lower Depths*. I handed it back to Lanford and said, "It reminds me of *Lower Depths*. You've really written a contemporary *Lower Depths*; it's an amazing play!" I could have been talking Chinese, because Lanford had no real education and didn't know anything about the history of drama. I said, "It will take a really brilliant director to do this play." Subsequently, I said my goodbyes and went home. Sometime later Lanford was given a date by Ellen Stewart to do the play at La Mama and Michael Powell, who was Lanford's roommate, came up to me at the Caffe Cino and said, "I can't understand why you don't like *Balm in Gilead*. I think it's so brilliant." I said, "What do you mean 'don't like it?' I think it's the best original play I've ever read! I think it's a work of genius!" He said, "Well, Lanford said you didn't like it." And I said, "I told him it needed a brilliant director to bring it off. Didn't he understand I was talking about myself? I want to direct it." Michael said, "No, I don't think he understood that." Michael went and talked to Lance and said, "He really wants to do the play." So Lance came over and sort of interviewed me at the Caffe Cino.

Bryer: You probably were a bit resentful of that; after all, at this point you had a better reputation in some ways than he did.

Mason: No, I was perfectly capable of giving him all the answers because I had them, and I knew he didn't have any. So we cleared up the thing about *Balm in Gilead*. I said, "I told you it needed a brilliant director. I didn't mean the play was in any kind of trouble. I meant that it was so good that it needed someone wonderful to realize it, and I couldn't see any alternative to myself." So he said, "OK, then I want you to direct it." And I jumped on it; I think it almost became physical. I grabbed him. Lanford had a very bad reputation as a playwright at the Cino— he was very interfering and was a mess at rehearsals. So I grabbed him and I said, "OK, but there are going to be certain rules from the very beginning that I must lay down. You will not speak to the actors. I am the director and only I will speak to the actors. If you have anything to say to them you talk to me." He said, "OK." I think he was stunned; nobody had ever come out with the kind of force he was always giving out. Then we went through casting and came to the first rehearsal. The first thing I do at my first rehearsal is to divide the play into beats. I use the beats subsequently to design a rehearsal schedule that allows me to approach the play in terms of its actions and to discover organically through that what movement we need. A beat, as I use it, is sort of like a French scene.

We had cut the play from fifty-six actors down to twenty-eight, and I started going through the script with all twenty-eight actors there, giving them the scene divisions that I had devised. Lanford sat there and listened to me mark the beats in the play, and because I'm an absolute purist about this sort of thing, some of the beats ended after the third sentence in the middle of a paragraph and then the fourth sentence began a new beat. He sat there and his mouth dropped open, because when he saw what I was doing he would sort of calculate, "Oh, I know when the next beat is." And damned if I didn't hit every one of them! He was truly amazed. He immediately felt, this man really understands my play because I had identified the same beats he knew were there. We had a very successful rehearsal period. We were all over the town; we had no permanent rehearsal space so we were stealing rehearsal space wherever we could. We rehearsed for a while in the CBS offices at night, because we had a friend who worked for CBS and he would get us in at night. We rehearsed some at the Actors Studio where Lanford was a member of the playwrights' unit and I was a member of the directors' unit. Suddenly here I was in my Mecca, because I'd started out worshipping Kazan and Brando and so forth and there I was.

Bryer: Died and gone to heaven!

Mason: Died and gone to heaven indeed! We actually performed the first scenes of the play at the Actors Studio. We opened at the La Mama in January of 1965 and it was the first full-length play ever done off-off-Broadway; it was also the first play ever to be published from off-off-Broadway. La Mama, like Cino, would only run a production for a week at a time but we were such a huge hit that Ellen, faced immediately with a sellout in the first week, held us over so we were the first play ever to run a second week. Lanford came to me, I remember, one night while we were playing at La Mama and said, "We've really got to hold these people together; this is a great ensemble. I've never seen ensemble acting before; I've heard about it, I've read about it, but until I saw your production I'd never known what it was. These people are an ensemble and we have to keep them together. Let's keep them and make a theatre out of them." Well, I was from Northwestern, all my friends were stars and I really expected Broadway to discover how wonderful we all were. That was the way things were done. Crawling around an off-off-Broadway cockroach-infested basement was not my idea of theatre. So I said, "I know what you mean, but we can get paid for doing this. This is our life, this is our career, this is our calling; we're artists and we deserve to be supported." But the eventual formation of Circle Repertory really grew out of our first experience on *Balm in Gilead* and Lanford saying, "We've got to hold these actors together and have a company" and he would write the plays and I would direct them. I just couldn't see doing that in January of 1965.

I didn't mention that there was another little grace-note to our meetings at the Caffe Cino. Having read *Balm in Gilead* in October, sometime in November he wrote a play called *The Sand Castle* and one night at the Caffe Cino, after the other show was over, whatever it was, Lanford said, "I've written this new play. Do you want to hear it?" I said, "Yes" and we read *The Sand Castle* and I just flipped out. I thought *Balm in Gilead* was good but I thought *The Sand Castle* was genius. If I ever had any doubts about Lanford Wilson as a writer, they were put to rest with *The Sand Castle*. So when he offered me *Balm in Gilead* and when I had been so rough on him, I accepted with this provision: I said, "The play I want to direct is *The Sand Castle*, but I will do *Balm in Gilead* if you will promise me *The Sand Castle*." He said, "OK." *The Sand Castle* was unlike anything I had ever read— music and dancing and realism and people talking to the audience. It was only an hour long but you felt like you'd been through a play by Eugene O'Neill.

Bryer: How long after all this took place did you actually start Circle Rep?

Mason: Not for some time after that. It was after we did *Home Free!* and *Lady Bright* in London and after we did *Gingham Dog* at

New Dramatists and *Untitled Play* at the Judson Poets Theatre. By this time also we had met Tanya Berezin, who was Rob Thirkield's girlfriend. We had had a limited engagement of *Home Free!* and *Lady Bright* at the Mercury Theatre in Nottingham Gate in the spring of 1968 so we didn't play very long, despite great reviews. We only played for a month or six weeks because we already had an engagement to play in Edinburgh. If we hadn't had to go on to Edinburgh it probably would have run for a year in London. Lanford never came over to see them. We were the toast of the town. We came back to the United States sometime in the summer of 1968 and had all these great reviews, so I went to Jules Irving who was then running Lincoln Center. I said, "Look at these reviews. We're a theatre company and we're looking for a home. You have a little theater downstairs that you're not using at all. Why don't you really be innovative and bring the American Theatre Project to Lincoln Center?" When we were going to London, we had taken the name the American Theatre Project because we weren't sure enough of ourselves to call ourselves a company.

Bryer: Who was the company at this point?

Mason: It was essentially based on the people who had first been in *Balm in Gilead* through *The Sand Castle* and through a couple of revivals as well.

Bryer: It was a core of about how many people?

Mason: I can tell you really specifically: Claris, Michael Powell, Charles Stanley, David Groh and Tanya were the five people who went to England together. It was those people plus a few others that had been in other plays, like Rob Thirkield. Jules Irving said, "Wonderful, do a production." We started rehearsing *Spring Play* by William Hoffman.

Bryer: Who later wrote *As Is*?

Mason: Yes, we knew Bill from the Caffe Cino. He was a poet back then. We were three weeks into rehearsal with *Spring Play* and Actors' Equity stepped in and said, "We will not allow a workshop production to occur on this stage." So we got trapped between Actors' Equity and Lincoln Center. Unfortunately the whole thing had been designed around doing it in this little space downstairs at Lincoln Center that seats 299. Equity found us a space called the New Theatre which is no longer there, up on East 46th, or 47th. So suddenly we were in this theater that was twenty-six rows deep—we were packed —and Jules Irving came to the opening night to see our work. It was a disaster, an utter disaster. You couldn't hear anything beyond the first six rows! After this, like with Northwestern Productions, I said, "Well, fuck it, this is too much for me; I don't want to do this anymore. I'm going to get out."

That was in the late summer of 1968. In the spring of 1969 my father died in Amarillo. I came back from the funeral and my life was absolutely falling apart. I wasn't pursuing the theatre, nothing was happening really—zip. Lanford and I both were over visiting Rob Thirkield and his new wife Tanya Berezin. It was June of 1969 and we had a call from Dr. Harry Lerner, who was Rob's psychiatrist and had also been my therapist for a while a few years before. He called and said, "I know you've got a theatre company and I've found this wonderful space that I think you ought to come look at." Lanford and Rob and I hopped in a taxi and the three of us went uptown to 83rd and Broadway to the second floor and saw this big empty space above a shoestore. It had awful acoustics, the echoes were terrible and once again—as when Lanford had suggested that we should form a theatre company—it seemed just much too primitive for my taste, having played London and all. I said, "No, this isn't what we want. We want to start a theatre somewhere, but this is not it."

Bryer: By this time you were a little more willing to stay with theatre?

Mason: No, I had really decided not to do any more theatre, but the reason I decided was that I felt I couldn't create miracle after miracle going around from one off-Broadway house to another off-Broadway house. If I was going to do theatre, I needed a place. Dr. Lerner now had called with a place.

Bryer: And that might have changed your whole attitude?

Mason: Oh, absolutely, totally. It did. The three of us agreed this was not what we wanted, so we told Dr. Lerner, "No thanks, we're not going to take it." And he said, "It's only five hundred dollars a month, so I'm going to take it with my CIRCLE, Metropolitan Area Council for International Recreation, Culture and Lifelong Education, C-I-R-C-L-E." And we said, "Oh, if you're going to take it, maybe we can use it until we find a place that we like." And he said, "OK." So on July 14, Bastille Day, in 1969, we had a big party to which we invited everybody that we knew in the theatre who was good. At this party we announced the formation of a new theatre company, at that point still to be called "The American Theatre Project." This theatre company came on the heels of Kazan and Whitehead both being fired from Lincoln Center and the basis of it was that we wanted a theatre that was run by artists, not by a board of directors. We would do new plays and there would be interdisciplinary crossovers from acting to directing to writing, to break down the walls that existed between the various disciplines. Beginning in August of that year, we started our workshops. Rob led one workshop that was called "Exploration," and I led one called "Methods." We offered workshops all the time. If you had an evening job you could come in the afternoon; if you had an afternoon job you could come in the evening. We trained from August of 1969 until I guess it was February or so of 1970, when we finally mounted our first production, a new play by David Starkweather.

Bryer: Lanford told me that right from the start you took the position that anybody who showed up and wanted to stay with things pretty much was part of the company if they felt in sympathy with you and you felt in sympathy with them.

Mason: Yes, but you understand this was an incredibly rigorous workshop. They had to attend something like seventeen hours a week. Anybody who would come and do the seventeen hours was in.

Bryer: And your initial core expanded as a result of this? You attracted people to this new company that had not been part of the original La Mama and Caffe Cino scene?

Mason: The original people really had boiled down to Tanya, Lanford, Rob and me.

Bryer: The actors who eventually became the core of Circle Rep beyond the people you just mentioned were those who went through those first workshops and survived.

Mason: Yes, that's right. We had David Starkweather who was one of the Cino playwrights and Doric Wilson and Lanford Wilson and we had a poetess named Helen Duberstein. I don't think we had any other writers as such.

Bryer: What was the first of Lanford's plays that you did?

Mason: We didn't do a play of Lanford's until the second season. Lanford had written a little one-act play called *Sextet (Yes)* and we did that. I think that was our first Lanford Wilson play.

Bryer: One of the things that Lanford said to me when I asked him what effect meeting you had had on him as a playwright was that your interest in Stanislavski and in working from within in acting had sent him to reading that sort of stuff. He said it led him to try to find out more about what was underneath his characters. Do you agree?

Mason: I never thought of that particular aspect, but a couple of things do occur to me. He had an enormous influence on me in two very important respects. One is that all my background had been in terms of classic theatre. I felt that contemporary drama, new plays, were not good enough. I had been raised on Chekhov and Ibsen and Euripides and, for me, those were the kinds of writers that I wanted to direct. Lanford was the one, not only through his own plays but through his philosophy, who made me aware of how important a contemporary writer writing about our world is. Of course, it changed my life, because it became all about producing and directing and presenting new plays.

    And the other important way he changed me was, as I mentioned earlier, it was really Lanford's saying that we must have a theatre company that was very important ultimately in the realization of Circle Repertory being founded, four years after he first started urging me. Although he is rather shy about it, saying he didn't have much to do with it at the beginning, he did. I'd say it was the third and fourth year before he really started getting involved. But the first year he was there at all of our important functions and it was Lanford's idea that we should get a group of actors together and keep them together. So he deservedly is considered one of the four founders because he was very important and still is. But one of the ways in which I affected him I think was not so much in terms of acting or Stanislavsky but in terms of dramatic literature. I knew Ibsen and Chekhov and Shaw and Pirandello and quite a few others, and Lanford was really quite ignorant about the history of world drama. Because of our meeting, some of his spontaneous enthusiasm rubbed off on me and some of my stuffy academic standards rubbed off on him. As a result he read all the great plays subsequently. My classicism worked well as a balance to his sense of light and free creativity.

Bryer: Then it was a sort of mutual synergy, wasn't it? His modernism rubbed off on you and your classicism rubbed off on him.

Mason: That's right. A director serves different functions, really, for different writers and some of that has to do with providing a sense of balance. Tennessee Williams's work was so extravagantly lyrical, what he needed from me as a director was to bring him down to the ground and root him in reality. William Inge was very grounded and he, I thought, needed to be liberated, to be set free, to be more lyrical, to allow his heart to sing a little more. What I try to do in a William Inge play is to try to let it soar, let it sing. I don't know really how I would define what I do with a Lanford Wilson play, except that my sense of classical order and his sense of life are a very good balance for each other. In terms of our working together, it's now got to the point where you can hardly tell where the directing ends and the writing begins and vice versa. I frequently will jump in and say, "Instead of saying that, you should say this!" I feel quite free to do that and if Lanford doesn't want to change the line, he'll say so, believe me. But generally he'll say, "Yeah, that's good, that's fine." Or if he sees a staging possibility that I haven't seen, he's not shy at all about making that contribution. Role playing, in our relationship to each other, has really virtually ceased to exist. We create as a team.

Bryer: There is so much ego usually in a director-writer relationship, with so much ego investment in the words as opposed to the production. You must have gotten beyond that, haven't you?

Mason: Yes. I think the lack of ego is certainly a very important part of it. It's interesting because both Lanford and I have tremendous egos. I have certainly been accused of arrogance in my time; I think I'm a rather arrogant person in some respects, but we are temperamentally very similar. That arrogance and that self-effacing quality alternate of course, and so Lanford is always able to catch me when I'm being too arrogant, and I'm always able to suggest when he could be a little more forthcoming. It is a good balance.

Bryer: Has your working relationship changed much over the years?

Mason: It's just gotten better. At the beginning Lanford was not really that aware of the actor's process, and so when we did our first production together, *Balm in Gilead*, I really laid down very strict rules to him and I would not allow him to speak to the actors and instead he watched me work. He has told me and told other people that watching me was like watching a magician. He thought that I must be using a wand or something because he didn't know how I got these people to do those wonderful things. He didn't know at the beginning but I think he does have a very real appreciation of it now. I think, in fact, by the end of *Balm in Gilead* he really did fully understand the miraculous process of creation that an actor goes through. I don't know of anybody in the theatre, certainly no other playwright, who is as appreciative of actors as Lanford Wilson. Lanford wants to know where this genuine talent comes from and how people use it and how they develop it. And I think over the years he has learned a lot about how actors approach a role. Of course, part of the thing at Circle Rep was that we insisted everybody learn everybody else's craft. So Lanford acted on our stage and directed for us as well. There's nothing like experiencing someone else's trip.

Bryer: What are your thoughts about why the two of you work so well together? You've worked with lots of other playwrights. What's different about working with Lanford?

Mason: I came to New York really having grown up on Tennessee Williams, Tennessee's play being the first I had directed. I felt very very close to Tennessee's writing. And Tennessee had had Kazan for his director. So here I was a junior Kazan with no Tennessee Williams. When I saw *Home Free!* the first time, I knew that I was in the presence of an extraordinary writer. Then *The Madness of Lady Bright* only confirmed what I already thought—and then to come upon the big plays! We have a lot in common: we're both from small towns, he from Ozark, Missouri, or Lebanon, and me from Luling, Texas. We both had divorced childhoods—yet he grew up with his mother and only came to deal with his father much much later; I grew up with my grandparents and then ended my years in high school with my father. There's something about being on your own, not having parents, not having the usual life. He had a bunch of brothers and sisters which I did not have. So I'm sure we were different in many respects as well. We were both poor kids, dirt poor, midwest essentially and southern midwest. We diverged in our education because I got a real education and Lanford sort of picked it up where he could, but going through all that early off-off-Broadway stuff together was important too. The reason why we're so compatible also has to do with the shared vision. My vision of the theatre and Lanford's vision of the theatre are very close to identical.

Bryer: And that is?

Mason: I don't know if Lanford would say this or not, but for me the theatre's about people in relationship to their environment and to each other. Their behavior is based on their needs and wants and desires and longings, and their secrets are written in that behavior. As a result of the friction between the inner drives and the external forces of social environment, behavior emerges, and it is behavior which is most fascinating and wonderful in the theatre. We're both interested in the human scale of life on stage. Both Lanford and I also have a great appreciation of music. Stanislavsky says, "All art is striving to become music." We put that up over the door at Circle Rep, at the first party we had on Bastille Day, 1969. In the theatre that means the music of language, the poetry of language. What I love about Lanford is that he has got an ear which captures what seems to be normal speech but he writes it so beautifully. Lanford captures the music of our speech in a way that is probably better than we speak, a lot better, but at the same time it never sounds stilted or awkward.

When I started, my heart was with Tennessee Williams but then when I met Lanford I realized that my talents might even be better suited to Lanford because I always felt I had to compensate for Tennessee's excesses and I don't feel that I have to compensate for Lanford's excesses at all. In fact, if anything, I have to encourage him: "Go ahead! Do that! Take that dramatic emotion!" But some of the most remarkable dramatic moments in Lanford's plays that I get a lot of credit for directorily are there in the conception right from the beginning. Other moments Lanford had no idea were there. There's the moment in *Hot l Baltimore* when Jackie's discovered with Mr. Morse's sock and she screams, "*I got dreams, goddamnit! What's he got?*" It's an incredible moment; everything works up to this cry being forced out of her and she just cries out from her soul. Lanford had no idea that that would be the climax; he thought maybe it would be said quietly or something. I built it all up for that to be the climax, and after that a silence—there was absolutely nothing left to say. We sometimes become adversaries in a creative and positive sense. Adversaries are not always negative with each other; there is a creative adversarial relationship that is extremely stimulating.

Bryer: Can you give an example of that?

Mason: The two plays that come immediately to mind are *Angels Fall* and *Burn This*. Lanford in writing *Angels Fall* had a strong impulse towards the priest's point of view. He really felt that Dr. Don should not leave, that he was selling out. I took the opposite point of view. I said, "Lanford, if you make this play into a Catholic play, I'm not going to do it. I don't want to do a play that's full of mumbo jumbo. What are you saying—that we all should turn to God? I'm not going to say that." So I fought him all the way through *Angels Fall* to make Don's case stronger and stronger, and I think by the time we finally got there you have the priest and the professor struggling over this man's soul. At the end he does go off; I kept trying to get Lanford to see. He would say, "He's just doing it for the money!" and I would say, "Lanford, yes he's going to get money. All that's true, but he may find the cure for cancer. You want him to throw his life away with these God-damned Indians where he can do no good, just to make himself be Dr. Schweitzer?" I think Dr. Don had a higher calling, frankly, than to stay on the reservation and be a good little Indian. I kept after Lanford to make that struggle more equal, and I think it helped the play enormously.

In *Burn This*, I think Lanford was in love with the character of Pale. It's almost a fantasy character—frightening, rough, dangerous, even repulsive almost, but magnetic, sexual, vibrant, with all the primitive urges that such a person elicits. He was very turned on by Pale, based on people that he's known in his own life, and that he wishes would come into his life and take him away from all this. I found that Lanford was romanticizing Pale to an extent that I just didn't buy. I was very concerned about the end of the play. I think that Anna is making an inevitable decision. I don't think that she has any choice; this is something that she has got to go through. But I look upon it like a trip to the dentist; Pale is going to be a very painful experience for her. For me it was not a romantic comedy at all, it was the story of an artist really learning to open herself to the suffering that she had closed herself off from. Obviously, Robbie is buried so deep in her heart that she never has really had any way to take that and turn it into work until she meets Pale, and Pale just upsets her world so much she is able finally to do the dance that she meant for Robbie. Pale gave her life content as it were; she already had the form, she just didn't have the content, something to be an artist about.

Bryer: Those are very interesting examples. Can you think of any others like them?

Mason: Those two stand out. I did take him to the mat on *Talley's Folly*. When he finished *Talley's Folly* he really thought it was a perfect little play and I came to it with my dramaturgical objections and said, "No suspense," and he was really pissed at me. Nobody wants to be dragged back to work when he thinks he's done. And I made him go back to work on it and kept after him until he did the revisions that made *Talley's Folly* what it is today.

Bryer: What kinds of revisions?

Mason: Matt knew Sally's secret from the beginning so there was no drama.

Bryer: Like the revision of *Home Free!*, wouldn't you say—the giving away of the end before the end?

Mason: That's right. Lanford has a tendency to do that, to be anti-dramatic.

Bryer: Because he doesn't want to cave into the notion of suspense; he wants to be "different?" And you of course as the director have to see it in terms of the ability to get a through line?

Mason: Exactly. I'm so corny and he's not. And it's a good balance. Lanford has been good about teaching me to be a little more tasteful, but I think I've been good for Lanford in saying, hey, when it's dramatic, be dramatic!

Bryer: What do you think are the advantages and disadvantages in a long-term director/playwright relationship? The advantages are obvious, I guess, and we've talked about them. Are there any disadvantages?

Mason: Not that I'm aware of so far. No, to work with Lanford is an absolute joy and delight. I remember long ago, about 1965 after I directed *Home Free!* off-Broadway, Michael Powell and I went up to the roof of my building and I said to him, "You know, I'm beginning to realize that if I never do anything else in my life than to help Lanford achieve what he can achieve I will live my life well." That's a humble kind of statement that I really genuinely felt in 1965 and that I still feel to some extent today. I think Lanford knows that and trusts that and I think that's why we're so close and such good collaborators.

There were two other plays I had something to do with dramaturgically. *The Gingham Dog* was written as a three-act play with some five characters and Lanford had submitted it all around. It was a well-made three-act play and nobody was doing it. He had given up on it, and had put it away. I said, "Let's drag that play out again," and he said, "Oh no, nobody wanted to do that play." But I took it home and went at it with a red pencil and I cut a character out, I changed it from a three-act play to a two-act play. I cut and pasted, cut and pasted and I took it to Lanford and said, "OK, I've reshaped your play entirely, but obviously I can't do this on my own. You'll see it's very very awkward; there are places where I've taken one scene and another and placed them next to each other when they don't fit, so you have to do something to get us from this point to this point." I had restructured the play with gaps that had to be filled in by him, and so he went back to the drawing board with that play and he rewrote it with my restructuring and it did quite well.

Bryer: And the other earlier play you'd had an effect on dramaturgically?

Mason: Ironically, it was a play that I haven't directed. Lanford had just come up with the plot on *The Rimers of Eldritch*; he had written the first act and I thought it was terrific. I loved it and he said, "Well, I can't figure out what happened. I'm telling this story and I don't know what happened!" So I just served as a sounding board really for him and the two of us figured out what the plot might be. I made a contribution of sorts to that play, although I don't feel that it has ever been as close to me as the ones that I've directed. But I do want to emphasize to you that if I talk about any kind of contribution that I have made to Lanford's writing, it is as a director and a friend, as his humble servant in a sense. By no stretch of the imagination would I ever want to take any credit for any of the things that he's done;

they're his wonderful plays. I'm very proud about pointing out a line or two here and there. Some of my lines, which have found their way into Lanford's plays, are words to be proud of.

Bryer: Has some of his directing found its way into your directing?

Mason: Oh, absolutely, no question about that. Lots of it. But I'm not going to identify any of that! I am always quick, however, to point out to people my line in *5th of July*. There was a moment when Nancy Snyder came down as Gwen in *5th of July* and she's inside making a telephone call while we're outside on the porch and of course we can see her there—it's a small theater at Circle Rep. I said, "Lance, she's got to say something; she just can't mime things, she has to say something." He said, "I'll think of something." They had just put in this new long distance dialing where you had to dial "1" to get a long distance number. So I said, "Gwen should say, 'What the fuck for, dial one?'" and Lanford said, "OK, fine," always thinking in the back of his mind that one day he would go back and provide the real line, but he just got lazy and didn't do it. We got to the first preview and that line, of course, brought the house down. So it became his line after that!

Bryer: Let me ask you a question that I asked Lanford. What happens to you as a director when you go to see other people's productions of a Lanford Wilson play?

Mason: It's a very difficult thing. I've always found that Lanford is far more generous about other productions than I have been. I saw *Fifth of July* in Seattle and they misinterpreted just about everything that could be misinterpreted. It's very difficult to see someone else redo your work. But it isn't always bad; sometimes I've actually seen some good productions.

Bryer: What about the feeling you get directing a revival of a play as opposed to a new play?

Mason: That's not the same at all, no matter how important the revival may be. When I did *A Streetcar Named Desire* at Arena Stage in Washington it was the first time as far as I'm aware that the play had been done in the round, and that's quite a challenge. And I was excited because I knew Tennessee would be able to come to see it. But that can't compare to doing a new play by Lanford Wilson. There's just no comparison. A new play by Bill Hoffman, a new play by Jules Feiffer, sure. I think I bring the same kind of feeling or concern, or care about those, just as much as if they were Lanford's.

Bryer: Do you think that there's any such thing as a Lanford Wilson or a Marshall Mason actor?

Mason: There has been in the past. For a long time he wrote roles for Trish Hawkins, who was just about his favorite actress and I was delighted to cast her again and again because I thought she was phenomenal. The two of us simply could not believe that anybody could be as good as Trish was. She didn't know how to lie on stage, she was always honest, she was always truthful; but she was mercurial and magic as well. On the other hand, there's someone like Helen Stenborg who has been in virtually everything. She was in *Rimers of Eldritch* for Lanford, in the original off-Broadway production, and of course he wrote Millie, the crazy waitress in *Hot l Baltimore*, for her, and then he wrote *5th of July* for her—and she's in his new play as well. With her there's that wonderful combination of feet on the ground and madness and spontaneity. But I guess in the long run if you really had to pick one, I would say that Tanya has been a real important person all along. Lanford was actually writing *Hot l Baltimore* with Tanya in mind for the role of Jackie, but she was pregnant at the time and couldn't do it. I loved Tanya's performance in *Angels Fall* so much. I think she really, in that performance, had all the things that a Lanford Wilson actor needs to have. Lanford adores Richard Thomas, as I do too; he's a great actor. We also obviously have enjoyed working again and again with Judd Hirsch, in *Hot l Baltimore* and *Talley's Folly*.

Bryer: Are there any qualities that you think all those people have in common?

Mason: Lanford likes that hard midwestern American stiff upper lip let's muddle through it all, balanced against the vulnerability of a Trish Hawkins—the interplay between those two things. Judd is a good example. On the one hand, you had a part like Bill in *Hot l Baltimore* where it's all internalized, a very quiet generous performance because it's all about everybody else. You notice Judd Hirsch because of the way he listens and that's wonderful; but on the other hand he can turn around and be utterly spectacular and have all his bag of tricks as in *Talley's Folly*. In writing *Talley's Folly*, Lanford was determined to give Judd a part that just let him use everything—all his talents at once: for mimicry, for verbal ability and what have you; but at the same time a wonderful pyrotechnical performance like that without being rooted in honesty would be really horrible. Lanford's least favorite actor of all time I think is an English actor named John Wood and he exemplifies everything that neither Lanford nor I appreciate in the theatre. I have one that's even less favorite for me that's in the same vein—Tim Curry, who did *Amadeus* on Broadway. I think what Tim Curry does for me is what John Wood does for Lanford! So that's an example of what we don't want to write for or direct.

Bryer: Let me close by just asking you what happened to send you to California away from New York, away from Circle Rep? I assume it's an amicable parting of the ways?

Mason: It's not a parting of the ways, really, at all. I'm in constant touch with Lanford; we talk usually once a week. I don't see it as any kind of parting of the ways and I don't think Lanford does either, or he wouldn't have let me go.

Bryer: Let me phrase it another way. What has the move to California meant for you positively?

Mason: I guess I really have to go back to what I mentioned to you at the beginning of this interview. Some of my greatest experiences in life have come from films, starting with *Pinky* and *The Young Lions* and so forth. As a child I grew up on films. It was something that I've always wanted to do. When I graduated from college I could have gone to work for Walt Disney, as an assistant director in his studio. I said if I go to Hollywood and do that I'll never be Kazan, so I went to New York to pursue the theatre because I believed in that. And unfortunately or fortunately or whatever, I became successful at what I was doing; I got trapped by my own success. I never intended to spend my entire life in the theatre; somewhere along the way I always had in mind doing films and I just kept putting it off and putting it off. Then one summer Neil Flanagan, who had been so important to Lanford and me both, died. Two weeks later Rob Thirkield died, and then about a month later, a third really good friend of Lanford's and mine died. When they all died that summer, I said life is not forever; if I'm going to do this, I'd better do it while I'm still alive. And let me tell you it takes a great deal of guts to turn your back on a successful life and say I'm going to go try something altogether new. I feel like Gauguin giving up banking and going to Tahiti! LA is such a foreign country to me in so many ways; just learning the ropes is a kind of horrifying lesson. I haven't gotten anywhere; I've been there three years and I'm nowhere.

Bryer: You don't have a track record in Hollywood.

Mason: Exactly, exactly.

Bryer: But you're still happy being there?

Mason: Yes. It goes all the way back to childhood. After years and years of being a stage director, the question of whether I have anything to say becomes important to explore before I reach the end of my life. There is a sense in which a film director, even if he is working on somebody else's screenplay, is much more expressive of his own experience in a film than on stage. On stage, my job is definitely secondary to the playwright's. It's the playwright's play that you're honoring and everything that I do is meant to honor that vision and to help it be heard. In film I think everything is really geared towards the director's expression. Even the script may change depending on what that director's vision is. It's a different relationship to the work and to the audience. I feel that if I went through my life and never tried it, it would be a terrible waste. I think it would be a sin not at least to explore what I might be able to accomplish. But it's a long, hard, difficult task. Going back to New York, which I do now frequently, is really necessary because I get so tired of being nobody in LA. I have to go back to New York to realize that I have accomplished a few things in my life!

A Lanford Wilson Bibliography

Martin J. Jacobi

Primary Works

I. Plays

Abstinence. Staged New York, 1988. New York: Dramatists Play Service, 1989.

———. In *The Best American Short Plays, 1990*. Ed. Howard Stein and Glenn Young. New York: Applause Theatre Books, 1991. 181–91.

———. In *The Best American Short Plays, 1990–1992*. Ed. Howard Stein and Glenn Young. Garden City, NY: The Fireside Theatre, 1992. 195–206.

Angels Fall. Staged Miami, FL, 1982; New York, 1982. In *Angels Fall*. New York: Hill and Wang, 1983.

———. In *The Best Plays of 1982–1983*. Ed. Otis L. Guernsey, Jr. New York: Dodd, Mead, 1984. 153–72.

Balm in Gilead. Staged New York, 1965. In *Balm and Gilead and Other Plays*. New York: Hill and Wang, 1965.

Bar Play. Staged Louisville, KY, 1979.

A Betrothal. Staged London, England, 1986; New York, 1987. In *A Betrothal*. New York: Dramatists Play Service, 1986.

——. In *The Best Short Plays, 1987*. Ed. Ramon Delgado. New York: Applause Theatre Books, 1987. 33–53.

The Bottle Harp. Staged New York, 1987.

Breakfast at the Track. Staged Philadelphia, 1984; New York, 1987.

Brontosaurus. Staged New York, 1977. In *Brontosaurus*. New York: Dramatists Play Service, 1978.

——. In *The Best Short Plays, 1979*. Ed. Stanley Richards. Radnor, PA: Chilton Book Co., 1980. 43–64.

Burn This. Staged Los Angeles, 1987; New York, 1987. In *Burn This*. New York: Hill and Wang, 1987.

——. In *Best American Plays: Ninth Series: 1983–1992*. Ed. Clive Barnes. New York: Crown, 1993. 270–300.

Days Ahead. Staged New York, 1965. In *The Rimers of Eldritch and Other Plays*. New York: Hill and Wang, 1967.

The Dying Breed. Staged New York, 1987.

Eukiah. Staged Louisville, 1991. In *More Ten-Minute Plays From Actors Theatre of Louisville*. Ed. Michael Bigelow Dixon. New York: Samuel French, 1992. 283–89.

The Family Continues. Staged New York, 1972. In *The Great Nebula in Orion and Three Other Plays*. New York: Dramatists Play Service, 1973.

5th of July (early version of *Fifth of July*). Staged New York, 1978. In *5th of July*. New York: Hill and Wang, 1978.

——. In *The Best Plays of 1977–1978*. Ed. Otis L. Guernsey, Jr. New York: Dodd, Mead, 1978. 239–60.

Fifth of July. Staged Los Angeles, 1980; New York, 1980. In *Fifth of July*. New York: Dramatists Play Service, 1982 (revised).

The Gingham Dog. Staged New York, 1968; Washington, DC, 1968; New York, 1969. In *The Gingham Dog*. New York: Dramatists Play Service, 1969.

———. In *The Gingham Dog*. New York: Hill and Wang, 1969.

The Great Nebula in Orion. Staged Manchester, England, 1971; New York, 1972. In *The Best Short Plays, 1972*. Ed. Stanley Richards. Philadelphia: Chilton Book Co., 1972. 49–74.

———. In *The Great Nebula in Orion and Three Other Plays*. New York: Dramatists Play Service, 1973.

Home Free! Staged New York, 1964. In *Balm and Gilead and Other Plays*. New York: Hill and Wang, 1965.

———. In *The Madness of Lady Bright and Home Free!* London: Methuen, 1968.

The Hot l Baltimore. Staged New York, 1973. In *The Hot l Baltimore*. New York: Dramatists Play Service, 1973.

———. In *The Hot l Baltimore*. New York: Hill and Wang, 1973.

———. In *The Best Plays of 1972–1973*. Ed. Otis L. Guernsey, Jr. New York: Dodd, Mead, 1973. 292–306.

———. In *The Obie Winners: The Best of Off-Broadway*. Ed. Ross Wetzsteon. New York: Doubleday, 1980. 441–549.

Ikke, Ikke, Nye, Nye, Nye. Staged New Haven, CT, 1972; New York, 1972. In *The Great Nebula in Orion and Three Other Plays*. New York: Dramatists Play Service, 1973.

Lemon Sky. Staged Buffalo, NY, 1970; New York, 1970. In *Lemon Sky*. New York: Dramatists Play Service, 1970.

———. In *Lemon Sky*. New York: Hill and Wang, 1970.

———. In *Best American Plays: Seventh Series*. Ed. Clive Barnes. New York: Crown, 1975. 337–68.

Ludlow Fair. Staged New York, 1965. In *Balm in Gilead and Other Plays*. New York: Hill and Wang, 1965.

The Madness of Lady Bright. Staged New York, 1964. In *Eight Plays from Off-Off-Broadway*. Ed. Nick Orzel and Michael Smith. Indianapolis: Bobbs-Merrill, 1966. 57–92.

——. In *The Rimers of Eldritch and Other Plays*. New York: Hill and Wang, 1967.

——. In *The Madness of Lady Bright and Home Free!* London: Methuen, 1968.

——. In *Gay Plays: The First Collection*. Ed. William Hoffman. New York: Avon, 1979. 177–97.

Miss Williams: A Turn. Staged New York, 1965.

The Moonshot Tape. Staged Arcata, CA, 1990. In *The Moonshot Tape and A Poster of the Cosmos*. New York: Dramatists Play Service, 1990.

The Mound Builders. Staged New York, 1975. In *The Mound Builders*. New York: Hill and Wang, 1976.

——. In *Plays From Circle Repertory Company*. New York: Broadway Publishing, 1986. 1–65.

No Trespassing. Staged New York, 1964.

A Poster of the Cosmos. Staged New York, 1988. In *Best Short Plays of 1989*. Ed. Ramon Delgado. New York: Applause Theater Books, 1989. 245–58.

——. In *The Way We Live Now: American Plays and the AIDS Crisis*. Ed. M. Elizabeth Osborn. New York: Theatre Communications Group, 1990. 63–75.

——. In *The Moonshot Tape and A Poster of the Cosmos*. New York: Dramatists Play Service, 1990.

Redwood Curtain. Staged Seattle, 1992; New York, 1993. In *Redwood Curtain*. New York: Hill and Wang, 1993.

The Rimers of Eldritch. Staged New York, 1966. In *The Rimers of Eldritch*. New York: Dramatists Play Service, 1967.

——. In *The Rimers of Eldritch and Other Plays*. New York: Hill and Wang, 1967.

———. In *The Off-Off-Broadway Book*. Ed. Albert Poland and Bruce Mailman. Indianapolis: Bobbs-Merrill, 1972. 135–60.

Sa Hurt? Staged New York, 1985.

The Sand Castle. Staged New York, 1965. In *The Sand Castle and Three Other Plays*. New York: Dramatists Play Service, 1970.
———. In *The Best Short Plays, 1975*. Ed. Stanley Richards. New York: Chilton Book Co., 1975. 122–76.

Say de Kooning. Staged Southampton, NY, 1983; New York, 1987.

Serenading Louie. Staged Washington, DC, 1970; New York, 1976. In *Serenading Louie*. New York: Dramatists Play Service, 1976.
———. In *The Best Plays of 1975–1976*. Ed. Otis L. Guernsey, Jr. New York: Dodd, Mead, 1977. 230–48.
———. In *Serenading Louie*. New York: Hill and Wang, 1984 (revised).

Sex Is Between Two People. Staged New York, 1965.

Sextet (Yes). Staged New York, 1971. In *The Sand Castle and Three Other Plays*. New York: Dramatists Play Service, 1970.

So Long at the Fair. Staged New York, 1963.

A Tale Told (early version of *Talley & Son*). Staged New York, 1981.

Talley & Son (revision of *A Tale Told*). Staged Saratoga, NY, 1985; New York, 1985. In *Talley & Son*. New York: Hill and Wang, 1986.

Talley's Folly. Staged New York, 1979. In *Talley's Folly*. New York: Hill and Wang, 1979.
———. In *The Best Plays of 1979–1980*. Ed. Otis L. Guernsey, Jr. New York: Dodd, Mead, 1981. 233–44.

——. In *Best American Plays: Eighth Series: 1974–1982*. Ed. Clive Barnes. New York: Crown, 1984. 158–81.

This Is the Rill Speaking. Staged New York, 1965. In *The Rimers of Eldritch and Other Plays*. New York: Hill and Wang, 1967.

Thymus Vulgaris. (Read as *Common Thyme*, New York, 1981.) Staged Los Angeles, 1981; New York, 1982. In *Thymus Vulgaris*. New York: Dramatists Play Service, 1982.

——. In *The Best Short Plays, 1982*. Ed. Stanley Richards. Radnor, PA: Chilton Book Co., 1982. 1–23.

——. In *The Best Short Plays 1982–1983*. Ed. Ramon Delgado. Garden City, NY: Doubleday, 1983. 3–26.

Untitled Play. Music by Al Carmines. Staged New York, 1968.

Victory on Mrs. Dandywine's Island. Staged New York, 1979. In *The Great Nebula in Orion and Three Other Plays*. New York: Dramatists Play Service, 1973.

Wandering: A Turn. Staged New York, 1966. In *The Rimers of Eldritch and Other Plays*. New York: Hill and Wang, 1967.

——. In *Collision Course*. Ed. Edward Parone. New York: Random House, 1968. 7–17.

——. In *The Sand Castle and Three Other Plays*. New York: Dramatists Play Service, 1970.

II. Other Works

"Acting Dangerously." Interview/article on Jessica Lange in *Mirabella*, April 1992: 41–42.

"Grape Performances." Article in *Mirabella*, April 1990: 48–50.

"If you can't stand honest theater, stay home." Article in *Springfield* (MO) *News-Leader*, 12 November 1989, sec. B: 5.

Introduction to Robert Patrick, *Robert Patrick's cheep theatricks!* New York: Winter House, 1972.

Last Exit to Brooklyn. Unproduced screenplay, adapted from the Hubert Selby, Jr., novel, ca. 1966.

"Meet Tom Eyen, Tom Eyen." Article in *Horizon*, July 1979: 43.

The Migrants. Television screenplay for "Playhouse 90," 3 February 1974.

"Observations of a Resident Playwright." Article in *New York Times* 23 April 1978, sec. 2: 5.

One Arm. Unproduced screenplay, adapted from a Tennessee Williams short story, 1969.

"'Our Town' and Our Towns." Article in *New York Times* 20 December 1987, sec. 2: 1, 36.

Review of *Howard Finster: Stranger From Another World, Man of Visions Now on This Earth* by Howard Finster as told to Tom Patterson; and *Howard Finster: Man of Visions* by J. F. Finster. *The Clarion* 15 (Spring 1990): 65–66, 68.

"Sam Found Out." TV skit produced on Liza Minnelli special on ABC, 31 May 1988.

Stoop: A Turn. Television screenplay on WNET, 1969. In *The Sand Castle and Three Other Plays*. New York: Dramatists Play Service, 1970.

Summer and Smoke. Libretto for an opera by Lee Hoiby, adapted from a Tennessee Williams play. Produced St. Paul, MN, 1971. In *Summer and Smoke*. New York: Belwin-Mills, 1972.

Taxi! Television screenplay for "Hallmark Hall of Fame," 2 February 1978.

Translator, *Three Sisters* by Anton Chekhov. Staged Hartford, CT, 1984; New York, 1986. In *Three Sisters*. New York: Dramatists Play Service, 1984.

"Trying to Discover Chekhov." Program note for Hartford Stage Company production of *Three Sisters*, March 1984.

Major Criticism

Barnes, Clive. "'The Gingham Dog,' Autopsy of a Marriage." *New York Times* 24 April 1969: 41.

Barnes's review, like most others, finds this play unsatisfactory. He says that "passages in the first act I found tautological to the point of tedium" although he does admit that "there was here a feeling for pain and a blunt honesty of expression that quietly moved me."

Barnett, Gene A. *Lanford Wilson*. Twayne's United States Authors Series. Boston: G. K. Hall, 1987.

Barnett analyzes the plays, through *Talley & Son*, by means of a broad, chronological survey. He identifies many of the commonly observed characteristics of Wilson's drama, including his experimental techniques, his dialogue of "lyric realism," and his thematic emphasis on family and loss, and he also identifies a large number of literary influences on the playwright. This book is at present the fullest discussion of Wilson's *oeuvre*.

——. "Recreating the Magic: An Interview with Lanford Wilson." *Ball State University Forum* 25 (Spring 1984): 57–74.

Wilson says that his experiences with *Death of a Salesman*, *The Glass Menagerie* and Ionesco's *The Lesson* were three early and important influences on his work. His first exposure to a production of Miller's play led him to want "to recreate some of that magic."

Bennetts, Leslie. "Marshall Mason Explores a New Stage." *New York Times* 11 October 1987, sec. 2: 3, 14.

This article provides information about Wilson's professional relationship with his director, Marshall Mason, and also Mason's thoughts about *Burn This*.

Berkowitz, Gerald M. *American Drama of the Twentieth Century.* London and New York: Longman, 1992. 135–39, 181–84.

Berkowitz devotes two brief sections of his survey to Wilson. The first deals with "the early plays" (through *The Mound Builders* [1975]), the second with the Talley plays, *Angels Fall* and *Burn This*.

Berkvist, Robert. "Lanford Wilson—Can He Score on Broadway?" *New York Times* 17 February 1980, sec. 2: 1, 33.

In this interview, Wilson claims that he is happier working with Marshall Mason and the Circle Rep than he would be on Broadway. He also comments on America's dismantling of its culture and says that many of his plays ask, "what are we losing and what is it doing to us?"

Blau, Eleanor. "How Lanford Wilson Writes with Actors in Mind." *New York Times* 27 January 1983: C15.

When Wilson has a vague notion of a character and a plot, he sizes up members of the Circle Rep company; the person he chooses helps the playwright define his character. His interest in people is said to be shown in their social, political and psychological contexts, and his plays emphasize the choices people make and the values that determine their choices.

Branam, Harold. "Lanford Wilson." *Critical Survey of Drama.* English Language Series, Volume 5. Ed. Frank N. Magill. Englewood Cliffs, NJ: Salem Press, 1985. 2095–103.

Branam says that Wilson often relies on bringing together disparate characters in an unusual setting, in lieu of standard plot development. He also wonders if Wilson's movement in his later work from "a prophetic to a priestly stance" suggests the development of a religious solution to the recurring thematic conflicts.

Busby, Mark. *Lanford Wilson*. Western Writers Series, 81. Boise, ID: Boise State Univ., 1987.

The book develops a number of thematic threads that occasionally conflict with one another, yet, as one of only two monographs on the playwright, it still has value. Busby links the playwright's personal history to the recurring themes of generational conflict and concern for the past. He also uses Leo Marx's *The Machine in the Garden* to argue that Wilson celebrates "the pastoral rather than the primitive ideal." Also included are references to a wide range of literary influences on Wilson.

Callens, Johan. "When 'The Center Cannot Hold' or the Problem of Mediation in Lanford Wilson's *The Mound Builders*." *New Essays on American Drama*. Ed. Gilbert Debusscher and Henry I. Schvey. Amsterdam: Rodopi, 1989. 201–26.

Callens sees the play as "about the problem of mediation: mediation beween different views; between past, present and future; between abstract contemplation and sense perception, utilitarianism and aestheticism; Science and Art; between the analytical and differentiating power of Reason and the synthetic and (re)creative power of the imagination."

Cameron, John C. "Isolation as Strategy for Characterization in the Family Dramas of Lanford Wilson." Ph.D. dissertation, Kent State University, 1986. Abstract in *DAI* 47 (March 1987): 3243A.

Cameron uses relationships between parents and children in arguing that isolation is the playwright's basic organizing principle for characterization. He analyzes *The Sand Castle, Lemon Sky*, and the three Talley plays. Included in appendices are two interviews with Wilson.

Chi, Wei-jan. "The Role of Language in the Plays of Mamet, Wilson, and Rabe." Ph.D. dissertation, University of Iowa, 1991. Abstract in *DAI* 52 (January 1992): 2327A.

The section on Wilson in this dissertation views him in the tradition of Chekhov and Tennessee Williams, calling his dramatic language "poetic in the sense that its evocative and suggestive qualities encourage the audience to participate actively in the interpretive process with their imagination."

Clurman, Harold. "Theater." *Nation* 5 March 1973: 313–14.

Clurman states that *The Hot l Baltimore* is a "slice of *life*, rather than a contraption of showmanship or aesthetic pretension." He continues by calling the play realistic and asserting that, despite what theatre connoisseurs continually tell us, realism still has much to offer. Clurman argues that attacks on realism mask critics' disgust with or fear of contemporary society.

——. "Theater." *Nation* 15 March 1980: 316.

Clurman remarks that Wilson has gotten beyond the thematic and structural limitations of many contemporaries, and that, as with much of Wilson's work, *Talley's Folly* is good natured but by no means ignorant in its acceptance of experience.

Cohn, Ruby. "Broadway Bound: Simon, Kopit, McNally, Wilson." *New American Dramatists 1960–1980*. New York: Grove P, 1982. 8–26.

Cohn states that Wilson's early plays are realistic sketches of sympathetic misfits. Like Tennessee Williams, Wilson is tender to his deviant characters; for instance, Cohn compares Lady Bright to Williams's Blanche DuBois. She also observes that *The Rimers of Eldritch* "dramatizes evil . . . with a suspense that is rare for Wilson."

Cooperman, Robert. "Lanford Wilson: A Bibliography." *Bulletin of Bibliography* 48 (September 1991): 125–35.

Unannotated but exhaustive listing of Wilson's published plays, plays in anthologies, other writings and stage productions, followed by a checklist of interviews and essays, articles and reviews about Wilson.

Dasgupta, Gautam. "Lanford Wilson." In *American Playwrights: A Critical Survey*, Vol. One. Ed. Bonnie Marranca and Gautam Dasgupta. New York: Drama Book Specialists, 1981. 27–39.

Dasgupta asserts that Wilson's "characters evoke the past in order to make their present lives more bearable." Perhaps the least positive of the overviews of Wilson's work, the article has few compliments to pay to any of the plays after the earliest. Dasgupta's readings of *5th of July* and *The Hot l Baltimore* as pessimistic appear to be unique.

Dreher, Ann Crawford. "Lanford Wilson." *Twentieth Century American Dramatists, Part Two, K-Z*. Vol. 7 of *Dictionary of Literary Biography*. Ed. John MacNicholas. Detroit: Gale, 1981. 350–68.

Dreher discusses major themes and the significance of structural and stylistic experiments, mentions the quality of his language and identifies numerous literary influences. She remarks on Wilson's ability to "represent universal truths through widely varying situations and characters."

Flately, Guy. "Lanford Is One 'L' of a Playwright." *New York Times* 22 April 1973, sec. 2: 1, 21.

Flately says that the perverted losers of Wilson's plays suggest a shambles of a childhood for the playwright. He also notes that *The Madness of Lady Bright* was the first homosexual play, predating *The Boys in the Band*.

Freedman, Samuel G. "Lanford Wilson Comes Home." *New York Times* 30 August 1987, sec. 6, part 2: 29, 63–64.

Wilson mentions in this interview that he overcame his writer's block in the early 1980's only after seeing Innaurato's *Gemini*, Mamet's *Glengarry Glen Ross* and Rabe's *Hurlyburly*. The playwright also calls the Talley plays "a side trip that took me away from the line of my work," and speaks about his goals when writing *Burn This*.

Garrison, Gary Wayne. "Lanford Wilson's Use of Comedy and Humor." Ph.D. dissertation, University of Michigan, 1987. Abstract in *DAI* 48 (August 1987): 254A.

This study discusses Wilson's use of comedy and humor through analyses of *Ludlow Fair*, *The Hot l Baltimore*, *Fifth of July* and *Talley's Folly*. The dissertation includes a biographical chapter, a chapter on the historical foundation of comedy from Aristophanes to twentieth-century American dramatists and three chapters on Wilson's work. According to Garrison, Wilson achieves comedy through characterization, language, and various comic devices such as running gags and topical sex.

Gottfried, Martin. "The Theatre: 'Lemon Sky.'" *Women's Wear Daily* 18 May 1970: 14.

Gottfried says that the "naturalistic" *The Gingham Dog* was a failure and with *Lemon Sky* Wilson has returned to what he does best and most naturally: a play of counterpointing thought, dream and reality. He calls Wilson one of the most talented writers in American theatre.

Gussow, Mel. "Lanford Wilson on Broadway." *Horizon* 23 (May 1980): 30–36.

Gussow notes that Wilson's plays are all about individualism and the importance of preserving history. He also makes the common observation that Wilson presents sympathetic portrayals of social misfits and outcasts, and claims that some of them "project such a purity of spirit—idealism honed to perfection—that in comparison, conformists seem like aliens."

———. "Lanford Wilson's Lonely World of Displaced Persons." *New York Times* 25 October 1987, sec. 2: 5.

In an interesting analysis of *Burn This*, Gussow says that the play describes the plight of the artist as one "destined to be a

watcher on the sidelines, at most a voyeur, but not someone who
can realize his own passions."

Haller, Scot. "The Dramatic Rise of Lanford Wilson." *Saturday
    Review* 8 (August 1981): 26–29.

Wilson talks about his primary concerns being relationships between parents and children, countrymen and business-
men, public trust and private action. He also provides information about his life and tells about his penchant for rewriting,
even after a play opens.

Harriott, Esther. "Images of America: Four Contemporary
    Playwrights." Ph.D. dissertation, SUNY, Buffalo, 1983.
    Abstract in *DAI* 44 (April 1984): 3065A.

This dissertation discusses Sam Shepard, David Mamet,
Charles Fuller and Lanford Wilson. The second chapter analyzes
Wilson's work through his preoccupation with the rootless and
impermanent—a preoccupation, Harriott argues, masked by a
deliberate cheerfulness. The third chapter is an interview with
the playwright. The author concludes that the four playwrights
share a similar view of the human condition despite a diversity
of contexts, themes and techniques.

Herman, William. "Down and Out in Lebanon and New York:
    Lanford Wilson." *Understanding Contemporary American
    Drama.* Columbia: U of South Carolina P, 1987. 196–229.

Herman limits his analyses to five plays—*Balm in Gilead,
The Rimers of Eldritch* and the three Talley plays. He observes that
Wilson is generally apolitical although sensitive to the
underclass. He also remarks that Wilson complicates his picture
of the American family by introducing important characters who
are alien to the traditional American.

Hewes, Henry. "The Theater: Birdlime and Bobby Socks." *Sat-
    urday Review* 11 March 1967: 30.

The Rimers of Eldritch is a "beautifully constructed effort to
present a complex portrait of the good and evil in a small

midwestern community." According to Hewes, Wilson seems to say that small-town social attitudes pervert natural sexual expression with both tragic and comic consequences.

———. "The Theater: Have Theater, Will Travel." *Saturday Review* 26 October 1968: 32, 67.

The Gingham Dog has as its most important quality the "honest representation of the reality of its situation"—a disintegrating interracial marriage. The play exhibits its integrity in the second act when the couple realizes that, although they love each other, there will be no reconciliation.

Hughes, Catharine. "From Taylor to Talley." *America* 18–25 July 1981: 35.

In a review of *A Tale Told*, Hughes notes that war is a central element in all the Talley plays. She quotes Wilson, who says, "I think we change most during war. . . . Recording those changes in direction is one of the large goals here." The Talley family, inexorably altered by each of the wars it has passed through, thus mirrors the often troubled past of the United States.

Jacobi, Martin J. "The Comic Vision of Lanford Wilson. *Studies in the Literary Imagination* 21 (Fall 1988): 119–34.

Jacobi argues that the earlier plays exhibit naturalistic or tragic elements because of the depiction of two interests that repeatedly conflict: sympathetic depictions of the traditions and values that have shaped American society, and compassionate portrayals of people not traditionally part of our society. The later plays, beginning with *The Hot l Baltimore*, harmonize these interests to produce mature comedy.

———. "Lanford Wilson." *Contemporary Authors Bibliographical Series: American Dramatists.* Ed. Matthew C. Roudané. Detroit: Gale, 1989. 431–54.

This bibliographic essay is organized according to the nature of the secondary sources on the playwright. Jacobi draws

from an extensive list of citations to describe the reception of
Wilson's work and to suggest areas for future research and publication.

Kakutani, Michiko. "'I Write the World as I See It Around Me.'"
    New York Times 8 July 1984, sec. 2: 4, 6.

Wilson says that Joe Cino's suicide made him decide to
turn from the darker visions of his earlier plays to the more
positive emphases in the later ones. He regards his plays as
"Baptist sermons," yet, wary of didacticism, he tries to ground
his examinations of social issues in intensely personal situations.

Kellman, Barnet, chair. "The American Playwright in the
    Seventies: Some Problems & Perspectives." *Theatre
    Quarterly* 8 (Spring 1978): 45–58.

In a roundtable discussion with six other playwrights,
Wilson comments on such topics as the value of off-Broadway,
writing for commissions, audience assumptions and expectations and the role of politics in playwriting.

Kerr, Walter. "When Best-Laid Plans Go Awry." *New York Times*
    15 November 1987, sec. 2: 5, 21.

The theme of *Burn This*—"we can't help loving those we
happen to love"—has been used already by the playwright in
Talley's Folly. Kerr praises Wilson's flair with words, his ability to
tease bizarre imagery along until it becomes as plausible as it is
startling and his humor; however, John Malkovich, as Pale,
overplays his role. Kerr suggests that the play be revised and
Malkovich be toned down.

Kissel, Howard. "Theatre: 'A Tale Told.'" *Women's Wear Daily* 12
    June 1981.

Kissel maintains that *Talley's Folly* presents a portrait of the
confrontation of two worlds—the urban Jewish and the rural
WASP; *Fifth of July* presents contemporary America in a mood of
self-doubt and comic bewilderment; and *A Tale Told* presents the
American ethos at a moment of supreme confidence—just as

World War II seems about to end—perhaps the last time that America has had so undiluted a sense of power.

Konas, Gary. "Tennessee Williams and Lanford Wilson at the Missouri Crossroads." *Studies in American Drama, 1945–Present* 5 (1990): 23–41.

Konas compares these playwrights' plays set in Missouri. The plays show protagonists confronting personal crossroads, which he sees as the plays' thematic dichotomies, and shows them making choices that have lifelong consequences. Dichotomies discussed include North/South, East/West, outsider/native and pillaging/preserving the land. The Missouri outsiders of both Williams and Wilson are most similar, Konas asserts, in that "they endure in the presence of a temptation to give up."

Kroll, Jack. "Love in a Folly." *Newsweek* 3 March 1980: 53.

Kroll remarks that the echoes of Chekhov in *Talley's Folly* make one realize that Wilson lacks Chekhov's vein of profound terror. The world of *Folly* could use a "nice deep abyss." Kroll also says that if this play is worth the Pulitzer it won, then *Fifth of July* is worth a Nobel Prize.

Leland, Nicholas F. "A Critical Analysis of the Major Plays of Lanford Wilson." Ph.D. dissertation, University of California, Santa Barbara, 1984. Abstract in *DAI* 45 (April 1985): 3030A.

This dissertation surveys ten major and fifteen minor works, up through *A Tale Told*. Leland argues that Wilson's vision develops from a pessimistic stance to a realistic optimism for the individual, that his earlier experimentalism merges with more traditional devices and that his roots are securely in his midwestern heritage.

Marowski, Daniel G., ed. "Lanford Wilson." *Contemporary Literary Criticism*. Vol. 36. Detroit: Gale, 1986. 458–66.

This citation includes a brief discussion of selected plays, including the observation that the concerns taken up in *The Hot l Baltimore* are typical of his works as a whole: a protest against the destruction of the past in the name of progress; the revelation of the poetic nature and humanity in "low-life" characters; and an affirmation of the importance of dreams. Marowski's piece is also very helpful because it includes a number of reviews by Frank Rich, Clive Barnes, Walter Kerr, John Simon and others.

Myers, Laurence D. "Characterization in Lanford Wilson's Plays." Ph.D. dissertation, Kent State University, 1984. Abstract in *DAI* 45 (April 1985): 3031A.

Myers asserts that Wilson uses characterization, drawn in terms of desire, moral stance and will, to illuminate his themes. He posits three kinds of characters in the plays: Conformists, Performers (non-conformists) and Devotees of the Past. Included in the dissertation is an interview with the playwright and Marshall Mason.

Novick, Julius. "Theater." *Nation* 29 November 1980: 588–89.

Fifth of July shows that Wilson is "sensitive to the genuine idealism, the shallowness and triviality and eventual disillusionment of the 1960's radicalism." And the play is all the more attractive because it concludes nothing about this time in American history.

O'Connor, John J. "Lanford Wilson's 'Lemon Sky.'" *New York Times* 10 February 1988: C26.

In this review of the "American Playhouse" television production of the play, O'Connor states that the cast (including Kevin Bacon and Lindsay Crouse) and some "uncommonly fine stages touches" make for a "terrific" production.

Oliver, Edith. "The Theatre: Off Broadway." *New Yorker* 17 May 1976: 125.

Oliver has written on almost all of Wilson's plays and this review of *Serenading Louie* is representative of her opinion of the playwright's work. She claims that unlike Edward Albee's presentations of marital discord, Wilson never convinces her that he knows what he is talking about. Furthermore, his writing in this play—as in almost everything except *Lemon Sky*—is synthetic.

Paul, John S. "Who Are You? Who Are We?: Two Questions Raised in Lanford Wilson's *Talley's Folly.*" *Cresset* 43 (September 1980): 25–27.

Wilson writes the "melting plot play," adding to the presentation of a single, fascinating character the use of a location containing characters who serve as a microcosm of society. Paul includes in this category *The Iceman Cometh, You Can't Take it With You, Bus Stop* and *Small Craft Warnings,* as well as *The Hot l Baltimore.* In such plays, plotting is secondary to the concern to find out who the characters are and how they have come to be where they are.

Pauwels, Gerard W. "A Critical Analysis of the Plays of Lanford Wilson." Ph.D. dissertation, Indiana University, 1986. Abstract in *DAI* 47 (November 1986): 1533A.

The playwright's works are presented as a cohesive body with a distinctive philosophical and aesthetic perspective. The seeming incoherence of the structures and of Wilson's career are the result, according to Pauwels, of the playwright's attempt to balance his perception of an irrational universe in which significant action is impossible, with a desire to present realistic images of the world. The dissertation also includes a summary of the contradictory critical responses to Wilson and of the influences on his work.

Peterson, William M. "Lanford Wilson's Classroom." *Confrontation* No. 48/49 (Spring/Summer 1992): 257–59.

Peterson describes Wilson's encounter and interview with a disabled Vietnam vet in a summer class he taught at the

Southampton campus of Long Island University. The student became the model for Kenneth Talley.

Rich, Frank. "Stage: 'Burn This,' by Wilson." *New York Times* 15
    October 1987: C23.

Pale is a latter-day Stanley Kowalski, and *Burn This* is "a cuter, softer version of *A Streetcar Named Desire* for the yuppie 1980's." Rich also says that in a play in which no pair of lovers has ever lived together, the voyeurism and disconnectedness of Larry "seem to say more about the playwright's feelings on loss and longing than the showier romance at center stage."

――. "Stage: 'Fifth of July,' Talleys 33 Years Later." *New York
    Times* 6 November 1980: C19

The play, Rich says, blends Chekhov and Mark Twain. It is about lonely and alienated characters who transcend their problems to face, at play's end, a more hopeful future. Specifically, it is about Ken Talley, a man who went to Vietnam to die and who is now, gradually, deciding to live.

――. "Theater: Wilson's 'Mound Builders.'" *New York Times* 1
    February 1986: 17.

In this review of the revival of *The Mound Builders*, Rich points out crucial concerns of the Talley plays that are here in embryonic form. The critic also compares Wilson to Chekhov (with *Fifth of July*), Tennessee Williams (with *Talley's Folly*) and Lillian Hellman (with *Talley & Son*).

Robertson, C. Warren. "Lanford Wilson." *American Playwrights
    Since 1945: A Guide to Scholarship, Criticism, and
    Performance.* Ed. Philip C. Kolin. New York: Greenwood P,
    1989. 528–39.

This bibliographic essay discusses the production history and occasionally the plots of Wilson's plays through *Burn This*. It also provides information on assessments of the playwright's reputation and influences, and an indication of the most important secondary sources.

Ryzuk, Mary S. *The Circle Repertory Company: The First Fifteen Years.* Ames: Iowa State UP, 1989.

This book contains biographical information about the four founders of the Circle Rep, traces the development of the company and thus Wilson's development as a playwright, and includes appendices on the company's rosters and the seasons' offerings. Also included are bibliographies and an index. Ryzuk provides a wealth of information about Wilson and his work, both before his association with the Circle Rep and since. The author quotes the principals frequently and at length, providing an angle on the company and on Wilson's work that is offered nowhere else.

Sainer, Arthur. "Lanford Wilson." *Contemporary Dramatists.* Ed. James Vinson. New York: St. Martin's P, 1973. 831–34.

Sainer argues that evil events and characters are almost entirely absent from the plays, and he calls Wilson's relationship to his characters that of a "tender observer." His first point seems overstated, although the second is frequently echoed by other critics.

Savran, David. "Lanford Wilson." *In Their Own Words: Contemporary American Playwrights.* New York: Theatre Communications Group, 1988. 306–20.

In an informative and wide-ranging interview, Wilson talks about his early career and influences as well as the six years he spent studying the construction of a "well-made play." The results of this study include *Talley's Folly, Talley & Son* and *Angels Fall.*

Schlatter, James F. "Some Kind of a Future: The War for Inheritance in the Work of Three American Playwrights of the 1970s." *South Central Review* 7 (Spring 1990): 59–75.

This essay examines *Fifth of July,* along with Shepard's *Curse of the Starving Class* and *Buried Child* and Preston Jones's *The Oldest Living Graduate,* in an effort to show that these three playwrights "attempt in their family plays of the mid and late

seventies to explore, however tentatively, possible avenues of
escape from [the] vicious circle of wandering and return
depicted by so many of our playwrights."

Schvey, Henry. "Images of the Past in the Plays of Lanford
    Wilson." *Essays on Contemporary American Drama*. Ed.
    Hedwig Bock and Albert Wertheim. Munich: Max Hüber
    Verlag, 1981. 225–40.

In this overview Schvey claims an essential thematic unity
for the plays from *Baltimore* through *Talley's Folly*, a concern for
the relationship of the individual and the past. Schvey also
provides brief yet insightful observations of particular works,
pointing out, for instance, significant areas of comparison
between *The Hot l Baltimore* and O'Neill's *The Iceman Cometh* and
Chekhov's *The Cherry Orchard*.

Sheed, Wilfrid. "The Stage: Relevant." *Commonweal* 29 April
    1966: 178.

In one of the more positive reviews of Wilson's early work,
Sheed remarks of *The Madness of Lady Bright* that, like *Death in
Venice*, homosexuality is not the focus; rather, the play is about
human loneliness and betrayal.

Schewey, Don. "I Hear America Talking." *Rolling Stone* 22 July
    1982: 18–20.

Through chatty encounters with the playwright at his office at the Circle Rep and his home in Sag Harbor, Schewey
reports on Wilson's early life and on such topics as the impetus
for his writing, the benefits of writing for particular actors and
actresses, and his play *Angels Fall*, which will be sharing a bill
with works by Tennessee Williams and Edward Albee.

Simon, John. "Demirep." *New York* 4 November 1985: 64, 66.

The two best active playwrights, Simon asserts, are
Shepard and Wilson. Wilson is the heir to Tennessee Williams
and better, if less original, than Shepard, since he is more literate,
disciplined, and humane. This is a review of *Talley & Son*.

——. "Mating Dance." *New York* 26 October 1987: 168–69.

In this review of *Burn This*, Simon identifies Wilson as at present "our soundest, most satisfying dramatist," and he offers comparisons with Shepard, Howe, Rabe, Mamet and others.

——. "Theater: All in the Family." *New York* 22 June 1981: 46–47.

A frequent and frequently positive reviewer of Wilson's plays, Simon claims that *A Tale Told* is less entertaining than *Fifth of July* and less enchanting than *Talley's Folly* but more commanding of respect. He compares the first Talley play to Chekhov, the second to Giraudoux and the last to Ibsen.

Tibbetts, John C. "An Interview with Lanford Wilson." *Journal of Dramatic Theory and Criticism* 5 (Spring 1991): 175–180.

Wilson reviews his life and his career and speaks of the Circle Rep process of play development.

Tucker, Martin. "A Running Log on Lanford Wilson." *Confrontation* No. 48/49 (Spring/Summer 1992): 245–56.

This is an account of three meetings with Wilson in November and December 1991, while he is preparing *Redwood Curtain* for its first production. The playwright speaks of his themes and his influences. Tucker also describes an early rehearsal of *Redwood Curtain*.

Weales, Gerald. "American Theater Watch, 1979–1980." *Georgia Review* 34 (Fall 1980): 497–508.

Weales claims that Wilson has always been "a child of American realism—popular theater division"—and that his forays into theatrical experimentation never impose on his realism. Weales also states that Wilson's portrayal of eccentricity is more sentimental and less sharp-tongued than Kaufman and Hart's, and that the violent and seedy subject matter and his preoccupation with loss are mitigated by his tonal softness.

——. "Stage: *Talley's Folly*: Lanford Wilson as Cyclist." *Commonweal* 28 March 1980: 182–83.

Weales asserts that, despite appearances, neither *5th of July* nor *Talley's Folly* has a happy ending: The characters of the former are mainly "spiritual, intellectual, physical failures" while those of the latter constitute a marriage of two sterilities. Except for *The Mound Builders*, none of Wilson's plays "find an intellectual frame strong enough to carry his sentimentality and easy irony."

Wetzsteon, Ross. "The Most Populist Playwright." *New York* 8 November 1982: 40–45.

The article quotes Wilson's observation that his plays are about putting his family back together or making a new one. It also asserts that Wilson's plays lack the bitterness and cynicism so prevalent in modern American drama; the playwright does not scorn America's corruption but mourns it, and with his "extraordinary empathy for ordinary people, he may be the last populist playwright."

Williams, Philip Middleton. "'A Comfortable House': The Collaboration of Lanford Wilson and Marshall W. Mason on 'Fifth of July', 'Talley's Folly', and 'Talley & Son.'" Ph.D. dissertation, University of Colorado, 1988. Abstract in *DAI* 50 (December 1989): 1487A.

This dissertation uses interviews with Wilson, Mason and other Circle Repertory Company members and drafts of scripts to examine "the background of the collaboration, the writing and staging process of the plays, and . . . the impact that these men have had on contemporary American theatre."

——. *A Comfortable House: The Collaboration of Lanford Wilson, Marshall W. Mason and the Circle Repertory Theatre.* Jefferson, NC: McFarland, 1993.

This is the published and slightly revised version of Williams's dissertation.

Witham, Barry. "Images of America: Wilson, Weller, and Horovitz." *Theatre Journal* 34 (May 1982): 223–32.

Witham's discussion of Wilson is limited to two pages on *Fifth of July*, about which he says that the playwright's vision is not a hopeless one, since Wilson's America is a garden, still capable of cultivation and renewal. "Seek out the values which endure," the play says to Witham, "and try to overcome the transitory, the sham, and the expedient."

Zinman, Toby Silverman. "Inside Lanford Wilson." *American Theatre* 9 (May 1992): 12–18, 63.

Interview in which Wilson talks at length about *Redwood Curtain*, about *Burn This* and about *Angels Fall*.

Index

PS
3573
I458
Z74
1994

Lanford Wilson.

$44.00